The Historical Bible

THE HEROES AND CRISES

OF

EARLY HEBREW HISTORY

FROM THE CREATION TO THE DEATH OF MOSES

THE HISTORICAL BIBLE

By CHARLES FOSTER KENT, Ph.D., Litt.D.

Professor of Biblical Literature in Yale University

ARRANGEMENT OF VOLUMES:

WITHDRAWN

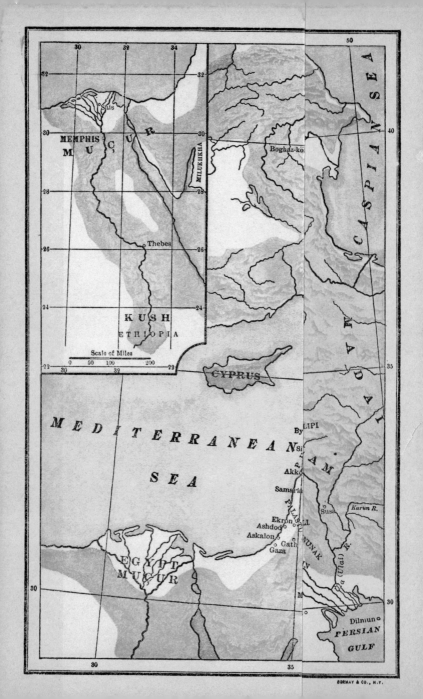

ORMAY & CO., N.Y.

The Historical Bible

THE HEROES AND CRISES

OF

EARLY HEBREW HISTORY

FROM THE CREATION TO THE DEATH OF MOSES

BY

CHARLES FOSTER KENT, Ph.D.

WOOLSEY PROFESSOR OF BIBLICAL LITERATURE IN YALE UNIVERSITY

WITH MAPS

CHARLES SCRIBNER'S SONS

NEW YORK   CHICAGO   BOSTON

COPYRIGHT, 1908, BY
CHARLES SCRIBNER'S SONS

Printed in the United States of America
O

PREFACE

Every man consciously or unconsciously makes his own working canon of the Bible. Sometimes this working canon includes everything that is found in the Scriptures, irrespective of relative values; sometimes it is pitiably limited, and fails to include many exceedingly important passages. To use the Bible intelligently and profitably it is important to realize that it is a great library, containing many different books, written by a great variety of authors, who lived in periods widely remote, and who wrote with diverse aims and points of view. Over twelve centuries lie between Moses and Paul, and each century contributed its part to the gradually growing records of God's revelation of his character and will in the experiences, the hearts and the minds of men.

The men of later ages, who have given us our present canons of the Old and the New Testaments, in their zeal to preserve all the existing records, included certain writings, which possess only a secondary historical and religious value. Sometimes, as in the case of the Gospels, they have also preserved three or four distinct yet parallel records of the same events; and sometimes, as in the case of the opening books of the Old Testament, they have closely blended together the older and later records into one continuous narrative.

The great service of modern, constructive biblical scholarship has been to distinguish and to restore the older records to their original form, and to make it possible again to study the heroic characters and stirring events in Israel's history as recorded by the earliest historians. In simplicity, literary beauty and historical value, the oldest history of Israel far surpasses the work of the later biblical historians. It includes practically all of the peerless narratives which have commanded the attention and moulded the faith and morals of humanity. When the later distracting parallels, the genealogical tables, the later Jewish traditions regarding the origin of institutions, and the popular legendary

PREFACE

material have been removed, there remains the heart of the Bible—clear, consistent, the earliest and noblest record of God's revelation of himself in the life of humanity.

The aim of the Historical Bible is to make this older, vital record available for popular reading and study. It also aims to arrange and combine with the earliest historical record the more important songs, prophetic addresses, laws, psalms, proverbs and epistles, so that the biblical writers will present in their own language the literature, history and religious belief of each succeeding age. This arrangement makes it possible to study the character, work and message of each great prophet, sage, or apostle in the full light of the events and conditions amidst which he lived and labored.

The translation is based on the oldest and best readings of the Hebrew, Greek, Syriac and Latin texts, and seeks to embody the constructive results of modern scholarship and discovery. It also aims to retain all that is best in the classic Authorized Version. It is hoped that by the means of a simple, dignified idiomatic translation the student may be directly introduced to the thought of the original writers and thus be largely relieved from the necessity of constantly referring to commentaries. The textual basis and the reasons for the different renderings adopted will be found in the corresponding sections of the author's *Student's Old Testament.*

The earlier system of dividing the text into sections and paragraphs has been adopted. The chapter and verse references, first added in the sixteenth century A.D., have been omitted because they distract the attention of the reader, and because they often make misleading divisions of the text. Those teachers and readers who desire to verify the chapter and verse references will find them printed in connection with the text in the corresponding sections of the *Student's Old Testament,* to which detailed reference is made in the Table of Contents.

To each general section of the biblical text have been added such brief connected historical, geographical and archæological notes as are necessary for the intelligent understanding of the biblical records. The purpose throughout has been to fix the attention on the biblical text itself and to put the reader in possession of those facts which are essential to its full understanding and appreciation.

The Historical Bible is intended for use, (1) as a text-book for college, seminary and preparatory school classes; (2) as a manual for teachers' training classes; (3) as a basis of study for general readers who desire to gain from the modern point of view a systematic knowledge of the

PREFACE

nistory, literature and teachings of the Bible; (4) as a text-book for senior and adult Bible classes.

For many years the conviction has been deepening that, if the alert young men and women of to-day are to be held in the Bible schools, they must be launched at the critical age of sixteen or seventeen upon a systematic course of Bible study which will hold their interest and attention, answer their critical questions, and give them the constant inspiration of definite and progressive achievement.

To give definiteness to the study a selected group of questions, with references for further study in connection with each section, are given in the Appendix. There is also being prepared for the use of Sunday-school teachers a special manual with suggestions regarding the method of presentation and application of the practical truths and principles illustrated by each general section.

To Mr. Charles Scribner I am under great obligation for many valuable suggestions in developing the plan of the series, and to Miss Ruth D. Sherrill and to Professor Irving F. Wood, of Smith College, for aid in revising the proofs.

C. F. K.

YALE UNIVERSITY.
May, 1908.

CONTENTS

INTRODUCTION

CONTENTS

CONTENTS

CONTENTS

CONTENTS

CONTENTS

THE HEBREWS IN THE WILDERNESS AND EAST OF THE JORDAN

CONTENTS

CONTENTS

LIST OF MAPS

INTRODUCTION

I

THE OLD TESTAMENT WORLD

I. The Influence of Environment. The character and history of a people are largely determined by the nature of the land in which they live. Mountains, valleys, desert, sea, cold and heat inevitably and indelibly mould the life of men. The fundamental characteristic of the Semitic race, to which the Hebrews belong, is its openness to the influence of environment. The striking contrast between the small, wizened Jew of Jerusalem, who has lived for centuries under an oriental despotism, and the tall, stalwart Jew of Spain, where conditions have been more favorable, is a familiar illustration of this susceptibility to external influences. To understand early biblical history it is therefore necessary to know the birthplace and home of the Hebrews and the races with which they came into closest contact.

II. The Scene of Earliest Human History. No portion of the earth's surface has more marked and significant characteristics than that limited territory in southwestern Asia which was the scene of the earliest human civilization and the background of Old Testament history. Its general form is that of a triangle. It is bounded on the west by the Mediterranean Sea, and on the east by the Zagros Mountains, which rise on the eastern bank of the Tigris River. Its southern base runs from the head of the Persian Gulf about twelve hundred miles across the northern end of the Red Sea and the Nile to the Desert of Sahara. Its centre is the great Arabian Desert, which occupies nearly half of this Old Testament world and ever dominated it. Nearly three-fourths of this entire area is either desert or dry, rocky, treeless pasture land. No high mountain ranges cut across this vast level expanse, which is hemmed in on its three sides by sea and mountains and burning sands.

III. The Lower Tigris-Euphrates Valley. In the eastern part of this natural home of the nomad are the flat, alluvial plains of the lower

1

Tigris and Euphrates rivers. Here, natural conditions all favored the development of an early and sturdy civilization. The Tigris, which flows thirteen hundred, and the Euphrates nearly eighteen hundred miles from their mountain sources before reaching the sea, brought down each year rich deposits of earth, and floods of water to irrigate the fertile soil. The clay of the river banks furnished the bricks from which were made temples, palaces and fortresses. The channels of the rivers and the intersecting canals were the highways of the merchant. The attractiveness of the territory and its exposure to attack on every side forced its inhabitants early to unite in common defence and to build up a strong and aggressive civilization.

IV. **Mesopotamia.** To the north, the Tigris and Euphrates are separated by the great level plain of limestone and selenite, commonly known as Mesopotamia. The arid pasture lands gradually merge into more fertile mountain regions in the north and west. Except, however, at a few favored sites beside the rivers, this ancient land of Aram simply supports a wandering, nomadic population. It is the connecting link between the richly productive lands along the lower waters of the Tigris and Euphrates, and the series of elevated plateaus and fertile valleys and coast plains that skirt the Mediterranean Sea.

V. **Syria and Palestine.** The eastern Mediterranean coast-land, known in later times as Syria and Palestine, was divided by natural barriers of desert, river and low mountain range into seven or eight distinct divisions. Each of these had its different products and interests. No one great river provided the background for a strong, centralized, conquering civilization. Instead, the Orontes, the longer of its two chief rivers, after flowing to the north only about one hundred and fifty miles, finds its way into the Mediterranean; while the Jordan, rising not far from the Orontes, flows a little over a hundred miles in the opposite direction to lose itself in the Dead Sea, far below the surface of the earth. About four hundred miles long from north to south and from seventy-five to one hundred wide, this little world, like ancient Greece, was, by virtue of its peculiar physical contour and character, destined to support many petty, independent, warring peoples, engaged in a great variety of occupations, and representing many different stages of civilization.

VI. **The Nile Valley.** The third large fertile area in the ancient Semitic world was the lower Nile valley. That remarkable river, fed by the melting snows and great lakes in the heart of Africa, flows northward over three thousand miles into the Mediterranean. The last thousand miles it runs through a desert of rock and shifting sands; but out of this desert the river, by its deposits of rich black earth, has created an oasis which man's industry has transformed into a paradise. The real Egypt of the past, as of to-day, was but a ribbon of fertile river land, not more than eight thousand square miles in area. Shut in by desert sands on the east and west, its closest and almost only point of contact with the outside world was with Asia to the northeast. From northern Egypt the great highways of commerce ran eastward along the Mediterranean, through Canaan and Syria, to the populous valley of the Tigris and Euphrates.

VII. The First Chapter in Divine Revelation. Thus the encircling barriers of sea and mountain and desert bound closely together the ancient Semitic world and protected it from too early or too close contact with its more barbarous neighbors. Natural conditions along the lower waters of the Nile in the west, and the Tigris and Euphrates in the east, fitted these river basins to become the two earliest centres of human civilization. The favorable physical conditions also largely determined the character of that civilization. Palestine and Syria, standing midway between the Arabian desert, Babylonia and Egypt, were clearly destined in time to receive and absorb the powerful political, social and religious influences emanating from each of these older centres. In the geographical background of early Hebrew life, therefore, is written in clearest characters the first and in many ways the most suggestive chapter in the history of divine revelation.

VIII. The Original Home of the Semites. Northern Arabia appears to have been the original home of the primitive Semites. There they lived as nomads, roaming, as do their descendants, the modern Arabs, from place to place in search of water and pasture for their flocks and herds. Their wandering life made it easy for them, when the desert steppes did not supply enough to support their increasing numbers, to pass over and seek permanent homes in the more attractive river valleys that encircled them. This process of transition began long before the dawn of history and has gone on without interruption to the present day. Usually the transition was gradual, but at times great hordes rushed forth with the sword to conquer and rule their more civilized but less virile agricultural neighbors.

IX. Semitic Races of Arabia and Africa. The fertile plains of central and southern Arabia doubtless early attracted Semitic immigrants. There they built up a rich and advanced civilization. It was, however, so completely isolated that, except through the medium of trade, it made little impression on the rest of the ancient world. From this land later came the Queen of Sheba with her costly gifts. To this southern group of Semitic races belong the nomadic Arab tribes, the highly civilized Sabeans, the Mineans and the later Nabatheans. From southern Arabia colonists crossed the southern end of the Red Sea to Africa, and founded the nation of the Cushites or Ethiopians, of whom are descended the modern Abyssinians. Other Semites early found their way to the lower Nile valley and, mingling with the native races, are known to history as the Egyptians.

X. Babylonians and Assyrians. Originally the lower Tigris-Euphrates valley appears to have been occupied by a non-Semitic people, called by modern scholars the Sumerians. The ruins of their ancient cities testify to the greatness of their art and culture. Their oldest tablets contain references to the advance of Semitic peoples from the north and west. The invaders, who settled in the south, assimilating the art and culture of the conquered, were later known as the Babylonians. Those who later went farther north and found a home on the upper Tigris, ultimately figure in history as the Assyrians.

XI. Arameans. Other groups of Semitic nomads crossed the Euphrates into Mesopotamia and are later known as the Arameans. Most of them retained their wandering habits; some of them in the northwest built cities; others pressed on westward into Syria and Palestine. Largely as the result of their intermediate position between Babylonia and Assyria on the one side, and Syria, Palestine and Egypt on the other, the Arameans became the great overland traders of the ancient world.

XII. Amorites and Canaanites. Probably from northern Arabia, the common home of the early Semites, came the ancestors of the Amorites and Canaanites. The earlier immigrants settled among the hills of central Palestine. On the fertile plains, which run along the eastern Mediterranean and intersect the hills and mountains that lie between the sea and desert, the later immigrants found their homes. Here they developed an agricultural civilization, which was a reflection of that of Babylonia.

XIII. Ammonites, Moabites and Edomites. Centuries later there came from northern Arabia and Mesopotamia another wave of nomadic immigration, which brought to this western land the ancestors of the Ammonites, Moabites, Edomites and Hebrews. The Ammonites settled east of the Jordan in the border between tillable land and desert, retaining their older nomadic institutions and acquiring also the arts of agriculture. The Moabites found their permanent abode on the more fertile headlands east of the Dead Sea. In the narrow valleys and rocky hills south of the Dead Sea the Edomites established themselves, depending for subsistence chiefly upon their flocks and the plunder which they seized from passing caravans.

XIV. **Hebrews.** The ancestors of the Hebrews appear to have at first crossed the Jordan into Canaan and to have found a temporary abode in the unoccupied uplands. They retained, however, their nomadic habits, and gravitated in time into the country to the south of Canaan. Thence a part of them at least pressed on to the borders of Egypt. Their return and conquest of Canaan are recorded in their earliest traditions. Of all the Semitic races they were the last to find a permanent abode and to crystallize into a nation. About them and in their midst were kindred peoples whose institutions had been developing thousands of years. Compared with that of Babylonia and Egypt and Phœnicia, their history is modern rather than ancient. By race, as well as by virtue of conquest and geographical position, they were heirs of that which had already been acquired through countless centuries of human effort and experience. The second chapter, therefore, in the record of divine revelation is the history of the great nations that preceded and deeply influenced the Hebrews.

II

THE BABYLONIAN BACKGROUND OF EARLY HEBREW HISTORY

I. **The Dawn of History.** The combined evidence of archæology, anthropology and geology indicate that man has existed on the earth at least twenty-five thousand and possibly one hundred thousand years. Back of the highly advanced civilization, disclosed by the excavations in the oldest ruins, lie millenniums, marked by slow but progressive development. Human history began at about the same time in the two most favored centres of the ancient Semitic world, the lower Tigris-Euphrates and the Nile valleys. The oldest records found in Babylonia and Egypt may be approximately dated between 5000 and 4000 B.C.

II. **Early Babylonian Systems of Writing.** Babylonia was the first to evolve a civilization that burst its natural boundaries and became a conquering force throughout the Semitic world. As the earliest inscriptions and archæological remains reveal the life of that far-away age and people, the historian is impressed by the remarkable progress already made in the art of writing. All important events were recorded on stone or clay by means of picture-characters. Thus, for example, a star represented the gods and heavens, a circle the sun, the crescent moon growth, the arm strength, and the fore leg walking. By the combination of these signs even most complex ideas were expressed. In time these pictures were represented by conventional characters, consisting simply of straight lines ending in a wedge (Latin, *cuneus;* hence called, *cunei-form*), made in the plastic clay by the sharp corner of a cube in the hand of the scribe. Many of these signs were also used, not only to represent ideas, but syllables, so that it was possible with these to spell out individual words and to make the record clear and exact.

III. **Different Industries.** By careful cultivation and irrigation the lower Tigris-Euphrates basin was made to bear far more than the needs of the people required. The surplus gave the Babylonians the material with which to trade with surrounding nations. The ancient arts and crafts were also highly developed. Sculptors, brickmakers, smiths, including those who worked in gold and silver, jewellers, potters, carpenters, masons, miners, weavers and leather-workers, are all mentioned on the monuments. Most of these trades were also organized at that early day into guilds or unions.

IV. **Merchants and Commerce.** The rich products of that ancient world, and the great highways on land and water, which led southward to Arabia and India and westward to Phœnicia and Egypt, made the inhabitants of Babylonia a nation of traders. The merchants soon became a rich and powerful class in the community. Some also became bankers, loaning money at a high rate of interest (25 per cent. per annum and up), and transmitting their business to their children from generation to generation.

V. **Effect of Commerce on Institutions.** The needs of commerce gave a great impetus to the use of writing, for every important transaction was recorded. Thousands of such records remain to testify to the great activity of the early scribes. In time, trade also made necessary a fixed standard of value. The coinage of money came much later; but in ancient Babylonia bars and rings of gold and silver of standard weight were early used in trade. Half an ounce avoirdupois made a shekel, sixty shekels a mina, and sixty minas a talent. The needs of trade likewise led to the early development of law and judicial institutions in Babylonia. If commerce is to prosper, it must be protected. As business relations became more complex, thousands of cases of dispute arose.

The decisions constituted precedents which in time became the basis of laws. These were regarded as possessing divine authority and were rigorously enforced. The result was that in time individual rights were as carefully guarded by law in ancient Babylonia as they are to-day in America or Europe.

VI. **Scientific Knowledge.** In the field of the mechanical arts great progress had been attained. The lever, the inclined plane and the arch were in common use. The length of the solar year (365¼ days) was known, and eclipses were often accurately predicted. In other respects the scientific knowledge of the Babylonians was exceedingly crude. They knew little about the human body and the treatment of diseases. The earth was thought of as an inverted dish, resting in the great watery deep, and the firmament above as a larger inverted bowl. Beneath the firmament moved the sun and moon and stars. Above the firmament were the great encircling waters; above these the bright abode of the immortal gods; while in the dark, beneath the earth, dwelt the dead.

VII. **Organization of Society.** The unit of this ancient society was the family. The father was the head of the household. The mother of children enjoyed an honored place, and her rights as wife or widow were carefully guarded by law. In later times, when conquering kings returned with captives, the slave class increased very rapidly. Whether the slaves belonged to a family or a temple, they appear to have been well cared for, and could even hold property in their own name. The king was the supreme head of the state, the commander-in-chief of the army, the judge to whom disputed cases were ultimately referred, the chief priest of the nation, and the protector of his subjects. The nobles shared his authority. In return for their service and tribute, he divided the land among them. Within their own domain they ruled as petty kings, renting the land in turn to the common people who were their tenants.

VIII. **Period of Small City States (4500–3800 B.C.).** The earliest historical period in Babylonia may be dated between 4500 and 3800 B.C., and is known as the age of small city states. Six important cities were found in the south, Eridu, Ur, Lagash (Shirpurla), Uruk (Erech), Larsa, Isin or Nisin, and six in the north, Agade, Nippur, Sippar. Kutha, Kish and later Babylon. Each was originally independent and held sway over the adjacent territory. In this early day the non-Semitic Sumerian civilization was dominant in the southern group of cities; in the northern the Semitic type was beginning to gain the ascendency.

The earliest inscriptions tell of the bitter wars that were frequently waged between these two rival races. The stronger city states also began to extend their rule beyond their own natural limits. The most significant ruler of this early period is Lugalzaggisi (about 3900 B.C.), who conquered Ur and Larsa and called himself "King of Uruk, King of the Totality." He also states in his inscription that his god gave him tribute from the lower sea (the Persian Gulf) to the upper sea (the Mediterranean), indicating that even at this early date the influence of this eastern centre of civilization was beginning to be felt in distant Syria.

IX. **Period of Unification and Expansion (3800–2100 B.C.).** Separated by no natural boundaries and united by common interests, institutions and religion, it was inevitable that the different cities of the lower Tigris-Euphrates valley would in time unite under the rule of the strongest. If the chronology of the later Babylonian scribes can be accepted, it was about 3800 B.C. that such a union was established by the great Sargon I, king of Agade. Apparently rising from the ranks of the common people, he built up a mighty empire. The inscriptions tell of his conquest not only of Nippur, Shirpurla, Kish and Uruk, but also record his campaigns in Arabia on the south, Elam on the east, Armenia on the north, and the Mediterranean coast-lands on the west. This empire he handed down to his son Naram-Sin, one of whose inscriptions has been found on the distant island of Cyprus. A few centuries later the leadership passed to Shirpurla in the south; but for about five hundred years the ancient city of Ur, devoted to the worship of the moon god Sin, held sway at times over all Babylonia. Its earliest kings were famous for their building enterprises, as well as their conquests. At Ur they reared a temple to the moon god; at Uruk to the goddess Ishtar; at Larsa to Shamash, the sun god; and at Nippur they repaired the ancient temple of Bel. The rulers of the second great dynasty of Ur assumed the proud and suggestive title of "King of the Four Regions." Contemporary tablets indicate that they carried their conquests into Elam, Arabia and Aram. The city of Larsa then enjoyed a brief period of supremacy. About 2000 B.C. it fell before the Elamite invaders from the east, who made it the centre from which they ruled over the cities of southern Babylonia.

X. **Supremacy of Babylon (about 2100–1700 B.C.).** It was at this time of humiliation at the hands of foreign invaders that the city which gave its name to the lower valley of the Tigris and Euphrates, first came to the front. About 2100 B.C. a strong dynasty arose at Babylon. The founders of this dynasty appear to have come from northern Arabia. The new blood and energy, thus infused into the already old civilization of Babylonia, found its noblest representative in the great Hammurabi, whose reign of forty-three years must now, in the light of a recently discovered royal chronicle, be dated not earlier than 2100 and probably about 1900 B.C. His deliverance of the southern cities from the Elamite yoke left him master of Babylonia. His two titles, "King of Shumer and Akkad" (southern and northern Babylonia) and "King of the Four Corners of the World," imply that his authority extended beyond the Tigris-Euphrates valley. His chief glory, however, was as a builder and organizer. He enlarged the temples at Babylon and its western suburb Borsippa, and erected new ones at Larsa and Sippar. He connected the Tigris and Euphrates by a canal. For the purposes of irrigation he constructed the great Hammurabi canal along the Euphrates. He introduced improved methods of agriculture. At Babylon he built a vast granary.

XI. **Effects of Hammurabi's Policy.** To ensure justice to all his subjects, he caused to be compiled and set up in public the remarkable civil code of two hundred and eighty laws recently discovered in the ruins of Susa. This code anticipates, by nearly a thousand years, many of the principles that underlie the Old Testament laws. It reveals not only a just, but also a humane ruler, eager for the welfare of his people. By his wise policy Hammurabi developed and bound together all parts of his great empire. He was the real founder of Babylonia's political, commercial and religious supremacy. He made Babylon itself, even after it fell before foreign conquerors, the great centre of culture throughout the ancient world. Under his descendants, the rulers of the first Babylonian dynasty, the empire appears to have enjoyed, for over a century, peace and prosperity, largely as the result of his epoch-making work.

XII. **Decline of Babylonia and Rise of Assyria (1700–1100 B.C.).** During the later years of the first dynasty of Babylon the Kassites came down from the mountains to the northeast and conquered Babylonia. Their rule was maintained for several centuries. They adopted, rather than destroyed, the Babylonian culture which they found, so that its influence still went forth to all the world. Soon after the appearance of the Kassites (about 1700 B.C.), the subject city of Asshur on the west bank of the upper Tigris threw off the foreign yoke and laid the foundation of the great kingdom known as Assyria. Centuries of bitter, destructive conflict between the new power and the parent state followed,

9

in which Babylon gradually lost strength and prestige. About 1100 B.C. the great Tiglath-pileser I, king of Assyria, entered upon his victorious campaigns in Babylonia, Elam and Mesopotamia. He also was the first conqueror to lead an Assyrian army into Syria. During this long period of Babylon's decline, its ancient rival Egypt had become a conquering power and had succeeded to the political control of the rich territory along the eastern Mediterranean.

III

THE EGYPTIAN BACKGROUND

I. **The Beginnings of Egyptian History (3400–2900 B.C.).** Egypt's early history is closely parallel to that of Babylonia. It begins at about the same time, with a long period during which rival city states, and nomes or provinces, fought with each other, the stronger gaining a temporary supremacy over their weaker neighbors. By 3400 B.C. at least, the rule of Memphis was acknowledged throughout all Egypt. About this time may be dated the first of the thirty-three dynasties in the classification of the Egyptian historian Manetho, whose tables have been generally adopted as the basis of Egyptian chronology. At the very beginnings of its recorded history, the art and civilization of Egypt had also attained an exceedingly high stage of development.

II. **The Fourth Dynasty (2900–2750 B.C.).** The immunity from foreign attack which Egypt enjoyed during its earlier history, left its rulers free to carry out vast building enterprises. The greatest building dynasty was the fourth (about 2700 B.C.). Its kings penetrated the Sinaitic peninsula and opened the mines and quarries along the Red Sea. They also, in part, reclaimed the lands of the Nile Delta and built defences on the east to keep out Semitic invaders. Their crowning achievement was the construction of the great pyramids at Gizeh as royal tombs. The magnitude of their work and the remarkable organization of the empire, which it reveals, can only be appreciated when it is remembered that the Great Pyramid alone covers thirteen acres, is four hundred and eighty feet high, and contains nearly seven million tons of stone, transported from Syene, five hundred miles up the Nile.

III. **Twelfth Dynasty (about 2000 to 1800 B.C.).** The rulers of the twelfth dynasty accomplished for Egypt what the great Hammurabi did for Babylon. Seven powerful, long-lived kings succeeded one another

THE TWELFTH DYNASTY

Nubia in the south, with its rich gold mines, was conquered. Peaceful commercial relations were established with Syria and southern Arabia. The marshy district west of the lower Nile, now called *the Faiyum*, was drained, greatly increasing the productive area of Egypt. Many palaces and temples were built. The industries and local interests of the different provinces were developed. Contemporary inscriptions bear testimony to the noble spirit of justice and consideration for their subjects that actuated kings and princes. One ruler declares that he "marched through the country to overthrow evil, fixed the frontier of each township and placed the boundary stones as firm as the sky. He sought information from the books as to the irrigation district belonging to each town, and this was drawn up according to the ancient writings, because he loved truth so much." A noble also boasts: "No daughter of a citizen have I injured, no widow have I molested, no laborer have I arrested, no shepherd have I banished, no superintendent of workmen was there whose laborers I have taken away. In my time there were no poor, and none were hungry in my day. When the years of famine came, I ploughed all the fields of the province from the southern to the northern boundary. I kept the inhabitants alive and gave them food, so that none was hungry. I gave to the widow, even as to her who had a husband; I never preferred the great to the small."

IV. **Rule of the Hyksos (about 1650–1580 B.C.).** After the peaceful and prosperous days of the twelfth dynasty, civil war between the kings and their powerful nobles weakened the kingdom and invited foreign invasion. The invasion of Babylonia by the Kassites during the latter part of the eighteenth century B.C. was but the beginning of a general westward movement of the peoples of southwestern Asia. One important result of this same movement was that certain tribes from Syria, Palestine, and Northern Arabia were pushed on through the Isthmus of Suez and seized northern Egypt. Establishing themselves in the Delta, they soon brought southern Egypt also into subjection. For fully a century these so-called Hyksos kings maintained their rule, adopting many of the Egyptian institutions. In the end the native princes of Thebes rallied the south-land, and, after a half century of fierce fighting, succeeded in driving the invaders back into Asia.

V. **The Victorious Eighteenth Dynasty (1580–1350 B.C.).** The long training in warfare, the possession of the horse and chariot which the Hyksos first brought to the land of the Nile, the fear of subsequent invasions, and the newborn desire for military glory, all united in transforming the peaceful Egyptians into a conquering nation. Under the

11

leadership of the able kings of the victorious eighteenth dynasty (about 1600 to 1350 B.C.), the kingdom of Egypt suddenly expanded into an empire. The great conqueror Thutmose III, in a series of campaigns, subjugated Palestine and Syria, and carried the borders of his empire to the Euphrates. For fully a century Egypt ruled the eastern Mediterranean coast-land. By its prestige and alliances with Asiatic provinces it extended its influence still further, so that, while Babylonia and Assyria were engaged in mortal combat, Egypt was mistress of the western world. From all the subject states she exacted heavy annual tribute. The income from this source and the services of the captives of war made possible the huge building enterprises for which the eighteenth and following dynasty were famous.

VI. **The Nineteenth Dynasty (1350–1205 B.C.).** During the rule of the nineteenth dynasty, Egypt was confronted in northern Syria by a formidable foe, the Hittites, who came down from the mountains of eastern Asia Minor. After fighting with them for nearly twenty years, Ramses II concluded a remarkable treaty which established the boundary line between the two peoples a little north of Mount Hermon. The treaty left Ramses II free to develop the resources of his empire, and to fill Egypt from one end to the other with the monuments of his zeal as a builder.

VII. **The Transitional Twelfth Century B.C.** The beginning of the twelfth century B.C. is memorable as a great transitional epoch in ancient history. It saw the decline of the first Babylonian empire. In the west the second great world empire, Egypt, torn by civil wars within and attacked from without by northern hordes, entered its long eclipse. The same hordes broke the power of the Hittites in northern Syria, so that they soon disappeared. At the same time in the east, Assyria began to gather its forces for that series of conquests which ended in the mastery of the ancient Semitic world. From Mesopotamia the Arameans moved westward and southward to take possession of northern Syria. Along the shore from southern Asia Minor came the ancestors of the Philistines to break the power of Egypt and to find a home on the rich, rolling plains of southwestern Palestine. From Egypt certain Hebrew tribes went forth as fugitives, and began that memorable movement which led them at last to the land of Canaan and the possession of central Palestine. With the twelfth century the earliest chapter of human history which represented over three millenniums of magnificent achievement and splendor, closes, and a new era of political, intellectual, and religious progress opens.

IV

THE EARLY PALESTINIAN BACKGROUND

I. Data Concerning Early Syria and Palestine. Until very re-cently the early history of the third great centre of Semitic culture (Palestine and Syria) has been known simply from occasional references in the monuments of Babylonia and Egypt. These still remain the chief sources of information. This fact is in itself indicative of the dependent position held by this intermediate land. Recent excavations in Palestine, at ancient Lachish, Gezer, Taanach, Megiddo and Jericho, have yielded only two or three inscriptions, but they and the archæological remains have confirmed and supplemented the testimony of the monuments, and made it possible to trace, in outline, the early history of the land which is the immediate background of the Bible.

II. Early Babylonian Influence. Lugalzaggisi, one of the earliest conquering kings of ancient Babylonia, states that about 3900 B.C. his army reached the Mediterranean. It is probable that the point gained was simply northern Syria, and that the expedition was little more than a raid; but it means that even at this early date the leaven of Babylonian culture had entered the west-land. About two centuries later Sargon I followed with the conquest of the land of Martu, which is identified in later tablets with the land of the Amorites. In the Assyrian inscriptions Martu is the designation of Syria and Palestine. These early expedi-tions are significant, for their primary aim was apparently to open the highways for commerce, which was a far more important agent for the spreading of Babylonian civilization and ideas than the march of con-quering armies. It is probable that from the days of Sargon I these influences were felt in the more favored centres on the western Mediter-ranean coast.

III. Pre=Semitic Inhabitants of Palestine. The excavations in Palestine indicate that before the Semites entered it, the land was in-habited by a race of short stature, living in caves. The Bible also refers to an ancient people, east of the Jordan, whose name, Horites, appar-ently means cave-dwellers. They may well be survivors of the earlier prehistoric people, who were otherwise expelled or absorbed by the larger and more energetic Semitic immigrants.

IV. The Amorite Migration. Doubtless, Palestine attracted tribes from the Arabian desert at a very early date, but the first traces of an

13

extensive Semitic invasion came from about 2200 B.C. The Babylonian, Egyptian, and Northern Israelite records agree in calling this people the Amorites. The recurrence of the same proper names in contemporary writings coming from Syria and Babylonia, together with other indications, support, although they do not establish, the conclusion that the wave of Semitic invasion which swept from Arabia westward into Palestine about 2200 B.C., also carried the ancestors of Hammurabi, the founders of the first great dynasty of Babylon, eastward across the Euphrates. Certainly, from the days of Hammurabi, the frequent references in the Babylonian tablets to the Amorite country and the Amorites are indicative of the close relation which henceforth existed between the two lands and peoples. This close and continued relation alone explains the fact that a few centuries later the Babylonian language and cuneiform characters were employed by the governors of Syria and Palestine in writing even to their Egyptian sovereign. It was during the centuries following 2200 B.C. that Babylonian institutions, ideas, and customs were indelibly stamped upon the Semitic peoples in Palestine.

V. **Story of Sinuhit.** From Egypt there comes a popular romance, the *Story of Sinuhit*, which throws interesting light upon conditions in Palestine about 2000 B.C. The hero, a princely Egyptian refugee, fled eastward past the " Wall of the Princes," which guarded the northeastern frontier of Egypt. On the borders of the desert he was found by a Bedouin herdsman who introduced him to the hospitality of his tribe. These "sand wanderers," as they are called in the story, send him on from tribe to tribe until he reaches the land of Kedem east of the Dead Sea. Here he remains for a year and a half, until he is invited by the king of Upper Tenu to share with the other Egyptian refugees already there the hospitality of his court. The king of Upper Tenu appears to have been one of the Amorite rulers of central Palestine. Although the story is a romance, it gives the earliest detailed picture of the ancient Amorite civilization. Every possible honor was heaped upon the hero by the king of the land:

"He placed me at the head of his children, and married me to his eldest daughter. He let me choose from amongst his lands, from amongst choicest possessions on the frontier of another country. This was the beautiful land of 'Eva; figs and vines grew there, there were many sorts of wine and it was rich in honey, its olive trees were plentiful and all kinds of fruit grew on its trees. There was corn there and barley and herds without number. And there was yet more that happened to me from love to me, for he made me prince of a tribe of his country.

Then I had as much bread as I wanted, and wine for every day, boiled meat and roast goose, irrespective of the game of the country that I caught and carried off as spoil, and irrespective of what my own hounds brought me. . . . Thus I spent many years and my children became heroes, each the protector of his adopted tribe. The messenger who came from the court or went thither stayed with me; I gave hospitality to every one, and I gave water to the thirsty. . . . I subdued each people against whom I marched, I drove them from their pastures and from their wells; I captured their cattle and carried off their children."

VI. **Origin of the Canaanites.** Contemporary Egyptian inscriptions indicate that by the fourteenth century B.C. Semitic people called the *Kinahni,* or Canaanites, were firmly established on the coast plains of the eastern Mediterranean and in the valleys of central Palestine. This fact accords with the statement of the Northern Israelite historian in Numbers 13²⁹ regarding conditions before the conquest, *The Amorites were dwelling in the hill-country and the Canaanites by the sea and along beside the Jordan.* Deuteronomy 3⁹ also calls attention to a difference between the dialects of these two races. Although closely related and later blended, the two peoples appear to have been originally distinct. The references in the inscriptions favor on the whole the conclusion that the Canaanites represented a later wave of Semitic immigration similar to the earlier Amorite invasion. It seems exceedingly probable that the great western movement in the latter part of the eighteenth century B.C., which carried the Kassites into Babylonia and the Hyksos into Egypt, bore the ancestors of the Canaanites to Palestine. Possibly they were closely connected with the Hyksos conquerors who, when defeated, retired to southern Palestine.

VII. **Egyptian Conquest of Palestine.** The pursuit of the retreating Hyksos led the kings of the powerful eighteenth Egyptian dynasty to the conquest of Palestine. After a siege of five years they captured Sharuhen, the Hyksos stronghold in southern Canaan. Thutmose I carried the standards of Egypt to the Euphrates, laying tribute upon the peoples of Palestine and Syria; but it was Thutmose III who made this territory an integral part of the empire. In an inscription on the walls of one of the temples at Thebes he has given a detailed account of his campaigns, which furnishes a vivid picture of conditions in Palestine at that time. The decisive battle with the Canaanites was fought about 1480 B.C. at Megiddo on the plain of Esdraelon. The Egyptian record reveals the spirit of the conquerors and the cowardice of the natives:

"On the twenty-first day of the month, even the same as the royal coronation, early in the morning command was given to the entire army to advance. His Majesty went forth in his chariot of electrum, adorned with his weapons of war. His Majesty was in the midst of them, the god Amon being the protection to his body and strength to his limbs. When his Majesty prevailed over them, they fled headlong to Megiddo, as if terrified by spirits; they left their horses and chariots of silver and gold and were drawn up by hauling them by their clothes into this city, for the men shut the gates of this city upon them. The fear of his Majesty entered their hearts, their arms failed, their mighty men lay like fishes on the ground. The great army of his Majesty drew round to count their spoil. The whole army rejoiced, giving praise to Amon for the victory that he had given to his son, and they glorified his Majesty, extolling his victories."

VIII. **Egyptian Rule in Palestine.** The city of Megiddo itself was soon captured. In the same campaign the king of Egypt completed the conquest of Palestine. The tribute brought to him by the conquered peoples reveals their prosperity and culture. Flocks and herds, slaves, horses, chariots, armor, weapons, gold and silver vessels, embroidered garments, and inlaid furniture of wood and ivory are mentioned in the lists. On the plain of Esdraelon alone the king reaped a harvest of one hundred and fifty thousand bushels of grain. For the next three centuries, with only occasional lapses, the rule of Egypt was maintained in Palestine. Armies were frequently sent to put down local rebellions and little mercy was shown. Egyptian garrisons were stationed at strategic points. These were supported by the local princes who continued in most cases to rule over their petty states as vassals of Egypt. While they remained loyal, supplied troops to aid in putting down rebellions, paid the regular tribute, which was far from small, little else was required. The rivalry between them was intense, and when Egypt showed any signs of weakness, they were each ready to improve the first opportunity to revolt. In the cities on the coast plains, which were most open to Egyptian influence, the civilization of the Nile valley took root, but throughout the rest of Palestine it made little impression. Instead, Babylonian and local Semitic customs, laws, and ideas held undisputed sway.

IX. **Testimony of the el=Amarna Letters.** During the reign of the reformer king of Egypt, Amenhotep IV (1375–1358 B.C.), remarkably clear light is shed upon conditions in Palestine by the famous el-Amarna letters, sent to the king by his vassal princes and governors. Although written in the Babylonian language and script, they abound in words and expressions familiar to the Bible student because they reflect the dialect of Canaan which was later used by the Hebrews. Like the inscriptions of Thutmose III, they show that many of the towns which figure in later Hebrew history were already in existence. The Canaanite-Phœnician cities of Gebal, Beruta (Beirut), Tyre, Sidon, Joppa, and the inland towns of Hazor, Gezer, Ajalon, Jerusalem, Gath, and Lachish are among the most important (*cf.* map., opp. p. 73). Altogether nearly one hundred and fifty towns are mentioned, of which two-thirds can be identified.

X. **Letters from Jerusalem.** The letters written by Abdi-heba, the vassal king of Jerusalem, state that he had been raised to that position by Amenhotep, and that his authority extended over the adjacent territory, which was called the country of Jerusalem. Like many of the Palestinian governors of the period, he had been accused of treachery by his colleagues ruling in other cities, and while he strongly protests his own innocence he accuses them in turn. The chief burden of his letters is the request that the king of Egypt send an army at once to deliver his people and land from the insistent attacks of an invading people called the Habiri.

XI. **The Habiri.** The letters of the other Palestinian governors contain similar references to these invaders. Notwithstanding the similarity in name, they can hardly be identified directly with the Hebrews. Rather they appear to be the vanguard of that new western migration from northern Arabia and Mesopotamia which included the Aramean or Arabian ancestors of the Hebrews, the Ammonites, the Moabites, and the Edomites.

XII. **Decline of Egyptian Power.** After the death of Amenhotep IV, Egypt lost control of Palestine and Syria for fully fifty years. The ambitious kings of the nineteenth dynasty, however, recovered Palestine in 1313 B.C. and held it for a century. An inscription of Mernephtah, one of its last kings, contains the first contemporary reference to Israel. From the context it is clear that Israel represents a people, apparently without a definite country, but then living within or near the bounds of Palestine. Mernephtah mentions them simply to record his victory over them. Ramses III (1198–1167 B.C.), of the twentieth dynasty, also re-established the rule of Egypt over Canaan and the coast-land; but by the middle of the twelfth century B.C. all foreign barriers to the advance of the Hebrews were removed. With this date Israel's history as a nation begins.

XIII. **Israel's Heritage.** This brief outline suffices to suggest how broad and significant is the historical background of early Hebrew history. Many great kingdoms and empires had flourished for centuries and fallen into decay before the Israelites appeared in Canaan. Through all the centuries each important nation and civilization had left its deep imprint upon the land that was destined in divine Providence to be the home of the people through whom a unique message was to come to humanity. The roots of Israel's life run back to the beginnings of human society and civilization. All ancient history is a unit, of which the Bible records the later and, in many ways, the more important chapters.

V

ISRAEL'S RELIGIOUS HERITAGE

I. Prominence of Religion in Early Semitic Life. The preceding studies have revealed the aggressive conquering, colonizing and commercial tendencies of the early Semitic peoples. Of these three tendencies the commercial was undoubtedly the strongest; but there was a still more powerful force in that ancient life. That force was religion. The earliest rulers were the priests of the tribe or nation, and the basis of their authority was their claim that they were the representatives of the gods. Kings fought and carried their victorious standards into unknown lands, and colonists followed to complete the work of conquest, that the glory and prestige of their god might be increased. The greater part of the fruits of conquest and commerce went to glorify the temples and service of the gods. The policy of the state and the activity of the people were directed by their religious leaders. Priests also acted as scribes, teachers, authors and judges. It is also deeply significant that the oldest records found in Babylon and Egypt are almost without exception religious in theme and spirit. The earliest mounds are filled with the ruins of temples and the symbols of worship. Ancient art and science were also both inspired by religion.

II. The Semitic Instinct for Religion. Among the primitive Semitic peoples the fact that man is by nature a religious being, finds its strongest illustration. The dearest possessions and even human life were all sacrificed to the gods. Though the beliefs of these early peoples were often absurd and their rites crude and repulsive, their fervent devotion reveals the spirit of true worship; for the essence of worship is not the intellectual belief, but the attitude of the worshipper. It was inevitable that in such an intensely religious atmosphere the faith of hu-

18

manity should attain its earliest and most advanced development, and that out of it should ultimately spring the exalted religion of the Hebrew prophets and Jesus. Divine revelation is necessarily gradual and progressive, for each age and race can receive only the truth which it is capable of apprehending. In the life and religions of the Semitic peoples, whose traditions Israel inherited, it is now possible to study the earlier stages in that continuous process of divine revelation which has given us our faith of to-day.

III. Early Semitic Religions. The primitive Semites, and especially the Sumerians who preceded the Babylonians, worshipped many spirits of air, and earth, and water. It was a religion of dread, for the deities were for the most part believed to be malign. Man's chief effort was to avert their jealousy and anger; but as civilization and culture advanced and man began to master natural forces, the gods were thought of, more and more, as friends rather than foes.

IV. The Many Local Gods. When history dawned in ancient Babylonia and Egypt, each city state or tribe had its local deity, who, it was believed, made its fields productive, prospered its industries, protected the individual from sickness and misfortune and the city from calamity, fought with his people against their foes, and appointed and directed its judges and rulers. The interests of the god and his people were identical. The chief aim of religion was to establish and maintain the right relation between the divine king and his subjects. The entire city life centred about the temple. Thus, in ancient Babylonia, Sin, the moon god, who guided the caravans by night across the sandy wastes, was worshipped at Ur, and also at northern Haran, beside the desert; Ea, the god of the great deep and of hidden knowledge, at Eridu, near the Persian Gulf; Bel, the lord of earth, at the sacred city of Nippur; Shamash, the sun god, at Larsa and Sippar; the goddess Ishtar at Uruk; Nabu, the god of learning, at Borsippa, and Marduk at Babylon. At each of these different shrines nearly the same forms of ritual and sacrifice obtained, and the common Semitic myths and traditions were handed down; but in each of the different versions the local god figured as the hero.

V. Development of the Pantheon. When some one of the cities conquered the rest, and a united kingdom and in time an empire arose, the god of the ruling city became the supreme deity of the realm. The local gods, however, continued to be worshipped by their subjects, and wise kings like Sargon I and Hammurabi won the favor and loyalty of the conquered cities by building temples and paying homage to these local deities. The natural result of the union of all the cities of Babylonia under one ruler was a pantheon. As has always been the case, theology was strongly influenced by the existing political and social organization. When Hammurabi made Babylon the head of an empire, Marduk, the god of Babylon, took his place at the head of the pantheon made up of the gods and goddesses of the more important cities of the Tigris-Euphrates valley. The theologians of that early day set to work to recast the old myths so as to give the supremacy to Marduk, to define the functions of the different deities, and to trace relationship between them. Each god was also provided with a divine consort. Thus, for example, corresponding to Bêl was the goddess Bêlit. The result was a divine household, the prototype of the Greek Olympus.

Egyptian religions passed through the same stages, but more of the primitive worship of spirits and animals survived. Its theology and mythology were never so thoroughly systematized as the Babylonian, and its interest centred in the future rather than in the present life.

VI. Transfer of the Religious Centre to Palestine. During the imperial period the Babylonians and Egyptians developed an exceedingly elaborate ceremonial system. Religion was defined more and more in the terms of ritual rather than of life and deeds. Priest-craft and superstition gained the ascendency, with the sad result that these great religions ceased to develop and so perished. In the freer, fresher atmosphere of Palestine the vital elements in the old faiths were destined to come to full fruition. Conquest, commerce, and literature had carried Babylonian customs, traditions, and religion to this western land. The dominant Amorite-Canaanite civilization in Palestine, because of its common Semitic origin, was also especially receptive of this powerful influence which radiated for centuries from the Tigris-Euphrates valley.

VII. Religion of the Canaanites. Recent excavations, the Egyptian inscriptions, the el-Amarna letters, and the biblical references together give a definite picture of the Amorite-Canaanite religion which the Hebrews found in Palestine. Each city or tribe had its local baal or lord and a corresponding goddess. These were worshipped at the open-air high places on some commanding height within or near each town. About the shrine were the asherahs or poles and sacred stones or pillars. A row of seven of these pillars has recently been found in the ruins of the old Semitic sanctuary at Gezer. The altars on which the sacrifices were offered were of earth or baked clay or stone. Here the people assembled in springtime and autumn to celebrate the ancient Semitic festivals and to present their offerings. Here also the inherited religious traditions of the race were doubtless perpetuated. In the absence of favorable natural conditions and a strong central power to unite all these little city states into one kingdom or empire, the peoples of Palestine never developed a local pantheon. While polytheism prevailed there, it was not of the complex type found in Babylonia or Egypt under the empire. Also ritualism had not destroyed the possibility of ethical and spiritual progress. On the other hand, the gross immorality and degeneracy of the local cults made imperative the demand for a purer and nobler religion.

VIII. **Israel's Religious Heritage.** Thus through their Arabian and Aramean ancestors the Hebrews received the primitive religious ideas and institutions of the early Semitic races. From the Amorites and Canaanites, whom they in time conquered and absorbed, they inherited their early sanctuaries, and with these the beliefs and rites and traditions which had gradually been transferred to Palestine from Egypt and especially from ancient Babylonia. In their conception of the Deity and of men's duty toward him and their fellow-men, these pre-Hebrew races had made vast progress, as is demonstrated, for example, by the Code of Hammurabi or by many of the noble Babylonian hymns and prayers. A prophet nation, however, was demanded to separate the true gold from the dross of superstition, to conserve that which was vital and eternal in the older Semitic religions and to become the agent of a new and far higher revelation. Not by chance nor by arbitrary divine choice, but as the result of a character and inheritance and training, which can be studied in the full light of its unique history, Israel proved to be that prophet nation.

VI

THE OLDEST HISTORY OF ISRAEL

I. **The Gradual Growth of the Early Historical Books.** During the past two or three centuries biblical scholars have been gradually discovering the real character and origin of the earlier Old Testament historical books. Like the later books of Samuel, Kings, and Chronicles, they consist of quotations from earlier and shorter narratives. These valuable quotations have been skilfully combined and supplemented by successive editors or compilers. In this way all ancient Semitic histories gradually grew. Many of the Old Testament books have a literary history extending through hundreds of years. The fact that they are compilations enhances their value manifold; for in citing passages word for word from the oldest histories known to them, the compilers have preserved the earliest records instead of their own impressions of the distant events of which they wrote. A careful study of the evidence of composite authorship found in each book also makes it possible to collect and combine these citations from the older histories and thus largely to recover the priceless originals.

II. **Evidences of their Composite Character.** The internal evidence regarding the origin and literary history of the opening books of the Old Testament consists in general: (1) of striking variations in the vocabulary, idioms, and style of different sections in the same book. A comparison, for example, of Genesis 1^1–2^{4a} with $2^{4b\text{-}25}$ at once reveals marked contrasts in literary form. In the second passage different words and idioms are used to express the same ideas. The literary style of the first passage is precise, formal, generic, and repetitious; in the second it is vivid, concise, picturesque, and flowing. (2) Very different ideas of God and his relation to the universe and man are found in different parts of the same book. Again, the opening chapters of Genesis well illustrate this point. In the first passage the Deity is presented as a God of spirit, majestic, omnipotent, issuing his decrees from afar. In the second and third chapters he is pictured as living and talking with the first man and woman, and as walking in the cool of the day to avoid the hot mid-day sun. The one passage, which always designates the Deity as God, is based on the mature theology of later Judaism; the other, which used the divine name Jehovah, or Yahweh, reflects the childlike beliefs of the primitive ancestors of the Hebrews. (3) Parallel and yet variant accounts of the same events abound. When these variant versions are compared, many minor inconsistencies appear. Thus the two accounts of creation in Genesis agree in emphasizing man's central position in God's universe, but in the one passage man is the last and in the other the first living thing to be created. In the order and method of creation the two versions also present the most striking variations (for the explanation of these, cf. § I $^{\text{vi-ix}}$). (4) Very different aims and points of view appear in succeeding narratives. Thus, for example, in Genesis 1^1–2^{4a} the primary aim is to establish the divine origin of the sabbath. In $2^{4b\text{-}25}$ it is to illustrate God's love and care for man. In the one narrative the point of view is the legal and priestly, in the other it is that of the prophet, interested only in ethical and spiritual truth (cf. for further illustration, § V).

III. **Contents of the Oldest History.** Fortunately, the oldest history of Israel is the one quoted most fully by the authors of the Old Testament historical books. It opens with the primitive story of creation in Genesis 2, which leads up to the account of man's fall in chapter 3. The origin of different institutions is then briefly given. The scattering of the human race over the face of the earth, as told in the story of the tower of Babel, is the introduction to the oldest Abraham narratives. The early stories of the patriarchs in turn introduce the primitive account of the experiences of the Hebrews in Egypt, in the wilderness during the settlement of Canaan, and as a united nation. When the extracts from this ancient history are collected and put together, the result is a brief, consistent, connected record of all the important events in Israel's many-sided life, down to the accession of Solomon. The unity of the whole indicates that in these quotations nearly all of the original history has been preserved.

IV. **Its Literary Characteristics.** Its literary style is that of the ancient story-teller: simple, vivid, concise, picturesque and dramatic. The vocabulary is large; each word is in itself a picture. The sound of many of them in the Hebrew is suggestive of the idea or action which they represent. Solemn plays upon words abound. The characters and scenes are pictured simply but graphically. The heroes and heroines are real men and women. Much of the story is told in the form of dialogues. The action moves on rapidly to the climax. The interest in the two or three principal actors in the story never for a moment flags. Oral transmission from story-teller to story-teller through long ages has evidently worn away all that is not essential; only that which is vital remains. The result is that these simple, early stories in charm and fascination are unsurpassed in all the world's literature.

V. **Its Religious and Ethical Ideas.** God is always spoken of in the language of primitive belief. Not only is he pictured as walking in the garden of Eden in the cool of the day, but he comes down to see with his own eyes the tower of Babel and to investigate the crimes of the men of Sodom. To the patriarchs and Moses he speaks by word of mouth. The terminology and mode of presenting the great truths regarding God's dealing with men are those of a poet. Concretely and directly in the language of life they convey their teachings. Back of the popular language is a sublime conception of the majesty and dignity of God. Over the great family of nations from the first he has exercised his benign yet omnipotent sway. But he is more than a supreme ruler, he is the personal Friend, Guide, Counsellor and Deliverer of his people, a God not only to be feared but loved. Loyalty and love to him are the beginning and the end of law and ethics. Religion is not abstract and formal, but a personal, vital relation.

VI. **Its Purpose and Value.** The historical purpose is prominent in this early history. It aims to trace briefly from their earliest beginnings the unfolding of Israel's life as a race and nation. The great crises and their significance are graphically portrayed. The interest in the heroes of the nation and their valiant achievements is that of a devoted patriot. The origin of Israel's social and religious institutions also commands attention. But a still broader and deeper purpose is everywhere evident, which reveals not only the patriotic historian, but the prophet. Israel's history is recounted, not because it was glorious, but because it effectively illustrates God's gracious attitude toward men, and the inevitable consequences of right or wrong acts. The selection of the narrative material is determined by this higher religious and ethical purpose. Much that would have been reproduced by a mere historian has evidently been ignored or else condensed into a sentence. Other narratives, containing little historical data, have been given a central place in the history, because they effectively illustrate and emphasize an important ethical or spiritual fact. Incidentally the author or compilers of this marvellous history have given a remarkably true picture of the life of early Israel; but the far greater value of their work lies in the universal and eternal truths which they have thus concretely and forcibly set forth.

VII. **Its Sources.** With this higher religious purpose in mind, it is not surprising that the early prophetic historians drew their illustrations from a great variety of sources. Sometimes they took from the lips of the people an old Semitic tradition, like the stories of the creation and the flood, handed down from their primitive ancestors through countless ages. Sometimes they drew from the cycles of stories transmitted by certain tribes from the nomadic period. Sometimes they utilized the popular heroic stories, retold for generations by father to son, or by the story-tellers at the great religious festivals. Often they found rich material in the traditions treasured at the ancient sanctuaries of Canaan. From the early collections of Israel's songs they frequently quoted long passages. For the later and more historical periods they had access to the popular traditions of their race. It is also evident that they freely recast, combined, and adapted this varied material to their prophetic purpose.

VIII. **The Place of Its Composition.** In this earliest Hebrew history the interest extends to the farthest bounds of Israel and even to the neighboring nations, but it is centred in Judah. In the patriarchal stories, Judah instead of Reuben figures as the first-born and the leader among the sons of Jacob. In the earliest version of the story of the spies, Caleb, the traditional ancestor of one of the southern tribes, also takes the place of Joshua the northern hero. These and other indications support the generally accepted conclusion that this early history is based on the traditions current in Judah, and that it was written by a prophet or group of prophets who lived and wrote in that southern kingdom. Hence it is called *the early Judean prophetic history*.

IX. **Its Date.** Statements like that in Genesis 36³¹, *before any king ruled over the Israelites*, clearly indicate that the history was written at least after Saul or David had ruled over Israel. The subjugation of the Canaanites, which was not completed before the reign of Solomon, is implied in many passages. The reference in Genesis 27⁴⁰ to Esau's shaking off the yoke of Jacob points to the revolt of the Edomites in the ninth century B.C. The spirit and theology of the history as a whole is that of the early monarchy. Doubtless a majority of the stories were current long before the days of David; but the historical allusions in the narratives themselves and in the other Old Testament books suggest that these stories were first committed to writing about 825 B.C. The immediate cause was probably the reformation, initiated by Elijah in Northern Israel, which under the leadership of Jehoiada the priest resulted, about 825 B.C., in the overthrow of Athaliah and the re-establishment of the religion of Jehovah in Judah. This noble history was supremely fitted to impress upon the mind of the nation the significance and importance of the covenant then "made between Jehovah and the king and the people that they should be Jehovah's people" (II Kgs. 11¹⁷, §LXXIII). It revealed the broad and deep historic foundations upon which that covenant was based, and set forth, in the light of Israel's remarkable national experiences, the eternal principles that must be observed by men or nations who would do the will of God.

X. **Later Additions.** The canonization of the Scriptures was first undertaken by Jews living long after the exile. The later Judean prophets who preserved the early history not only felt free but under obligation to supplement it by additional narratives and explanatory or archæological notes that seemed to them worthy of a place in it. Some of the most important stories in the Old Testament, as for example, the story of Cain and Abel, and the account of the flood, are later additions. They can usually be readily recognized by the slight variations in vocabulary and point of view. They all bear the marks of the same noble prophetic school, whose work extended through more than a century.

VII

THE LATER PARALLEL HISTORIES

I. **The Northern Prophetic History.** During the eighth century B.C. the prophets of Northern Israel also began to collect the national songs and traditions current in the north, and to weave them together into a connected history, parallel to that of the early Judean prophets. Many characteristic water-marks distinguish their work. Peculiar words and expressions are constantly employed. The mountain of revelation is called *Horeb* or simply *the mountain* instead of *Sinai*, as in the early Judean history; the inhabitants of Palestine *Amorites* instead of *Canaanites*, and the father of the twelve tribes *Jacob*, not *Israel*. *God* (*'elôhîm*), not *Jehovah*, is the early designation of the Deity. Ordinarily, he is represented as communicating with his people through his Messenger, instead of by word of mouth as in the older Judean stories. These northern or Ephraimite (using Hosea's designation of the northern kingdom) prophetic historians also recognize that the ancestors of the Hebrews were idolators (Josh. 24²), and that divine revelation was gradual and progressive. Living in an age when prophets, like Elijah and Elisha, gave commands to king and people, they naturally assign the commanding position throughout all their history of Israel to the prophets. Abraham, Isaac, Jacob, Joseph, Moses, Joshua, Deborah, and Samuel are their chief heroes, and these all figure in the prophetic rôle, overshadowing the priests and secular rulers.

II. **Its Purpose.** In the thought of the Northern Israelite prophetic historians Israel was from the first a theocracy. Its victories and achievements were attained not so much by human effort and natural means (as in the Judean history), but by divine interposition. Its disasters they trace directly to acts of apostasy. Their purpose is clearly instructive and religious rather than historical. They aim to show, by familiar illustrations drawn from Israel's experience, that disaster is the sure result of rebellion, and that peace and prosperity and the assurance of divine favor are the certain rewards of obedience to God's commands and the counsels of his theocratic representatives, the prophets.

III. **Its Contents.** Since its interest centres in the Hebrew theocracy, this northern prophetic history begins with Abraham. It records all the important events in Israel's life down to the establishment of the united monarchy under Saul. This independent version is in general closely parallel to and yet differs in many details from the Judean account. Each of these parallel prophetic histories has also preserved narratives peculiar to itself. Thus, for example, the account of the sacrifice of Isaac (Gen. 22), the making of the golden calf (Ex. 32), and the appointment of the seventy elders (Nu. 11[16. 17. 25-30]) are found only in the northern history, and the later additions made to it. Doubtless it was also originally far more complete than the present extracts from it in the Old Testament would suggest.

IV. **Blending of the Two Prophetic Histories.** When Northern Israel fell in 722 B.C., its literature became the possession of the southern prophets. The religious and didactic value of the northern history was recognized by some prophet or group of Judean prophets who lived in the dark days preceding the great reformation of Josiah in 621 B.C. The variant accounts of the same events were, however, distracting and not adapted to practical use. Accordingly, the two histories were combined. Naturally, the early Judean was made the basis, and this was supplemented by extracts from the northern history. If the two versions of the same narrative were closely parallel, they were joined together, so that, as for example, in the account of Jacob's deception to secure his father's blessing (§ XII), succeeding verses or sections were taken from the two different histories. If they could not be thus fused, the two versions were sometimes introduced independently, as are the two accounts of Isaac's deception regarding Rebekah in Genesis 12 and 26. If the variations in the two versions were too great, simply the one was quoted, and that was ordinarily the southern, for it was the form of the tradition most familiar to the Judean compiler. When there was but one version of a story, it was usually reproduced, whether found originally in the northern or in the southern history. The task of combining the two sources was carried through with great care, and the result was a composite narrative, abounding in minor inconsistencies and abrupt transitions in literary style and point of view, but representing that which was most valuable in the two histories.

V. **Point of View of Later Judaism.** The Babylonian exile fundamentally transformed the thought and point of view of the Israelite race. The law and ritual took the place of the earlier popular religion and the priest succeeded the prophet. The prevailing conceptions regarding the earlier history of the nation also changed. The seat of authority was found in the past, rather than in the divine revelations through the present experiences of the nation and the heart of the living prophet. The historical spirit was largely lost, and, instead, a tendency prevailed to idealize the early days of Israel's life, and to trace back to them the ideas and institutions so dear to later Judaism.

VI. **The Late Priestly History.** Under the influence of this new point of view and tendency, certain priests, probably originally exiles in Babylonia, wrote a brief history of their race. This history begins with the story of creation in Genesis 1, and traces the important incidents in Israel's experience to the conquest of Canaan. The literary style is that of a legal writer and stands in striking contrast to that of the earlier prophets. Chronological data and genealogies are common. The interest is directed not to the history of the nation, but to the origin of legal and ceremonial institutions. This is in accord with its general aim, which is to provide a fitting introduction to the laws. God is conceived of as the absolute, omnipotent, transcendent ruler of the universe, who realized his will in the life of his people, not so much by natural laws and the acts of men, as by a miraculous use of his divine power. Israel's earlier history has been so far idealized that no mention is made of the sins of Jacob, Moses, and the Hebrews. For the study of the theology and thought of later Judaism these narratives are of value; but the more reliable historical data and the vital messages adapted to universal human needs are found in the older prophetic narratives.

VII. **The Final Blending of the Prophetic and Priestly Histories.** The fusion of the late priestly with the earlier composite prophetic histories has given us five of the opening books of the Old Testament. Since the final compiler was a late priest, he has assigned the first place to the priestly narrative that comes from his own age. Its account of creation, because of its majestic character, furnishes a fitting introduction to the Old Testament. Its order of events largely determines that of the resulting composite history. The stories of Genesis and Exodus lead up to the laws which later Jewish tradition associated as a whole with Moses and Sinai. Numbers and Joshua trace the history of Israel to the conquest of Canaan, the land where subsequently the temple was reared.

VIII. **The Heart of the Old Testament.** The greatest service performed by the final compiler was, however, the preservation of the earlier prophetic history. Embedded in the midst of later traditions, laws, and editorial additions, this older record has in divine Providence survived almost intact the successive revisions to which it has been subjected. Now, in the light of modern biblical research, it stands forth as the earliest witness, to make known the essential facts of Hebrew history and, above all, to illustrate the great spiritual and ethical truths revealed to the Hebrew prophets. This earliest history of Israel and the later prophetic books, and those inspired by them, constitute the real heart of the Old Testament and the true introduction to the New. The primary object in the opening volumes of the *Historical Bible* is to recover and reprint this early prophetic history of Israel (with its important later supplements) that it may again be available for popular study and teaching. It is not a new, but the original Old Testament, which is thus restored and freed from the distracting parallels and scribal additions that through the ages have gathered about it.

THE BEGINNINGS OF HUMAN HISTORY

§ I. THE STORY OF MAN'S CREATION

In the day that Jehovah made earth and heaven, no plant of the field was yet on the earth, and no herb of the field had yet sprung up, for Jehovah had not caused it to rain upon the earth, and there was no man to till the ground; but a mist used to rise from the earth and water the whole face of the ground. *1. Conditions before man's creation*

Then Jehovah formed man of the dust of the ground and breathed into his nostrils the breath of life. Thus man became a living being. *2. Creation of man*

And Jehovah planted a garden in Eden far in the East, and placed there the man whom he had formed. And out of the ground Jehovah made to grow every tree that is pleasant to the sight and good for food, the tree of life also in the midst of the garden, and the tree of the knowledge of good and evil. And Jehovah commanded the man, saying, Of every tree of the garden thou mayest eat freely, except of the tree of the knowledge of good and evil; from it thou shalt not eat, for in the day that thou eatest of it thou shalt surely die. *3. Provisions for his development*

Then said Jehovah, It is not good for the man to be alone; I will make a helper suited to him. Therefore out of the ground Jehovah formed all the beasts of the field and all the birds of the heavens, and brought them to the man to see what he would call them; and whatever the man called each living creature that was its name. Thus the man gave names to all cattle and all the beasts of the field; but for the man himself there was found no helper suited to him. *4. His social needs*

Then Jehovah caused a deep sleep to fall upon the man, so that he slept; and he took one of his ribs, and closed *5. Creation of woman*

up its place with flesh. But the rib, which he had taken
from the man, Jehovah fashioned into a woman and brought
her to the man. Then said the man,

> This, now, is bone of my bone
> And flesh of my flesh.
> This one shall be called woman,
> For from man was she taken.

**Therefore a man leaves father and mother and cleaves to
his wife, so that they two become one flesh.**

I. **Literary Form and Character of the Story.** This narrative
gives the primitive answer to the question which every child of the human
race has earnestly and often asked. How were we made? How were
all living things made? Man is pictured as the first being to be given
life. Trees, beasts, and birds (of lesser importance than man) are made
later. Last of all, woman is created that man may have a suitable companion. Jehovah is thought of as a God who himself moulds the human
form from the dust, breathing into the clay his own life-giving breath.
This same God is represented as experimenting to find what companions
are best suited to man. Thus this ancient story reflects those ideas
about the universe and the origin of things which men held in the
childhood of the human race. There is little trace of that later belief
in an orderly gradual process of creation, in which God is thought of as
a sovereign spirit issuing his commands from afar (Gen. 1¹-2⁴ᵃ, *cf.*
Appendix I).

The literary style of the narrative, that of the earliest prophetic historian (*cf.* Introd. VI), is concise, picturesque, graphic and concrete.
Five short paragraphs tell vividly the story of creation and of Jehovah's
provisions for man. With a few strong strokes each scene and character
is clearly portrayed.

II. **The Original Introduction to the Biblical Story.** This earliest
Hebrew story of creation was placed after the later narrative of Genesis
1¹-2⁴ᵃ that it might precede the account of man's sin in chapter 3 (§ II)
which it introduces. From references to the early tradition made in
the poetic and prophetic sources one may infer that it originally told
how at first there was no earth or heaven but only chaos; how Jehovah
set fast the foundations of the earth and reared up its pillars in the waters,
and then spread out the canopy of the heavens, establishing the courses

of sun, moon and stars. All of these opening sentences have apparently been condensed by the compiler of the two accounts of creation into the statement, *In the day that Jehovah made earth and heaven.* At this point the story begins. No vegetation or life was on the earth, but a mist constantly rose from the earth to water the surface of the ground and thus make plant and animal life possible.

III. **Man's Creation.** Jehovah's presence and personal activity in the work of creation are strongly emphasized. By him the body of man was shaped out of the dust of the ground. What were the exact methods and the time required—whether a gradual process of evolution, extending through countless ages, or by the hand of God in a moment of time—is not stated. Doubtless the primitive story-teller, with his limited scientific knowledge, had in mind the simpler explanation. Then Jehovah breathed into the nostrils of the human form the vital force that made the moulded dust a living being. Thus the primitive belief in man's relationship to the Deity was reasserted in nobler form. That which gave mankind life was the breath of God within him. Hence, when that was withdrawn, his body returned to its native dust (§ II⁸).

IV. **Traditional Site of the Garden of Eden.** To meet man's physical and spiritual needs, Jehovah then planted a beautiful garden far in the distant East. A later compiler, perhaps familiar with Babylonian tradition, added a note to the effect that this garden was beside a river. This stream was probably the Persian Gulf, which was called by the Babylonians "the bitter river." As one ascended it, this river divided into four branches. Two of these were the Tigris and the Euphrates. The other two may have been (1) the modern Wady-er-Ruma, which extends far into Arabia, where the Assyrians placed the land of Havilah, and (2) the Kerkha, east of the Tigris. Or, in view of the incredibly vague geographical ideas held by the ancients, the Pishon may be identified with the Indus or Ganges, and Gihon with the Nile.

The original prophetic historian had, however, no interest in mere geography. It was the significance of the garden itself that commanded his attention. The garden provided for man a home, the fruit of the trees food, and the life-giving tree in its midst the possibility of enjoying unending life, while he dwelt beside it and could eat of its fruit.

V. **The Provisions for Man's Higher Needs.** The divine care did not cease, however, with provision for man's physical life. Beside the tree of life grew another tree, the fruit of which, as its name implied, gave to him who ate of it the knowledge of good and evil. This knowledge was to come, as the sequel shows, through experience. This tree of knowledge was hedged about by the divine command not to eat of its fruit under penalty of death.

Without wholesome and helpful companionship man's happiness and development would be incomplete. Among the Semitic peoples the name was supposed to represent the character of a person or thing. As the primitive man gave names to the beasts and birds, he established his dominion over them and voiced the impression which each made upon him. But none of these creatures satisfied his need of a companion and helper. Therefore, from man's own body a portion of bone and flesh was taken, and from this Jehovah fashioned woman. When she was brought to the man, he recognized her kinship with him. The name which she bore in the Hebrew, *ishsha*, woman, was, in sound at least, suggestive of innate relationship with *ishah*, her husband. This close kinship and the inborn needs of man and woman constitute the eternal basis of that marriage bond which leads a man to leave parents and to enter into the most intimate relation with his wife, so that they, indeed, become one flesh.

VI. **Aim and Teachings of the Story.** The primary aim of the narrative is to introduce the facts and characters which figure in the subsequent story of man's sin. It is the prologue to the great tragedy of human history. Briefly. but with inspired skill and authority, it sets forth the basal facts of history and religion. (1) Back of all the universe and the world, with its teeming life, is a personal Creator and Ruler. (2) Man is the highest product of God's creation, and the object of his tenderest care and solicitude. (3) Man's Creator is a God of infinite love, providing for his human child all that is best for his happiness and true development. (4) It was God's aim from the first to deliver man from everything that seems evil, such as pain, wearisome labor, and death. (5) The beauties of the natural world and the inhabitants of air and earth were all created for the sake of man. (6) Man and woman were made akin and yet different, that together they may fully meet each other's deepest needs. (7) The obligations of the marriage bond are absolute and sacred, because they are based upon the innate character of man and woman. (8) Temptation is not an accident in God's creation, or in itself an evil, but rather is absolutely necessary for man's moral development.

VII. **The Oldest Babylonian Account of Creation.** The different elements that enter into this story of creation are found in ancient oriental literature which existed centuries before the Hebrews became a nation. An old Sumero-Babylonian tablet tells of the time when all lands were sea and nothing had yet been made. Then Marduk built the city of Babylon (where he was especially revered), and made the gods, the spirits of earth. The poem adds:

> Marduk laid a reed on the face of the waters,
> He formed dust and poured it out beside the reed;
> That he might cause the gods to dwell in the dwelling of their hearts' desire,
> He formed mankind;
> With him the goddess Aruru created the seed of mankind.
>
> The beasts of the field and living things in the field he formed;
> The Tigris and Euphrates he created and established in their place;
> Their names he proclaimed in a goodly manner.
> The grass, the rush of the marsh, the reed and the forest he created,
> The lands, the marshes and the swamps;
> The wild cow and her young, the wild calf,
> The ewe and her young and the lamb of the fold.

As in the oldest Hebrew version of the story, man is created before the other living things.

VIII. **The Later Babylonian Version.** From the library of Asshur-banipal, who reigned over Assyria during the middle of the seventh century B.C., comes a later and more highly developed version. First, the firmament is created, then the heaven above and the great deep below. Then in the sky are placed the stars, moving in their fixed orbits, to determine the year and months.

> The moon god he caused to shine forth, and to him he entrusted the night;
> He appointed him as the luminary of the night to determine the days.

A recently discovered fragment of the sixth tablet of this epic tells of Marduk's purpose in creating man:

> My blood will I take and bone will I form,
> I will make man that man may . . .

I will create men who shall inherit the earth,
That the service of the gods may be established and their shrines
    built.

IX. The Later Biblical Account of the Creation. (*Cf.* for the
text Appendix I.) The priestly author of Genesis 1¹–2⁴ᵃ has accepted
the order and picture of creation which are given in this later Babylonian
version, but he rejects the polytheistic and unworthy elements. He has
arranged the story in six great acts, which lead up to the divine origin of
the sabbath. Being a priest, he was supremely interested in this institution. God is represented as an omnipotent spiritual Ruler who
reveals his benign purpose at each stage of creation. Man, as in the
older Hebrew version, is the central figure; but he is created last rather
than first, thus completing the evolutionary process. He is made in the
image of God in that he is gifted, like his Creator, with intelligence and
will, and is given authority to rule as God's viceroy on earth.

X. Other Creation Stories. The literature of the Phœnicians,
and Egyptians indicate that they also were acquainted with the common
Semitic tradition. Most primitive peoples have their myths which explain the origin of the natural world, and in many of these myths there
are striking parallels to the Semitic version. Of them all, the Persian
tradition presents the closest analogies to the early Hebrew narrative.
It tells of a region of bliss where dwelt two beings, subsisting only on
fruit, until they were tempted by a demon to disobey God's commands.

XI. The Tree of Life. Among the Babylonians it was a common
belief that certain heroes, as for example, the Babylonian Noah, were
granted immortality, and were allowed to dwell forever "in the distance
at the confluence of the streams," in a blessed abode guarded by scorpion
men.

Many analogies to the tree of life, the fruit of which was believed to
give immortality to the eater, can be traced. The hero of a very ancient
Babylonian story, after long searching and countless trials, finds the
plant called "the restoration of old age to youth," but fails to attain
immortal life, for the precious plant is snatched away by a serpent.
A legend has also been found on a Palestinian tablet of the fifteenth
century B.C. which tells of a fisherman Adapa who was admitted to the
dwelling place of the gods, and, having learned their secrets, was offered
"the food of life," which conferred immortality.

XII. The Tree of Knowledge. Trees also figure in the thought of
the ancients as a medium of revelation. To Moses the call to service

came in connection with the burning bush (§ XXI[1]). A famous divin-ers' tree was found in the days of the Judges near Shechem (§ XXXVII). The movement in the balsam trees was the divine signal to David to go forth to battle (§ XLIX[4]). The oaks of Dodona and the laurels of Delos and Delphi were consulted even by kings and philosophers in ancient Greece. The Arabs believe to-day that the box-thorn some-times utters prophetic words. Hence a tree, the fruit of which gave the eater knowledge of good and evil, was perfectly consistent with the belief of the East.

XIII. **The Story of Eabani.** An old Babylonian poem also tells of a primitive hero, Eabani, who was created by a goddess from a bit of clay. Clad only in the long locks of hair which covered his body, he ate and sported with the wild animals in a state of savagery. To lure him from his strange companions a beautiful woman was sent to him, and by her charms she wooed him from his barbarous life. The resemblance of this early Babylonian hero to the man of the Hebrew story is strikingly close. These various analogies in the thought and traditions of the East at least suggest that there lies back of the marvellous biblical story of the garden in Eden an older Semitic original which has been adapted by the Hebrew prophet to illustrate his noble spiritual messages.

§ II. MAN'S SIN AND ITS CONSEQUENCES

Now the man and his wife were both naked, yet felt no shame. And the serpent was more subtle than all the beasts of the field which Jehovah had made. *1. Man's original innocence*

And the serpent said to the woman, Hath God really said, ' Ye shall not eat from any tree of the garden ? ' The woman replied to the serpent, From the fruit of all the trees of the garden we may eat; only of the fruit of the tree which is in the midst of the garden, God hath said, ' Ye shall not eat from it, neither shall ye touch it, lest ye die.' Then the serpent said to the woman, You shall not surely die; for God knoweth that in the day you eat of it your eyes shall be opened, and you shall be like gods, knowing good and evil. *2. The voice of temptation*

Now when the woman saw that the tree was good for food, and attractive to the sight, and desirable to make one wise, she took of its fruit and ate, and gave also to her husband with her and he ate. *3. The act of sin*

4. Effect of sin Then the eyes of both of them were opened, so that they knew that they were naked; therefore they sewed fig-leaves together and made themselves girdles. But when they heard the sound of the footsteps of Jehovah, as he was walking in the garden in the cool of the day, the man and his wife hid themselves from the presence of Jehovah among the trees of the garden.

5. Fatal excuses And Jehovah called to the man and said to him, Where art thou? And he said, I heard the sound of thy footsteps in the garden and I was afraid, because I was naked; so I hid myself. Then he said, Who told thee that thou wast naked? Hast thou eaten of the tree from which I commanded thee not to eat? And the man said, The woman whom thou didst place beside me, she gave me from the tree and I ate. When Jehovah said to the woman, What is this thou hast done? The woman replied, The serpent beguiled me and I ate.

6. Explanation of serpents' habits Then Jehovah said to the serpent, Because thou hast done this,

> More accursed shalt thou be than all animals,
> And more than all the beasts of the field.
> On thy belly shalt thou go,
> And dust shalt thou eat,
> All the days of thy life.
> Enmity will I set between thee and the woman,
> And between thy offspring and her offspring.
> He shall bruise thee on the head,
> And thou shalt wound him on the heel.

7. Consequences of the woman's sin To the woman he said,

> I will make thy pain great in thy pregnancy,
> With pain shalt thou bring forth children.
> Yet toward thy husband shall be thy desire,
> And he shall rule over thee.

8. Of man's sin But to the man he said, Because thou hast hearkened to the voice of thy wife and hast eaten of the tree concerning which I commanded thee, saying, 'Thou shalt not eat from it':

38

Cursed shall be the ground because of thee,
By painful toil shalt thou eat from it all the days of thy life.
Thorns and thistles shall it bring forth for thee,
    And thou shalt eat the herb of the field.
    By the sweat of thy brow shalt thou eat bread,
    Until thou return to the ground,
    Because from it thou wast taken;
        For dust thou art,
        And to dust shalt thou return.

Therefore Jehovah sent him forth from the garden of 9. God's
Eden to till the ground whence he was taken. But Jehovah benign
made for the man and his wife tunics of skin, and clothed care
them.

I. Literary Form and Origin of the Story. This narrative is the immediate sequel to the preceding story of the creation. In two marvellous scenes it presents the great tragedy of tragedies in human history—the loss of man's happy, natural relation with God through deliberate disobedience to the divine command. Like the great Teacher of Nazareth, the prophetic author of this marvellous story was dealing with the deepest experiences of human life. His problem was to make clear and plain even to children the nature of that inner struggle which we call temptation. He accomplishes his end by the use of the simple story and dialogue. Attention and interest are fixed from the first on the experiences of a certain man and woman. The story has all the personal charm of those fascinating popular tales which come from the ancient East. Its prologue, the primitive story of creation (§ I), was old centuries before the days of Moses. In the first scene the actors are the serpent, the woman, and the man. In the dialogue between the serpent and the woman is brought out vividly the struggle that raged in her own mind between her natural inclinations and her sense of duty. In the second scene Jehovah appears. The acts and motives of the man and woman, and the terrible consequences of sin are portrayed so concretely and dramatically that even the youngest and simplest reader can fully appreciate them. The thoughtful reader, however, soon discovers that the marvellous biblical narrative is far more than a mere record of the experiences of a primitive man and woman. Like the inimitable parables of Jesus, it is a chapter from the book of life. It is in every respect historical because it is absolutely true to human experience.

The closest parallel to this account of man's fall is the late Persian story of the man and woman who were influenced by the evil spirit, Ahriman, to disobey and deny God, to cut down trees, to kill animals, and thus to lose their original innocence.

II. The Character of the Serpent. The serpent is clearly not, as Milton has taught us, the Satan of later Jewish theology. It is rather the animal, which, because of its silent, secretive, venomous habits was generally regarded as the wisest and at the same time the most treacherous foe of man. It was, therefore, most natural that of all the creatures in the garden the serpent should be the one chosen to voice the temptation in the heart of the woman. This choice may also be due to the influence of an older Babylonian tradition.

III. The Real Nature of Temptation and Sin. The dialogue between the serpent and the woman brings out clearly the various forms which temptation assumes. The serpent's first question implies a doubt concerning Jehovah's goodness and wisdom. The woman's answer shows that she fully understands the meaning of the divine command. Then follows the questioning of Jehovah's warning and a strong appeal to the woman's curiosity. It is clearly an oriental woman, with her characteristic mental and moral limitations, that the ancient storyteller has in mind. The appeal to her curiosity, therefore, is well-nigh irresistible. There is also an implied dare in the serpent's words.

The issue is clear. On the one side was the definite divine command not to eat. Her noblest impulses of love and gratitude prompted the woman to obey that divine command. On the other side were the natural cravings of appetite, the promptings of the æsthetic sense (for the fruit was attractive), of curiosity, and the desire for knowledge and power. All of these motives were in themselves worthy. Under other conditions they would have inspired noble and right actions, and yet to the woman of the story they were temptations, because they impelled her to turn her back upon the nobler and diviner impulses of gratitude, love and duty which she owed to Jehovah. The story well illustrates the significance of the Hebrew word for sin, which means *missing the mark*. In missing the mark of implicit obedience set clearly before her the woman sinned.

The man's temptation assumed a very different form, but one which appealed as strongly to him. He himself would doubtless have waved aside the whisperings of the serpent; but when the wife, whom Jehovah had given him as his companion and helper, had eaten the forbidden fruit, he felt that he had a sufficient excuse for disobeying the divine command. Thus with him the choice was between the nobler dictates of duty and the promptings of appetite, the desire for knowledge and a false chivalry. In following his baser impulses the man also missed the mark set before him and thus sinned.

IV. **The Effects of Sin.** The inevitable consequences of sin are truly and graphically set forth in the story. Sin brought knowledge to man and woman, but a knowledge which destroyed their former innocence. Cowardice and a desire to avoid the presence of Jehovah took the place of their previous glad confidence. While their sin blinded their vision and reared a high barrier between them and Jehovah, residence in the garden was intolerable.

And yet, as Jehovah sought the guilty pair, his words were not those of condemnation. Rather his questions invited that frank confession which would have at once dispelled the barrier which sin had raised. But they made a fatal mistake and sinned doubly in excusing their sin and in trying to shift the responsibility. The man said, "The woman gave me from the tree"; the woman said, "The serpent beguiled me." Thus, their lack of repentance made it impossible for even the infinite God to forgive them.

The ancients regarded all misfortune as the result of the divine displeasure. The snake, wriggling through the dust with no legs on which to walk, the deadly enemy of mankind, beaten to death by its foe, or in turn striking its fatal fangs into the heel of its assailant, seemed to primitive peoples to be especially afflicted by God, and, therefore, to rest under the shadow of some great crime. Hence the early story-teller naturally connected the unfortunate peculiarities of serpent kind with the act of the serpent in tempting Eve to disobey Jehovah.

The grievous pains of childbirth and the subjection of the oriental woman to her husband are likewise traced to sin. Man's painful struggle to wrest food and a livelihood from the rocky earth, and death, the sad but certain end of that struggle, are likewise attributed to rebellion against the divine command. The fate of man and woman is not so much a penalty, as the inevitable effect of their sins unconfessed; for, according to the representation of the story, banishment from the garden was necessary, because they had forfeited their title to it. Even they themselves were eager to escape from the presence of Jehovah. Banishment meant a struggle for food, suffering, and ultimate death, for they could no longer eat of the life-giving tree in the midst of the garden.

V. **The Element of Hope.** The gloom of this tragedy of human tragedies is relieved by one bright ray of hope. As the man and his wife go forth to learn in the school of pain and hardship the lessons of life, the divine care still attends them, providing the garments needful in their new and harsh environment—an earnest that they are not beyond the pale of God's love and forgiveness.

VI. **Aim and Teachings of the Story.** The prophet's first aim was clearly to teach the origin, nature, and terrible consequences of sin. Incidentally he retained the popular explanations of certain striking facts in the natural world, as for example, the habits of serpents, the pains of pregnancy, and the necessity of laborious toil. He was, however, preeminently a religious teacher. Even the pseudo-scientific explanations are only concrete illustrations of his central teaching that all pain and affliction are ultimately but the effect of sin. Among the many religious teachings with which this marvellous story abounds may be noted: (1) Innocence does not become virtue until it is tested and proved by temptation. (2) If the testing is to be effective, the temptation must be of a character to appeal to the individual tested. (3) Sin is not God's but man's creation. (4) To sin is to act in accord with the baser and more selfish rather than the nobler and diviner motives. (5) An act of sin destroys a man's peace of mind and purity of thought. (6) Sin unconfessed is a sin constantly committed, and it absolutely prevents even God himself from forgiving the unrepentant sinner. (7) In keeping with the law of cause and effect, sin brings its own inevitable punishment. (8) The worst effect of sin is the severing of the normal, harmonious relations between God and the individual. (9) Most of the pains and ills of life are the result of some one's sin. (10) Man must learn in the school of pain and toil the lesson of obedience. (11) Even though guilty and unrepentant, man is still the object of God's unceasing love and care.

§ III. THE STORY OF CAIN AND ABEL

1. Occupations of Cain and Abel

Now the man called his wife's name Eve, because she was the mother of all living beings. And the man knew Eve his wife, and she conceived and bore Cain. And she also bore his brother Abel. Abel was a keeper of sheep, but Cain was a tiller of the ground.

2. Their offerings

Now in course of time it came to pass, that Cain brought some of the fruit of the ground as an offering to Jehovah. And Abel also brought some of the firstlings of his flock and of their fat. And Jehovah looked favorably upon Abel and his offering; but for Cain and his offering he had no regard.

Therefore Cain was very angry and his countenance fell. And Jehovah said to Cain, *3. Cain's anger and Jehovah's counsel*

> Why art thou angry?
> And why is thy countenance fallen?
> If thou doest well, is there not acceptance?
> But if thou doest not well,
> Does not sin crouch at the door?
> And to thee shall be its desire,
> But thou shouldst rule over it.

Then Cain said to Abel his brother, Let us go into the field. And while they were in the field, Cain rose up against Abel his brother and slew him. *4. The first murder*

And when Jehovah said to Cain, Where is Abel, thy brother? he said, I know not; am I my brother's keeper? Then he said, What hast thou done? the voice of thy brother's blood crieth to me from the ground. Now, therefore, cursed art thou; away from the ground, which hath opened its mouth to receive thy brother's blood from thy hand. Whenever thou tillest the ground, it shall no longer yield to thee its strength; a fugitive and wanderer shalt thou be on the earth. *5. Conviction and condemnation of Cain*

Then Cain said to Jehovah, My punishment is greater than I can bear. Behold, thou hast driven me out this day from the face of the ground, and from thy face shall I be hid; and I shall become a fugitive and a wanderer on the earth; and it will come to pass, that whoever finds me will slay me. *6. His complaint*

But Jehovah said to him, *7. Divine decree and sign for his protection*

> Not so! if any one kill Cain,
> Vengeance shall be taken on him sevenfold.

So Jehovah granted Cain a tribal mark, that any one finding him should not kill him. Thus Cain went out from the presence of Jehovah and dwelt in the land of Nod [Wandering].

THE STORY OF CAIN AND ABEL

I. The Background of the Story. The story of Cain has all the literary charm and picturesqueness peculiar to the Judean prophetic writers; but it is complete in itself and has no vital connection with the stories that immediately precede and follow. Its background is the settled land of Palestine, where herdsmen and tillers of the soil live side by side. The worship of Jehovah and the institution of sacrifice have already been established. The land is peopled by tribes whose vengeance Cain the murderer fears. The significance of the tribal mark is also fully recognized. The Cain of this story is evidently not the Cain of the ancient genealogy (§ IV). The identity of the name doubtless explains why the two independent traditions have been joined together in Genesis 4.

II. Origin of the Story. No Babylonian or Egyptian parallel to this story has yet been discovered. The closest analogy is found in the Roman tale of Romulus and Remus; but even here the resemblance is only in general theme. The present story probably originated in or near Palestine. In its oldest form, Cain and Abel apparently represented tribes or nations. This conclusion alone explains Cain's fear of blood revenge, for only the tribe of the murdered man would seek to slay the murderer.

Possibly the story is based on some otherwise forgotten chapter in Israel's early history. Certain scholars have sought to identify Cain with the Kenites, the nomadic tribe, which in Israel's early history shared the worship of the same tribal god. The story states, however, that Cain was not a nomad but a tiller of the soil. Cain is perhaps to be identified with the agricultural Canaanites. During the early days, after the Hebrew shepherds emerged from the wilderness, they lived side by side in Palestine with the older inhabitants of the land. The Hebrews, however, increased rapidly in numbers and possessions. Prosperity was ever regarded by the ancients as clear evidence that the Deity looked with favor upon the offerings of his people. Finally, in the days of Deborah (§ XXXVI) the Canaanites were defeated and dispossessed. Some of the survivors were absorbed by the Israelites and others became wandering traders.

Whatever be the origin of the story, the prophet who has preserved it recognized its value as an illustration of certain vital religious truths, and adapted it to his noble purpose. By treating Cain and Abel as individuals, he has given to the story that personal quality which greatly enhances its interest and value.

III. The Reason why Cain's Offering was Rejected. Both Cain and Abel brought regularly, as gifts to Jehovah, the respective products

44

of their labor. The growing prosperity of Abel and the waning fortunes of Cain soon showed that the younger of the two brothers enjoyed Jehovah's favor. This favor was not due to the nature of his offerings, but rather, as the sequel indicates, to his nobler spirit and character.

The jealousy and anger of Cain were soon revealed in his sullen, lowering countenance. Then there came to him the divine counsel, Hast thou any cause for anger? If thou doest what is right, thou wilt surely enjoy Jehovah's favor. But if not, then temptation, which thou shouldst conquer, and the consequences of sin shall ever dominate thee. The Greek and Hebrew versions of the Old Testament differ in their rendering of the closing words of Jehovah, and the original meaning is not clear. The translation given above appears to be the meaning of the Hebrew and Latin texts. This interpretation is also true to human experience, as well as to the implications of the context.

IV. **Cain's Crime and its Punishment.** But Cain was already mastered by his passions, and was therefore irresponsive to the divine voice. Luring his brother out into the open field, he treacherously murdered him.

Even to the bloody murderer Jehovah came, as to the man and woman in the garden, with a question that invited frank confession; but Cain's reply was one of denial and defiance. It also disclosed his inner motives. True to the criminal type, he repudiated all responsibility to society. Having by his deliberate act severed his connection with his fellow-men, he had made himself an outlaw. The ancient law of blood-revenge demanded the shedding of his blood. The very ground was a witness of his crime. No longer should it yield to him its richest products. Rather as a fugitive, he must wander up and down the face of the earth, ever haunted by the dread that the avenger of blood would suddenly overtake and slay him.

V. **Meaning of the Mark of Cain.** Not in contrition, but appalled by the severity of the judgment that had fallen on his guilty head, Cain asks that he may not be sent forth to a foreign land, where, according to the thought of his day, he would be beyond the pale of his God's protection. The guardian of each man in the ancient East was his tribe or clan. The knowledge that each and all the members of a tribe were pledged to avenge any wrong done to one of its number stayed many a murderous hand in the past, as it still does to-day in the life of the desert. To be deprived of the tribal protection meant that any man might with impunity slay the accursed outcast. It is this fate that Cain bewails.

Again God's mercy far surpasses that of men. Upon the cringing but unrepentant criminal, he places the tribal mark that proclaimed, as does the tattooing or method of cutting the hair among the Arabs to-day, that he was still a member and under the protection of a powerful tribe. Cain bears the mark of Jehovah's own people, who are thus under obligation, not only to spare but also to avenge in full measure any wrong done to him. The land of wandering (Nod), may be an allusion to the nomadic life of the desert or to that of the itinerant traders, who were called by the Hebrews, Canaanites.

VI. **Aim and Teachings.** As in the preceding story the prophet's main aim is to present the origin, nature, and consequences of sin. At many points it supplements the story of man's fall. Chief among the vital prophetic truths illustrated by the sad story are: (1) Mere formal worship is not necessarily acceptable to God. (2) It is the spirit and character of the offerer, not the offering, that the Lord regards. (3) Temptation comes in connection with the acts of worship, as well as in the other relations of life. (4) God patiently endeavors to point out to the offender the right way and to influence him to follow it. (5) Great crimes are committed only by men whose characters have been gradually debased by lesser sins. (6) Man is a free agent: God surrounds him with good influences, but does not remove from him the possibility of committing the most heinous crimes. (7) The man who repudiates his responsibility as his brother's keeper allies himself with Cain. (8) Guilt unconfessed cuts a man off from his fellows and makes him an outcast from society. (9) God's mercy to the guilty is infinitely greater than that of man.

§ IV. THE TRADITIONAL ORIGIN OF EARLY SEMITIC INSTITUTIONS

1. Origin of the family

Adam knew his wife and she conceived and bore a son and called his name Seth, for she said, God hath given me offspring.

2. Of worship

To Seth also was born a son, and he named him Enosh. He was the first to call on the name of Jehovah. And the man [Enosh?] knew his wife and she conceived and bore Cain, and said, I have got a male child with the help of Jehovah.

3. Of city life

Now Cain dwelt east of Eden. And Cain knew his wife, and she conceived and bore Enoch. Cain also built a city and called the city Enoch after his son's name.

46

And to Enoch was born Irad, and Irad begat Mehujael, and Mehujael begat Methushael, and Methushael begat Lamech. And Lamech took to himself two wives: the name of the one was Adah [Light], and the name of the other was Zillah [Shadow]. *4. Of polygamy*

And Adah bore Jabal [Shepherd]; he was the father of those who dwell in tents and with cattle. *5. Of nomads*

And his brother's name was Jubal [Ram's Horn]; he was the father of those who handle the harp and pipe. *6. Of musicians*

And Zillah also bore Tubal-cain [Smith]; he was the father of all those who forge copper and iron. And the sister of Tubal-cain was Naamah [Grace]. *7. Of metal workers*

And Lamech said to his wives: *8. Of blood-revenge*

> Adah and Zillah, hearken to my voice,
> Wives of Lamech give ear to my saying.
> > A man I slay for wounding me,
> > Yea, a youth for bruising me.
> > If Cain be avenged sevenfold,
> > Lamech shall be seventy and seven.

And Lamech begat a son; and he called his name Noah [Comfort], saying, This one will comfort us in our work and in the toil of our hands, because Jehovah hath cursed the ground. And Noah was the first tiller of the soil to plant a vineyard. *9. Of vine culture*

And when he drank of the wine, he became drunken, and lay uncovered within his tent. *10. Of drunkenness*

Then Canaan saw the nakedness of his father and told it outside to his two brothers. But Shem and Japheth took a garment and laid it upon both their shoulders and went backward to cover the nakedness of their father, their faces being turned away so that they did not see their father's nakedness. *11. Of Canaanite degeneracy*

When Noah awoke from his wine and learned what his youngest son had done to him, he said, *12. Of Canaanite slavery*

> Cursed be Canaan;
> May he be a servant of servants to his brothers.

13. Of the superiority of the Semites

Also he said:

> Blessed of Jehovah be Shem;
> Let Canaan also be a servant to him.
> God enlarge Japheth
> And let him dwell in the tents of Shem.
> Let Canaan also be a servant to him.

I. **Literary Form and Character.** Most primitive peoples connected the more important events in their early history with the names of certain traditional heroes. In the thought of later generations the names of these heroes represent the periods during which each lived. The tendency to join them together in genealogical tables was also common. Since they bridged the centuries and connected the past with later events, these genealogical lists were often preserved long after the stories regarding the different heroes had been forgotten. In the present narrative several traditions have been retained. Usually only the names remain. The crude form and naïve point of view of the narratives prove that they are extremely old. The song in [8] is a superb example of popular poetry. Two balanced lines of four beats each are followed by four lines, each with three measured beats or accents.

II. **Origin of the Genealogical List.** Certain names in the opening genealogical list have been identified with Babylonian originals. The Babylonian records also contain a list of ten antediluvian kings or dynasties representing a total period of four hundred and thirty-two thousand years. In the later priestly list of Genesis a definite number of years is assigned to each of the ten antediluvians. This was probably due to the influence of the older Babylonian tradition. While Genesis 4 also contains the names of ten heroes, their order is different. This disarrangement apparently resulted from the addition of the later story of Cain and Abel, which made Cain a son of the man and woman of chapter 3. It would seem that in the present case the late priestly tradition, in making Seth the first and only son of Adam, and Enosh his grandson, had preserved the original tradition (*cf.* St. O.T., I, §III) This order is confirmed by the parallel Babylonian list, in which Amelon, the Babylonian equivalent of Enosh is third and Ammenon, the equivalent of Cain is fourth.

III. **Babylonian and Phœnician Traditions Regarding the Origin of the Arts.** The origin of the early arts and institutions greatly interested the ancients. The Babylonian inscriptions state that the great gods, Ea, the lord of wisdom, and Marduk, the creator, brought culture to mankind. The Greeks attributed the discovery of fire to Prometheus. The fragmentary Phœnician traditions contain the closest parallels to the Hebrew. These trace the origin of the different arts and inventions to individual heroes.

One Phœnician story states that a son of the first man and woman built Tyre, and made huts out of the reeds, rushes and papyrus. Another son (*Ousoos*) was the first to make garments from the skins of animals, and boats from the trunks of trees. Among the descendants of the first son were also six pairs of brothers, who like the sons of Lamech, were the inventors and patrons of different arts and occupations. Their names are also significant of their professions. Thus Hunter and Fisherman developed hunting and fishing. The second pair (of whom one apparently bore the name, *Smith*) discovered the arts of working iron and of making fishing tackle, as well as of navigation, magic and divination. The third pair (of whom one was named, *Artificer*), discovered how to make bricks and roofs. From the fourth pair were descended those who make courts and enclosures to houses, and who till the soil. The fifth pair were the traditional fathers of village and pastoral life. The sixth pair discovered the use of salt. Apparently these closely parallel Phœnician and Hebrew stories come from earlier Canaanite or possibly Babylonian originals.

IV. **Interpretation of the Genealogical List.** The Northern Israelite prophetic, as well as the late priestly group of narratives, trace the revelation of the sacred name, Yahweh (or as it is commonly written Jehovah) to the days of Moses (*cf.* Ex. 6; § XXI[3]). The present early Judean prophetic narrative, however, assigns the beginning of that formal worship to the days of Enosh, the traditional grandson of the first man. While the later narrators may be more exact in their technical historical statement, the early prophets declare, with true insight, that man has worshipped God from the first, even though the theological beliefs of the primitive worshipper were crude and defective.

Cain, the artificer, was naturally regarded as the first to build a city. In the priestly list of Genesis 5, Enoch, Cain's son, and the corresponding Edoranchos in the Babylonian list, stand in the seventh place, still further confirming the conclusion that the name of Cain, which represents an advanced civilization, was originally found nearer that of Lamech than of Adam.

V. **Origin of the Enoch Tradition.** In the prophetic narrative nothing but the names of Enoch and of the three heroes that follow have been preserved. The priestly parallel of Genesis 5²⁴ adds that, *Enoch walked with God and was not, for God took him.* Like the Babylonian hero of the flood, he was believed to have been borne beyond the waters of death, there to enjoy immortality. Enoch is the Hebrew equivalent of Edoranchos, who is probably to be identified with Enmeduranki, a pre-historic king of Sippar, a city devoted to the worship of the sun god Shamash. A recently discovered tablet states that the sun god called Enmeduranki to intercourse with himself, gave him the tablet of the gods, initiated him into the secrets of heaven and earth, and taught him the art of divination (*cf.* Zimmern, *The Bab. and Hebrew Genesis*, pp. 43 *ff.*). This knowledge he transmitted to his descendants, and thus became the traditional father of an hereditary guild of Babylonian diviners.

Later Jewish thought made Enoch the one through whom the secrets of heaven and the future were revealed, as is well illustrated by the composite Book of Enoch. The earlier priestly writers purified and spiritualized the ancient story; but, apparently under the influence of the older tradition, they assigned to this Babylonian worshipper of the sun god three hundred and sixty-five years, corresponding to the number of days in the solar year.

VI. **The Lamech Stories.** To Lamech and his sons the Hebrew traditions attribute the origin of polygamy and of the three different occupations of primitive life. As with the Greeks, shepherds and musicians are closely associated. They are descended from a common mother whose name, meaning *Light* or *Dawn*, is especially appropriate; while the son of Zillah (*Shade*) is the traditional ancestor of the grimy smiths, whose services were most highly esteemed in these early days.

Unfortunately, the prophet has given us none of the popular stories regarding Naamah the gracious. Instead he has reproduced from the lips of the people the ancient song of blood-revenge, sung boastfully to his wives by the victorious warrior, probably as he returned from some victorious foray against a hostile tribe, possibly, also, as he brandished a sword forged by Tubal-cain. Its thought is, Each and every injury to myself or clan will be requited in fullest measure. "An eye for an eye and a tooth for a tooth," is at the foundation of many of the ancient laws found in the Code of Hammurabi and the Old Testament. "Do to others as they do to you" is still the law of the desert. In striking contrast to these barbarous standards are the teachings of the Hebrew prophets and Jesus.

VII. Meaning of the Earliest Tradition Regarding Noah. The story of Noah, the tiller of the soil, was originally independent of the preceding, as well as of the more familiar story of the flood. In the priestly genealogy of Genesis 5, Noah is the oldest son of Lamech, and nothing is said of his other illustrious brothers. The popular etymology of the name Noah, which really comes from a root meaning *to rest*, is characteristic of the early prophetic writers. Noah they regarded as the inaugurator of a new epoch in which the curse upon man was to be mitigated. The original object of the story was to explain the fate of the Canaanites; but the prophet who reproduced it was seeking to bring out the evils of intemperance and moral depravity. The illustration is striking and effective. Under the influence of wine the aged father is a pitiable object of warning.

A later editor, familiar with the genealogical table of Genesis 10, has here introduced into the Hebrew text the name of Ham, although the following sentences show that the original contained only that of Canaan. He is the traditional ancestor of the highly civilized Canaanites, whom the Hebrews found in possession of central Palestine. His fundamental lack of moral sense, as revealed in his attitude toward his father, is typical of that gross immorality which weakened the physical and national character of the Canaanites and ultimately proved their ruin.

Shem is the personification of the dominant Semitic peoples, and especially of the Hebrews. Japheth, as its meaning, *far extended* or *distant*, suggests, represents the trading peoples of the eastern Mediterranean, and especially the Phœnicians, with whom the early Hebrews made commercial alliances. The act of Shem and Japheth reveals a far higher moral sense, and also that filial piety which is strongly emphasized by all oriental peoples.

The curse and blessings which follow are based upon the established facts of history. Although in the form of predictions, they represent the deeper prophetic interpretation of these facts. The enslavement of the Canaanites is the inevitable result of their innate moral depravity. The Hebrews and their allies are supreme because of their superior moral ideals and character.

VIII. Aim and Teachings. As has already been noted, to explain the origin of the various arts and institutions is the common aim of all these stories. They record in the language of tradition the beginnings and development of human civilization. They are forerunners of the modern sciences of history, religion, anthropology and sociology. They emphasize that unity of the human race, the basis of which is one common Creator and Father. The concluding story also illustrates certain profoundly vital religious truths: (1) Excessive indulgence debases and disgraces even the strongest and noblest characters. (2) Innate character and thoughts will surely be revealed by acts. (3) He who is immoral and depraved, even though he may have outward culture, will surely in the end become the slave of others. (4) He whose instincts and ideals are noble and pure will become a ruler of men. (5) Blessed are the pure in heart, for they shall enjoy God's favor.

§ V. THE STORY OF THE GREAT FLOOD

1. Union between divine and human beings

Now it came to pass when men had begun to be many on the face of the ground, and daughters had been born to them, that the sons of God saw that the daughters of men were fair, and they took to themselves as wives whomsoever they chose.

2. Jehovah's disapproval

Then said Jehovah, My spirit shall not abide in man forever, inasmuch as he is only flesh; therefore his days shall be one hundred and twenty years.

3. Origin of giants

The Nephilim [giants] were on the earth in those days, for when the sons of God came in to the daughters of men, they bore children to them. These were the heroes who were famous in olden time.

4. Penalty for man's guilt

When Jehovah saw that the wickedness of man was great in the earth, and that every purpose in the thoughts of his heart was only evil continually, it was a source of regret that he had made man on the earth, and it grieved him to his heart. Therefore Jehovah said, I will destroy from the face of the ground man whom I have created, for I regret that I have made mankind.

5. Directions to make the ark

But Noah found favor in the eyes of Jehovah. Therefore he said to Noah, Make thyself an ark of cypress wood; rooms shalt thou make in the ark, and thou shalt smear it within and without with pitch. And this is the plan according to which thou shalt make it: the length of the ark shall be three hundred cubits, its breadth fifty cubits, and its height thirty cubits. A window shalt thou make for the ark, and a cubit in height shalt thou make it; and the door of the ark shalt thou set in its side. With lower, second, and third stories shalt thou make it.

THE STORY OF THE GREAT FLOOD

Later Judean Prophetic

Then Jehovah said to Noah, Enter thou and all thy house into the ark; for thee have I found righteous before me in this generation. Of all clean beasts thou shalt take to thee by sevens, male and his mate, but of the beasts that are not clean by twos, a male and his mate; and of the clean birds of the heavens, seven by seven; to keep offspring alive upon the face of the earth. For after seven days I will cause it to rain upon the earth forty days and forty nights; and every living thing that I have made will I destroy from off the face of the ground.

And Noah did according to all that Jehovah commanded him.

And it came to pass after the seven days that the waters of the flood came upon the earth. Then Noah, together with his sons and his wife, and his sons' wives, entered into the ark, because of the waters of the flood. Of clean beasts, and of beasts that

Late Priestly Version

And God said to Noah, I will establish my covenant with thee; and thou shalt enter the ark, thou, and thy sons, and thy wife, and thy sons' wives, with thee. Also of every living thing of all flesh, two of every kind shalt thou bring into the ark to keep them alive with thee; a male and a female shall they be. Of the birds after their kind, and of the cattle after their kind, of every creeping thing of the ground after its kind, two of each shall come to thee, that they may live. Take also of all food that is eaten, and gather it to thee, that it may be for food for thee and for them. **6. Command to enter the ark**

Thus did Noah; according to all that God commanded him, so did he. **7. Its execution**

And Noah was six hundred years old when the flood of waters was upon the earth. In the six hundredth year of Noah's life, in the second month, on the seventeenth day of the month, on the same day, **8. Beginning of the flood and the entrance into the ark**

All the fountains of the great deep were broken up
And the windows of heaven were opened.

On that very day Noah, and Shem and Ham and Japheth, the sons of Noah,

53

are not clean, and of birds, and of every thing that creeps upon the ground, there went in two by two to Noah into the ark, a mate and his mate, as Jehovah commanded Noah. And Jehovah shut him in.

and Noah's wife, and the three wives of his sons with them, entered into the ark, together with every beast after its kind, and all the cattle after their kind, and every creeping thing that creeps on the earth after its kind, all birds of every species. And they went in to Noah into the ark, two by two of all flesh in which is the breath of life. And those that entered, went in male and female of all flesh, as God commanded.

9. Extent and effects of the flood

And the rain was upon the earth forty days and forty nights, and the waters increased and bore up the ark, and it was lifted high above the earth. All in whose nostrils was the breath of life, of all that was on the land, died. Thus Jehovah destroyed every thing that existed upon the face of the ground, both man and animals, and creeping things, and birds of the heavens, so that they were destroyed from the earth; and Noah only was left and they that were with him in the ark.

Then the waters rose high, and increased greatly upon the earth; and the ark moved on the face of the waters. And the waters rose higher and higher over the earth, until all the high mountains that were under the whole heaven were covered. Fifteen cubits above *their* tops rose the waters, so that the mountains were completely covered. Then all flesh died that moved upon the earth, including birds, and animals, and every creeping thing that creeps upon the earth, and all mankind.

10. Cessation of the flood

But it came to pass at the end of forty days that the rain from heaven ceased, and the waters

Thus the waters rose high above the earth for a hundred and fifty days. Then God remembered Noah, and all the beasts, and all the animals that were with him in the ark; and God caused a wind to pass over the earth, so that the waters began to subside; the fountains also of the deep and the windows of heaven were closed; and at retired continually from off the land.

the end of the hundred and fifty days the waters decreased. And the ark rested on the seventeenth day of the seventh month upon the mountains of Ararat. And the waters decreased continually until the tenth month; on the first day of the tenth month were the tops of the mountains seen.

Then Noah opened the window of the ark which he had made; and he sent forth a raven, and it kept going to and fro, until the waters were dried up from off the earth. And he sent forth from him a dove to see if the waters had subsided from off the face of the ground; but the dove found no rest for the sole of its foot, and it returned to him to the ark—for the waters were on the face of the whole earth—and he stretched forth his hand and took her and brought her to him into the ark. Then he waited seven days more and again sent forth the dove from the ark. And the dove came in to him at eventide; and, lo, there was in her mouth a freshly plucked olive leaf. So Noah knew that the waters had subsided from off the earth. And he waited seven days more and sent forth the dove; but it did not return to him again. Then Noah removed the covering of the ark and looked, and behold, the face of the ground was dry.

And it came to pass in the six hundred and first year, on the first day of the first month, the waters were dried up from off the earth. And on the twenty-seventh day of the second month the earth was dry. Then God spoke to Noah, saying, Go forth from the ark, together with thy wife, and thy sons, and thy sons' wives with thee. Bring forth with thee every living thing that is with thee of all flesh, even birds and cattle, and every creeping thing that creeps on the earth; that they may swarm over the earth, and be fruitful and become numerous upon the earth. So Noah went forth and his sons, and his wife, and his sons' wives with him. Every beast, every creeping thing, and every bird, whatever moves on the earth, after their families, went forth from the ark

11. Disappearance of the flood

55

THE STORY OF THE GREAT FLOOD

12. The
divine
prom-
ise

And Noah built an altar to Jehovah, and took of every clean beast, and of every clean bird, and offered burnt-offerings on the altar. And when Jehovah smelled the pleasant odor, Jehovah said in his heart, I will never again curse the ground because of man, for the purpose of man's heart is evil from his youth; nor will I again smite every thing that lives, as I have done.

> While the earth remains,
> Seedtime and harvest,
> Cold and heat,
> Summer and winter,
> Day and night
> Shall not cease.

And God spoke to Noah and to his sons with him, saying, Behold, now I establish my covenant with you, and with your descendants after you, and with every living creature that is with you, the birds, the animals, and every beast of the earth with you of all that have gone out of the ark, even every beast of the earth. And I establish my covenant with you that all flesh shall never again be cut off by the waters of the flood, and that never again shall there be a flood to destroy the earth.

I. Literary Form of the Flood Story. The oldest Hebrew account of the flood is not altogether complete, because the final compiler of Genesis has closely blended it with the late priestly version, which he made the basis of the composite narrative. The dimensions of the ark were probably the same in both versions. To illustrate how two originally complete and variant accounts of the same event have frequently been combined in the Old Testament, and how the two independent stories can be recovered, they have been printed here in parallel columns. The composite narrative of the flood is prefaced by what was originally an independent tradition regarding the origin of the race of the Nephilim or giants. According to Numbers 13[33] they still survived in the days of the settlement of Canaan, indicating that this earlier tradition knew nothing of the flood. In its present form the story is incomplete. It has been joined to the story of the flood because it suggested one of the reasons for Jehovah's disfavor and the signal judgment which followed.

II. Origin of the Story Regarding the Sons of God and the Daughters of Men. This tale has been called an example of "unassimilated mythology." The Hebrew prophet has simply reduced to its briefest possible form the popular tradition regarding the origin of the giants, who were believed to have lived in Palestine in ancient times. As the result of a natural psychological tendency, most early peoples believed that the older races conquered by their ancestors were of gigantic stature. Herodotus states that the Egyptians were the only race that did not hold this belief. Recent excavations in Palestine have shown, however, that the early cave-dwellers, who preceded the Semitic immigrants, actually averaged only a little over five feet in height.

III. **Ancient Parallels.** The closest parallels to the story of the unions between divine and human beings come from the Persian and Greek mythology. Persian tradition states that Ahriman and his fallen angels entered into similar relations with the daughters of men. In Greek mythology the Titans are the result of such unions. In his familiar dialogues Plato says: "Do you not know that the heroes are demigods? All of them spring either from the love of a god for a mortal woman or of a mortal man for a goddess." On the basis of the ancient Hebrew narrative, later Christian thought developed the elaborate doctrine of the fall of the Satan, which Milton has idealized in his immortal cantos.

IV. **The Oldest Babylonian Story of the Flood** (cf. St. O. T. I. pp. 373–8). The biblical versions imply that the scene of the story of the flood was in the East. The method of constructing the ark was also characteristically Babylonian. The Assyrian inscriptions prove convincingly that the common Semitic tradition of the flood is of Babylonian origin. The oldest and best preserved version is found in the eleventh tablet of the great epic which begins with the account of creation. Recently discovered fragments of an older version prove that the story was current in Babylonia at least as early as 2000 B.C. A few extracts will suffice to illustrate the close parallels to the biblical version. The Babylonian Noah first narrates how the great gods determined to destroy by a flood the ancient city of Shurippak, beside the Euphrates. But, Ea, the lord of wisdom, to save his faithful worshipper, warned him:

> Man of Shurippak, son of Ubara-tutu,
> Construct a house, build a ship;
> Leave goods, look after [thy] life,
> Forsake possessions, and save [thy] life!
> Cause all kinds of living things to go up into the ship.
> The ship which thou shalt build,—
> Let its form be long;

> And its breadth shall equal its length.
> On the great deep launch it.
> I understood and said to Ea my lord:
> "Behold, my lord, what thou hast commanded
> I have reverently received and will carry out."

Then follows Ea's directions in response to the question, What answer shall I give to the city, the people, and the elders?

The next day Parnapishtim, the Babylonian Noah, began his work.

> On the fifth day I laid the frame of the ship.
> According to the plan, its sides were one hundred and twenty
>   cubits high.
> The border of its roof was likewise one hundred and twenty
>   cubits in breadth;
> I traced out its form, I marked it off,
> I built six decks on it,
> Thus I divided it into seven stories,
> Its interior I divided into nine compartments.
> Plugs [to keep out] the water I drove in from within.
> I provided a rudder-pole and supplied what was necessary;
> Six sars of pitch I poured over the outside,
> Three sars of bitumen I poured over the inside.

He then goes on to recount in detail the supply of provisions—oil, wine, oxen, and lambs—which he took on board, and to tell of the great feast with which he celebrated the completion of his work.

After taking on all his possessions of gold and silver and living creatures, he adds:

> I brought on board my family and household,
> Cattle of the field, beasts of the field, the craftsmen,
> All of them I brought on board.
> Shamash had appointed a time [saying],
> "When the lord of darkness at evening shall send down a de-
>   structive rain,
> Then enter into the ship and close the door."

When the appointed time came, he entered the ship and closed the door and entrusted the ship to his captain.   The description of the tempest that follows is especially striking:

> When the first light of dawn shone forth,
> There rose from the horizon a dark cloud, within which Adad
>   thundered,
> Nabu and Marduk marched at the front,
> The heralds passed over mountains and land;
> Nergal tore out the ship's mast,
> Ninib advanced, following up the attack,
> The spirits of earth raised torches,
> With their sheen they lighted up the world.
> Adad's tempest reached to heaven,
> And all light was changed to darkness.

Even the gods are terrified and "cowered like dogs at the edge of the heavens,"

> The gods, bowed down, sat there weeping
> Close pressed together were their lips.
> For six days and nights
> Wind, flood and storm overwhelmed the land.
> But when the seventh day arrived there was an abatement of
>   the storm, the flood and the tempest,
> Which (like a host) had contended;
> The sea became calm, the tempestuous wind was still, the flood
>   ceased.

> Then I looked for the race of mortals, but every voice was
>   hushed,
> And all mankind had been turned to clay.
> As soon as the light of day appeared, I prayed
> I opened a hole so as to let the light fall upon my cheeks,
> I bowed down and sat there weeping,
> Tears flowed down my cheeks.

> I looked in all directions, toward the border of the sea;
> After twenty-four hours an island rose up,
> The ship approached the mountain Nisir,
> The mountain Nisir caught the ship and held it fast.
> So also during the five succeeding days, it held fast the ship.

THE STORY OF THE GREAT FLOOD

When the seventh day arrived,
I sent forth a dove and let it loose,
The dove went forth, but came back;
Because it found no resting-place, it returned:
Then I sent forth a swallow, but it came back;
Because it found no resting-place, it returned.
Then I sent forth a raven and let it loose.
The raven went forth and saw that the waters had decreased
It fed, it waded, it croaked, but did not return.

Then I sent forth everything in all directions, and offered a sacrifice,
I made an offering of incense on the highest peak of the mountain.
Seven and seven bowls I placed there,
And over them, I poured out calamus, cedar wood and fragrant herbs.
The gods inhaled the odor,
The gods inhaled the sweet odor,
The gods gathered like flies above the sacrifice.

The god Bel, who had been especially active in causing the flood, was enraged to find that any man had escaped destruction. Ea, however, placated him by urging that it was wrong to destroy all mankind, righteous and evil alike.

Then Bel took his counsel,
And went on board the ship,
Seized my hand and led me up,
Led up my wife also and had her kneel beside me,
Touched our shoulders, stepped between us and blessed us
"Formerly Parnapishtim was human;
But now Parnapishtim and his wife shall be gods like us,
And Parnapishtim shall dwell in the distance, at the confluence of the streams."
Then they took me and made me dwell in the distance, at the confluences of the streams.

V. Similarity Between the Oldest Babylonian and the Oldest Hebrew Accounts. The parallels between this version of the Babylonian story recorded in the tablets from the great Assyrian library, founded in the middle of the eighth century B.C., and the later Judean prophetic account, current in Judea during the same century, are exceedingly close. In each a special revelation is given to the hero of the story. Animals, as well as people, are taken into the ark; the flood is caused by an extraordinary downpour of rain; seven is the favorite number; all living things on the earth are destroyed; birds are sent out three times before it is found that the waters have subsided. After disembarking, the hero of the flood offers a sacrifice, the sweet savor of which wins divine favor and the assurance that mankind will never again be destroyed by a great flood. These analogies are too many, and too striking, to be explained as mere coincidences.

VI. **The Later Babylonian Version.** The Chaldean priest Berossus, quoted by Eusebius, has preserved a later version of the same Babylonian story. Xisuthros, the hero, was the last of the ten ancient Babylonian kings. To him Kronos appeared in a dream and informed him that at a certain date men would be destroyed by a flood. He commanded him to bring all the sacred writings and bury them at the city of Sippar, and then to build a ship and go aboard it with all his possessions and nearest friends. He was also to provide food and drink, and take with him all kinds of quadrupeds and birds. If he was asked where he was going, he was to say, To petition the gods to bless mankind.

Accordingly he obeyed, and built a ship fifteen stadia long and two in width, brought all aboard as commanded, including his wife, children, nearest friends, and the pilot. When the flood began to recede, he sent out a bird, but this found no place to rest, and so returned to the ship. After some days he sent forth another bird. This returned, but with mud on its feet. When he sent forth the third it returned not. Then he knew that land had emerged, and, taking off the cover of the ship, he found that it had stranded on a mountain of Armenia.

After he had disembarked with his wife, daughter, and pilot, he kissed the earth, built an altar, made an offering to the gods, and then disappeared. When he did not return, the others set out to find him, calling his name. They never saw him again, but a voice from heaven commanded them to fear the gods, since it was because of his reverence for the gods that Xisuthros had been taken to dwell with them. The same honor was also granted to his wife, daughter and the pilot.

VII. **Similarity and Contrast Between the Later Babylonian and Hebrew Versions.** This later version illustrates the variations that the tradition had undergone as the result of transmission during

three or four centuries among a literary people like the Babylonians. It is also noteworthy that the later biblical version is most closely parallel to this later Babylonian story. In both the hero was the tenth in his line and was famous for his piety; the destruction was universal; and the ark was stranded on a mountain in Armenia, which is identified in the later biblical version with Mount Ararat. These striking analogies suggest, as do the stories of the creation, that the Jewish priests in Babylonia were influenced by the version of the tradition which they then found current in the land of the exile.

The variations between the Babylonian and biblical versions of the story are equally instructive, for they definitely illustrate the influence of transmission among the Hebrews and the nature of the work of Israel's inspired prophets and priests. Instead of many rival deities, one God rules supreme over mankind and the universe. No traces remain of the grotesque heathen elements in the Babylonian versions, such as the deception of mankind, the conflicts between the gods, and their fright at the extent of the flood. The only possible exception is the statement that Jehovah smelled the sweet savor of the sacrifice. Even here the biblical version is far removed from the gross picture of the gods gathered like flies above the sacrifice. The biblical versions alone give a just cause for the great judgment, and reveal a benign rather than a capricious purpose behind even the seeming calamities of human history. In the hands of Israel's teachers the ancient story has received a universal and ethical interpretation.

VIII. **History of the Common Semitic Flood Story.** In the light of these different versions the history of the tradition may be tentatively traced. It may have originally been suggested simply by the annual floods and fogs which inundate the Tigris-Euphrates valley. More probably, as the earliest Babylonian story indicates, it was based on the memory of a great local inundation, caused perhaps by a hurricane sweeping up from the Persian Gulf at the time of the spring floods, inundating not only the city of Surippak, but the entire Euphrates valley. Possibly it may have been due to a sinking of the land. Apparently, the only survivors were a few who escaped in a ship which was driven by the winds until it grounded on the low hills north of Babylonia. The mythological elements would naturally be added later, and in time the tradition would grow until it became, as in the later biblical versions, a universal destruction. In this connection it is suggestive that the latest biblical version, the priestly, represents the flood as lasting a full year instead of sixty-eight days (as in the earlier), and as covering the tops or the highest mountains, that is rising to a depth of fully five miles above the ordinary level of the sea.

IX. Transmission of the Babylonian Story to the Hebrews. The channels through which the Babylonian tradition could find its way to Palestine were many. Possibly it was brought from Mesopotamia by the Aramean ancestors of the Hebrews. It may have been received through the Canaanites, who were in possession of many Babylonian traditions when the Hebrews entered the land. The close analogies between the Judean prophetic version and the one current at the same time in Assyria suggest that the conquering armies of the great empire brought it, together with the many other religious ideas and institutions, which gained acceptance in Judah during the reign of Ahaz and especially that of Manasseh. If so, this would explain why the flood story was not found in the early, but only in the later, Judean prophetic narratives.

X. Flood Stories Among Other Peoples. Flood stories in variant forms are found among most primitive peoples (*cf.* Hastings' D. B., article, *Flood*). The only races who do not have them are those living in Africa and central and eastern Asia. The resemblances between these different stories seem to be due to similar local causes and psychological tendencies, rather than to descent from a common tradition. Often the original basis of the story was a great inundation or the subsidence of large areas of land. Sometimes it was suggested by the recurring floods of springtime. Among island and coastland peoples, the tradition was based on the fact that their ancestors came on boats over the great sea. The discovery of geological evidence that the sea had once covered elevated areas also fostered the growth of the tradition.

XI. Meaning of the Story Concerning the Sons of God. In the light of its many parallels the meaning of the biblical narrative is clear. The opening story takes us back to the misty past to which was traced all that was extraordinary. It reflects the primitive belief that the gods had bodily forms and passions, and that the demi-gods, descended from them, entered into marital relations with humankind. In the popular thought of the prophet's day, the giants, who figured in their ancient traditions, were believed to be the offspring of such unions. The effect of myths like these was not wholesome. In Greek mythology the example of the gods was often far from moral. The text is obscure, but it was apparently to correct this immoral implication that the prophet introduced the ancient story. Since man has shown his frailty by thus going astray, God's life-giving spirit will not always remain in him to keep him alive. Rather the length of his life shall be limited to one hundred and twenty years.

XII. Interpretation of the Oldest Biblical Story. When Jehovah found that the ideals and aims of mankind were base, he realized with sorrow that his hopes and benign provisions for the development and happiness of humanity were being ruined by human sin. Hence, nothing remained but to destroy the evil, and begin again with the noblest type of man. Noah, who by his character and acts had won Jehovah's favor, was selected for the new beginning.

Accordingly he was instructed to make a box-like boat, about four hundred and fifty feet long, seventy-five feet broad, and forty-five feet high. Like the Babylonian houses and barges, it was to be made water-tight by means of bitumen. It was apparently to be lighted by an aperture about eighteen inches in height, running along under the projecting roof. Being smaller than the Babylonian ship, it had only three instead of seven stories.

When the ark was completed, Noah was instructed to enter it with his household, and a pair of each of the species of animals and birds regarded by the later Hebrew law as unclean. Of the clean animals and birds seven were to be taken, that ample provision might thus be made for the needs of sacrifice. In the parallel priestly version two of each species suffice, for the later priests taught that sacrifice began with Moses.

After Noah had complied with the divine command, the rain poured down for forty days until all living things on the land were destroyed. Noah, and those with him, alone survived to perpetuate the original work of creation. When, at the end of the forty (in the late priestly version, one hundred and fifty) days the rain ceased and the waters began to subside, Noah sent forth a raven, which because of its predatory habits, did not return. The statement that he waited seven days before sending out the dove a second time implies that the compiler, in combining the two versions, has left out the fact that Noah also waited seven days before he first sent out the dove. The Babylonian order—a dove, a swallow, and then a raven—is the more natural, as well as the older; but nothing could surpass the picturesqueness of the Hebrew prophetic narrative, especially the picture of the dove returning to the anxious waiters at eventide with the freshly plucked olive leaf in her bill.

The selection of Noah to inaugurate a new era did not prove a mistake. His first act, on emerging from the ark, was to express his thanksgiving and adoration by sacrifice. A huge holocaust, consisting of victims of every species of clean beast and bird, was offered. As the placating savor of this offering, that symbolized gratitude and devotion, rose to heaven, Jehovah's promise was given that he would never again be led by man's evil propensities to visit universal judgment upon the earth.

XIII. Aim and Teachings. The late priestly story of the flood culminates in the new covenant, sealed by the rainbow, in accordance with which God promised never again to destroy mankind by a flood. He also renewed man's commission to rule over all living things, and permitted him to eat animal as well as vegetable food, provided only he abstained from eating the blood. The prophetic version likewise closes with a promise of Jehovah's mercy and care, but its primary aim is spiritual and ethical, not legal. It emphasizes, as do the preceding stories, the terrible and inevitable consequences of human sin and the greatness of God's goodness.

Among the more important truths illustrated by the ancient story in its prophetic form are: (1) Man's freedom and responsibility. Even though it was his supreme desire, Jehovah could not make men virtuous. (2) The ultimate aim of creation is the moral and spiritual evolution of man. (3) Evil men and evil acts thwart the divine purpose. (4) In the divine economy of the universe, men or nations, or generations, that thus thwart God's purpose, have no permanent title to life. (5) Righteousness delivereth a man or a nation. (6) The worship and devotion of mankind are pleasing to God. (7) God is eager to surround men with all that is conducive to their highest development and happiness.

§ VI. THE TRADITIONAL ORIGIN OF THE NATIONS

Now the whole earth was of one language and of one speech. And it came to pass as they journeyed from the east that they found a plain in the land of Shinar [Babylonia], and dwelt there. Then said they one to another, Come, let us make bricks and burn them thoroughly. And they had brick for stone and bitumen for mortar. *1. Original unity of the race*

They also said, Come, let us build us a city and a tower, with its top in the sky; thus let us make ourselves a name, so that we may not be scattered abroad upon the face of the whole earth. But Jehovah came down to see the city and the tower, which the children of men had built. *2. Building a city and tower*

Then Jehovah said, Behold they are one people and they all have one language; and this is the beginning of their achievement, but henceforth nothing, which they purpose to *3. Jehovah's disapproval* do, will be too difficult for them. Come, let us go down and there confound their language, that they may not understand one another's speech.

4. Origin of different ent races

So Jehovah scattered them abroad from thence upon the face of all the earth; and they ceased building the city. Therefore they called its name Babel [Confusion], because there Jehovah confounded the language of the whole earth, and there Jehovah scattered them over the face of the whole earth.

5. Sons of Noah

And the sons of Noah, who went forth from the ark, were Shem, Ham, and Japheth. These three were the sons of Noah, and to them were sons born after the flood, and of these was the whole earth overspread. And Ham was the father of Cush, Mizraim [Egypt], and Canaan.

6. Eastern peoples

And Cush begat Nimrod; he began to be a mighty one in the earth. He was a mighty hunter before Jehovah; therefore it is said, Like Nimrod, a mighty hunter before Jehovah. And the beginning of his kingdom was Babel, Erech, Accad, and Calneh, in the land of Shinar. Out of that land he went forth into Assyria and built Nineveh, Rehoboth-Ir, Calah, Resen, between Nineveh and Calah (that is the great city).

7. Southern peoples

And Mizraim begat Ludim, Anamim, Lehabim, Naphtuhim, Pathrusim, Casluhim, and Caphtorim (whence went forth the Philistines).

8. Palestinian peoples

And Canaan begat Sidon, his first-born, and Heth. And afterward the families of the Canaanite were spread abroad, so that the boundary of the Canaanites was from Sidon, as far as Gerar (to Gaza), *and* as far as Sodom and Gomorrah and Admah and Zeboim, to Lasha.

9. Arabian ancestors and kinsmen of the Hebrews

And children were also born to Shem, the father of all the children of Eber, the elder brother of Japheth. And Arpachshad begat Shelah, and Shelah begat Eber. And to Eber were born two sons: the name of the one was Peleg [Division], for in his days was the earth divided; and his brother's name was Joktan. And Joktan begat Almodad, Sheleph, Hazarmaveth, Jerah, Hadoram, Uzal, Diklah, Obal, Abimael, Sheba, Ophir, Havilah, and Jobab; all these were the sons of Joktan. And their dwelling place was from Mesha, as far as Sephar, the mountain of the East.

And Peleg begat Reu, and Reu begat Serug, and Serug begat Nahor, and Nahor begat Terah. And Terah begat Abraham, Nahor, and Haran; and Haran begat Lot.

I. The Two Explanations of the Origin of Languages and Races.

These narratives contain two distinct explanations of the origin of the different languages and races. The older is a simple story in the style of the early Judean historians. The other is what purports to be a genealogical list, but is in reality a table of the nations known to the Hebrews in the period just before the Babylonian exile. It is the immediate sequel of the later Judean prophetic account of the flood and clearly comes from the same source.

The genealogical table in its final form in Genesis is supplemented by names from a later priestly table. The sons of Japheth, the distant northwestern and western peoples living in Asia Minor and Greece, the Phœnician colonies skirting the Mediterranean, and the Elamites and the Arameans, are thus added. These are the nations with whom the Israelites became acquainted during and after the period of the exile. The principle of arrangement is nominally ethnological, but in reality it is also geographical, and from the point of view of Israel. The nations not closely related to the Israelites are given first, then their nearer relatives, the Canaanites, and last of all their Aramean ancestors and Arabian kinsmen.

II. Origin of the Story of the Tower of Babel.

The background of the story of the Tower of Babel is Babylonia, and the tradition was doubtless inherited by the Hebrews from their Semitic ancestors. It is probable that it originated outside Babylonia, for a Babylonian writer would not have stopped to explain that the building material was brick and that bitumen was used for mortar. He would have known that the lofty mound, about which the tradition centred, was not reared in rebellion, but as a temple site in devotion to the service of the gods. He would also have known that the true derivation of the word Babylon is *Bab-il, Gate of God*. The popular derivation given in the story is probably from the Aramaic word *babil, confusion*. All these indications suggest that the tradition was handed down to the Hebrews from their Aramean forefathers, who lived near and yet outside Babylonia.

The Tower of Babel, which aroused the wonderment of the desert passers-by, and probably gave rise to the tradition, may have been the *zikkurat*, or pyramid-like mound of earth, on the west of the Euphrates, now known as *Birs Nimroud*. It is the foundation of the great temple of Êzida in Borsippa, the western suburb of Babylon. Nebuchadrezzar states in one of his inscriptions that it had been partially built by an earlier king, but its top had not been set up, and it had fallen into disrepair. Nebuchadrezzar himself restored it.

The other possible site is the mound of Babil, on the east of the Euphrates in the ruins of Babylon itself. It probably represents the remains of the great temple of Marduk, with its huge pyramid-like foundation. Either of these imposing ruins would have profoundly impressed all passers-by. The fact that the mound of *Birs Nimroud* early gave the impression of incompleteness favors on the whole its identification as the original Tower of Babel. Also at the basis of the tradition is the popular memory of the greatness of the early Babylonian empire, with its capital at Babylon. It was natural that the same centre should be regarded, as the point from which the human race dispersed over the earth. The popular explanation of the motive for building the tower recalls the Greek tradition of the attempt of the Titans to mount up into heaven.

In the prophetic table of the nations, Noah, with his three sons, Shem, Ham and Japheth, corresponds to Hellen of early Greek tradition, whose three sons, Æolus, Dorus, and Ion, were the ancestors of the three great branches of the Hellenic race.

III. **Meaning of the Story of the Tower of Babel.** Like the narrative of the sons of God and the daughters of men (§ V) the story of the Tower of Babel is placed in the dim, misty age of tradition. The land of Shinar is the early Hebrew name for Babylonia (*cf.* 10¹⁰ 14¹· ⁹ Is. 11¹¹ Zech. 5¹¹ Dan. 1²). It may be a variation of the old Babylonian name *Shumer*. On the level plain of Babylonia any elevation seemed lofty by contrast. The great mounds, which the Babylonians reared with infinite toil to be the foundations of their temples, still stand as monuments of human achievement. In the extent of its ruins Babylon, even after thousands of years, is impressive. The chief impression, however, that the ruins of the ancient mounds made on the mind of the Semites who viewed them from afar, was that the spirit and purpose which prompted their builders were sinful. They were symbols of the pride and self-sufficiency of early man and of God's destructive judgment. The different languages, which constituted a troublesome barrier between races and nations, were also regarded as a punishment for some sin of their primitive ancestors. The very name of Babylon was associated in the mind of ancient Arameans and Hebrews with the similar word meaning *confusion*. All these varied elements have evidently entered into this story.

The point of view and conception of God are those of primitive men. "Let us go down" may be a remnant of the old polytheistic form of the tradition. Possibly the expression is used, as in Genesis 3^{22}, because the Deity is thought of as standing at the head of the divine hierarchy, even as he is pictured in the prologue to the book of Job. The popular explanations of the ruined tower, of the derivation of the word Babylon, and of the origin of languages are supported by neither history nor philology. It is rather the deeper religious principles that underlie the story in its Hebrew form that have an abiding value. The unity of the entire human race and the universal fatherhood of God were vital facts which other nations were very slow to perceive.

IV. The Hamitic Races. In the later Judean prophetic table, which explains the origin of the various nations by descent from the different sons of Noah, Ham stands as the ancestor of the three peoples who developed the earliest civilizations: the Babylonians, the Egyptians and the Canaanites. The derivation of the word Ham is not certain. It may be from the Semitic root meaning *hot* or *burned*, or from the native designation for Egypt which comes from *ḳam*, meaning *black*. In Psalms 78^{51} $105^{23, 27}$ and 106^{22} it refers simply to the Egyptians.

In the parallel priestly list, and usually in the Old Testament, Cush refers to the Ethiopians; but here Cush apparently stands for the Kassites (Babylonian, *Kashshu*), who from their home east of the Tigris came down and conquered and ruled over the lower Tigris-Euphrates valley for many centuries (*cf.* Introd., II^{XII}). They were of non-Semitic origin, but the memory of their political supremacy evidently led the Hebrews to regard them as the people from whom were descended the founders of the ancient Babylonian and Assyrian cities and empires.

V. Nimrod the Mighty Hunter. The identification of Nimrod is still uncertain. The statement that he was a son of Cush favors the conclusion held by some, that he is Nazimurudash, one of the later Kassite kings, whose achievements may have given him this prominent place in Hebrew tradition. The reference to Nimrod's reputation as a mighty hunter has suggested that he is to be identified with Gilgamesh, the mythological hero of the great Babylonian epic, in which are found the stories of creation and deluge. In this epic he is depicted as a famous hunter, and many of his feats in slaying dangerous wild beasts are recounted. Tradition also states that he delivered Babylonia from the rule of the Elamites. Erech, mentioned as one of the four Babylonian cities over which Nimrod first held sway, was, according to the Babylonian epic, the city of Gilgamesh. The name of Nimrudu has not yet been found on the monuments of Babylonia and Assyria, so that this identification still remains only an exceedingly plausible conjecture. Evidently the Hebrew traditions regarding Nimrod were much more detailed than the extract given by the biblical narrator. His object was simply to explain the origin and meaning of the popular proverb, *Like Nimrod, a mighty hunter before Jehovah.*

VI. The Old Babylonian and Assyrian Empires. The testimony of the monuments regarding the history of the great empires of Babylonia and Assyria has already been given in the Introduction (chap. II). Erech is the Babylonian Uruk on the southern bank of the lower Euphrates. Accad (Babylonian, *Akkad*) is mentioned in an inscription of the twelfth century B.C. as a city, as well as the name of the district which figured in the old Babylonian title, *King of Shumer and Akkad.* It was somewhere in northern Babylonia. Calneh has not yet been identified.

Although Assyria developed much later than Babylonia (Introd. II[XII]), in the biblical tradition their growth is represented as almost contemporary. The statement is true, however, that Assyria was an offspring of the older Semitic state. The old Assyrian capital Asshur (the present *Kal'at Sherghat*, sixty miles south of Nineveh) is not mentioned. The later capitals, Calah, situated at the point where the upper Zab flows into the Tigris, and Nineveh, eighteen miles further up the Tigris, were the cities best known to the Hebrews in the age when the present table took form. Sennacherib, in the latter part of the eighth century B.C. first made Nineveh the permanent capital of the empire. Rehoboth-Ir means *broad places of a city*, and is apparently the Hebrew equivalent of the Assyrian *rebit Nina*, the designation of the northern suburbs of Nineveh. Resen has not yet been identified, but from the description it would seem to have been a southern suburb of Nineveh, connecting the two capitals, so that in the mind of the biblical writer, they, with their outlying towns, are regarded as a single great city.

VII. The Egyptians. Mizraim (literally, *the two Egypts*, probably including upper and lower Egypt) is the usual Hebrew designation of the land of the Nile. The "sons" of Egypt are the southern peoples known to the Hebrews through war and commerce. The Ludim appear in the days of Jeremiah and Ezekiel as archers in the Egyptian army (*cf.* Jer. 16[19] Ezek. 27[10] 30[5]). Their home was probably on the border of Egypt. The Anamim, Naphtuhim, and Casluhim have not been identified. The Lehabim are probably the Libyans who lived to the east of Egypt. The Pathrusim are the inhabitants of Pathros, the southland of upper Egypt. The Caphtorim are the people of Caphtor, regarded by the Hebrews as the homeland of the Philistines (*cf.* Am. 9⁷ Dt. 2²³ Jer. 47⁴). Caphtor is probably to be identified with the Egyptian *Kefto*, the name of a people living originally in Cilicia and Cyprus.

VIII. **The Canaanite Races.** The "sons" of Canaan are the peoples whom the Hebrews found in possession of Palestine. That the present list is an ethnological rather than a genealogical table is illustrated by the fact that the city of Sidon is called the first-born of Canaan. Sidon, being the oldest important Phœnician city, here represents the Phœnician branch of the Canaanite race. Heth is the biblical name of the great Hittite nation that held northern Syria in the centuries preceding the advent of the Hebrews. Although their racial origin is still in doubt, it is clear that there was in reality no close relationship between them and the Canaanites. The author probably had in mind the few survivors of the earlier race. These had been so thoroughly assimilated by the Canaanite races of Palestine that a later scribe has at this point added in the Hebrew a list of the local tribes inhabiting Palestine. The original table, however, simply defined the territory occupied by the Canaanites living outside Phœnicia. It extended southward from Sidon along the shore to Gerar, southeast of Gaza. Its eastern boundary was the line extending from Sodom and the neighboring cities, probably at the south of the Dead Sea, to Lasha, which may be but a scribal error for Laish or Dan (§ XXXIV), at the northern end of the Jordan valley.

IX. **The Hebrews and their Arabian Kinsmen.** Shem means *name* and his "sons" are the ancestors and tribes closely related to the people of name or renown, the Hebrews. Eber is here not only the eponymous ancestor of the Hebrews but also of certain other Arabian tribes. The genealogy of his eldest son Peleg is reserved to the last, for it introduces the immediate forefathers of the Hebrews. The author apparently finds in the name Peleg, which means *division,* an allusion to the division of the human race into different races, as recorded in the story of the Tower of Babel. From the other brother, Joktan, are descended thirteen tribes living in southern Arabia. Some of them can be identified. Sheleph is a place in the province of Yeman, still bearing the corresponding Arab name. Hazarmaveth is the modern district of *Hadramaut,* east of Aden and bordering on the Indian Ocean. According to the Arabs, Uzal is the ancient name of the present capital of Yeman. Sheba is the designation of a rich commercial people living in southwestern Arabia. Their inscriptions and the ruins of their temples and cities testify to their advanced civilization. Through the medium of trade it frequently touched that of the Hebrews. Ophir was perhaps a seaport on the east coast of Arabia through which the products of India reached the Semitic world, or else it is to be identified with *Abhira* at the mouth of the Indus (*cf*. § LVIII). Havilah was somewhere in central or northeastern Arabia. The territory of these different peoples appears to have extended from the bounds of the central Arabian tribe of Massa to the south coast of Arabia. The mountain of the east is probably the great frankincense mountains which extend east from the modern *Daphar*.

Only the late priestly version preserves the list of the immediate ancestors of the Hebrews, but it completes the genealogical connection between the list of Israel's neighbors and the forefathers of the chosen race. Some of the names in the list may be identified as tribal or place names. Serug is a city and district about thirty-eight miles west of Haran, mentioned in the Assyrian inscriptions and by the Arabic writers of the Middle Ages. *Til-Nahiri*, a place near Sarugi, may represent a survival of the name Nahor. These identifications confirm the testimony of the biblical narratives that the Aramean ancestors of the Hebrews came from the region in western Mesopotamia, lying to the east of the upper Euphrates.

X. **Aim and Teachings.** The chief aim is to trace the origin of the different races and to indicate Israel's place in the great family of the nations. The broader Semitic background of Hebrew history, and the vital connection between Israel's life and the powerful civilizations that preceded and influenced it are also suggested. In its origin Israel was not apart from, but rather a part of, the ancient Semitic world, and only in its true setting can its unique history be understood. While their ethnological knowledge was necessarily limited, the early Hebrews were deeply interested in their neighbors. This interest stands in striking contrast to the narrow attitude of most ancient peoples, who classified all outside their race as barbarians. The fundamental unity of all peoples and races is here assumed and concretely set forth. The basis of this unity is the common rule and fatherhood of one God. All the different nations are but different branches of the same great family. All men are, therefore, brothers. While nothing is here said of Israel's divine mission to the world, the essential foundations are thus laid for that great prophetic doctrine which gradually dawned upon the race.

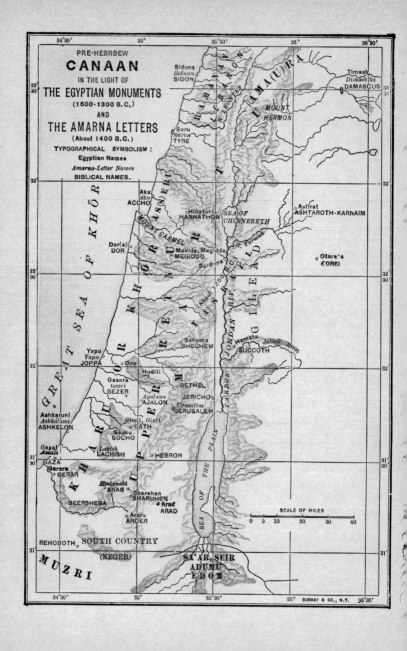

PRE-HEBREW
CANAAN
IN THE LIGHT OF
THE EGYPTIAN MONUMENTS
(1600-1300 B.C.)
AND
THE AMARNA LETTERS
(About 1400 B.C.)

TYPOGRAPHICAL SYMBOLISM:
Egyptian Names
Amarna-Letter Names
BIBLICAL NAMES.

SCALE OF MILES

0 5 10   20   30   40

BORNAY & CO., N.Y.

THE TRADITIONAL ANCESTORS OF THE HEBREWS

§ VII. ABRAHAM'S CALL AND SETTLEMENT IN CANAAN

Now Haran died before his father Terah in the land of his nativity. And Abraham and Nahor took for themselves wives. The name of Abraham's wife was Sarah, and the name of Nahor's wife, Milcah, the daughter of Haran, the father of Milcah and Jiscah.

<small>1. History of the house of Terah</small>

And Jehovah said to Abraham, Go forth from thy country, and from thy kindred, and from thy father's house, to the land that I will show thee, that I may make of thee a great nation; and I will surely bless thee, and make thy name great, so that thou shalt be a blessing. I will also bless them that bless thee, and him that curseth thee will I curse, so that all the families of the earth shall ask for themselves a blessing like thine own. So Abraham went forth, as Jehovah had commanded him, and Lot went with him.

<small>2. Abraham's call and departure for Canaan</small>

Then Abraham passed through the land to the district of Shechem, to the oak of Moreh [oracular oak or terebinth]. And the Canaanites were then in the land. And Jehovah revealed himself to Abraham, saying, To thy descendants will I give this land; and there he built an altar to Jehovah, who had revealed himself to him. And he removed thence to the mountain on the east of Bethel, and pitched his tent, having Bethel on the west, and Ai on the east. And there he built an altar to Jehovah and called upon the name of Jehovah.

<small>3. Experiences in Canaan</small>

Now Abraham was very rich in cattle, in silver, and in gold. And Lot also, who went with Abraham, had flocks and herds and tents, so that they could not dwell together. And when there was a strife between the herdsmen of Abraham's cattle and the herdsmen of Lot's cattle, Abraham said to Lot, Let there be no strife, I pray you, between me and you, and between my herdsmen and your herdsmen; for we are kinsmen. Is not the whole land before you? separate yourself, I pray you, from me. If you go to the

<small>4. Reason for the separation from Lot</small>

73

left, then I will go to the right; or if you go to the right, then I will go to the left.

5. Lot's choice Then Lot lifted up his eyes, and beheld all the Plain of the Jordan that it was well watered everywhere (before Jehovah destroyed Sodom and Gomorrah), like the garden of Jehovah, as far as Zoar. So Lot chose for himself all the Plain of the Jordan; and Lot journeyed east; and dwelt in the cities of the Plain, and moved his tent as far as Sodom. And the men of Sodom were exceedingly wicked and sinners against Jehovah.

6. Abraham at Mamre But Abraham moved his tent and came and dwelt in the plain of Mamre, which is in Hebron.

I. Literary Form of the Abraham Stories. The eleventh chapter of Genesis marks the transition from the common Semitic traditions to the stories regarding the traditional forefathers of the Hebrews. Throughout the rest of Genesis the narratives are chiefly personal and biographical. Many extracts are introduced from the late priestly history. In chapter 14 is found what appears to be a late Jewish tale, based on the memory of an invasion of the eastern kings far back in the days of Hammurabi (cf. Introd., II$^{x, xi}$); but most of the Abraham stories are taken from the early prophetic narratives. Each of these stories is, as a rule, a complete literary unit, bringing out like a flash-light picture some trait or incident in the life of the patriarch. Together they give an exceedingly life-like and majestic portrait of the character who stands at the beginning of Hebrew history.

II. Origin of the Stories. Except in the later Jewish story of Genesis 14, the setting and atmosphere of the Abraham stories are those of the wilderness, and of that peculiar type of nomadic life which may be studied to-day among the Bedouin tribes that wander up and down in the Arabian desert. The point of view and interest are also those of the nomad. It is probable that these stories were originally retold from generation to generation among the early Hebrews. At the same time it is evident that, like those of Babylonian or Aramean or Canaanite origin in §§ I–VI, they have been transformed and idealized. The idealization of Abraham's character was almost inevitable, since he was the revered forefather of the Hebrew race. Analogies might be cited from almost every chapter of human history; Sargon, Menes, Romulus and King Arthur are only a few of many classic examples.

In these marvellous stories associated with Abraham are voiced the

74

later hopes and ideals of the Hebrew race. Those aspirations for widely extended territory, teeming population, and great prosperity, which were realized in full measure in the days of David and Solomon, are here embodied in divine promises to Israel's traditional forefather. It was thus that the prophetic historians effectively taught the great truth that Israel's later glories were but the realization of God's gracious and eternal purpose.

III. **Abraham in Later Jewish Traditions.** The Abraham of later Jewish traditions is represented, sometimes as having been borne to heaven on a fiery chariot, there to receive to his bosom the faithful of his race, sometimes as the ardent foe of idolatry, and sometimes as the valiant warrior before whose sword even the great city of Damascus fell. In Genesis 14 he is a chivalrous warrior, as generous as he is brave and energetic, who, with his few followers, defeats the armies of Babylonia and Elam. The Abraham of the priestly historians is a faithful observer of the law through whom the covenant with his race, sealed by the rite of circumcision, is established; but the Abraham of the early prophets is the embodiment of their noblest ideals of faith and character.

IV. **The Prophetic Element.** It can never be absolutely decided, and fortunately it makes little difference how far these Old Testament stories are exact records of the experiences of a certain early nomadic chieftain. The real father of the faithful, the Abraham whose deeds and character and faith are perennial sources of inspiration to-day, as in the past, lived in the glowing hearts of Israel's early prophets. It is not strange that they have embodied in his biography many later beliefs and experiences of their race. Local traditions also traced to him the origin of several sacred places. Institutions which went back beyond the days of Moses were naturally associated with him or else with Isaac or Jacob. Thus the original kernel of tradition, under the varied national, institutional, and prophetic influences, gradually assumed its present form. Hence, these narratives are more than mere history: they are prophetic homilies, whose theme and illustrations are found in the past rather than the present or the future.

V. **The Two Names.** The final compiler of Genesis, in accord with the late priestly tradition of the covenant recorded in the seventeenth chapter, has designated the patriarch as *Abram* up to this point, and *Abraham* in the succeeding passages. In view of these late, arbitrary changes, it is impossible to determine which of the two forms of the name was used originally in the prophetic narratives. The same baffling difficulty also makes it impossible to prove or disprove the alluring hypothesis that certain of the traditions related originally to an Aramean ancestor of the Hebrews, who bore the name *Abraham*, and others to a Canaanite hero, *Abram*. The derivation of *Abraham* (*the father of a multitude*), offered by the late priestly writer in Genesis 17[5], is based simply on a similarity in sound to the Hebrew word (*hamon*) meaning *multitude*. It seems probable that the two forms are but dialectic variations of the familiar Hebrew name, *Abiram*, meaning, *the father is exalted* or *the lofty one is father*. The name has been found on a Babylonian tablet, coming from the reign of Hammurabi's grandfather. It was therefore used as an individual name at least as early as 2000 B.C. Since the form Abraham is always used elsewhere in the Old Testament (except in two late priestly quotations in Genesis), it has been restored in the text.

VI. **The Home of Abraham.** The oldest Hebrew records agree in the fact that Haran of Aram-Naharaim, in eastern Mesopotamia, was the original home of Abraham and, therefore, of the earliest ancestors of the Hebrews. In § XI[2] Abraham speaks of Aram as the land of his nativity (*cf.* also Gen. 22[20] 27[43] 28[10] 29[5] Dt. 27 Josh. 24[2, 3]). This overwhelming weight of testimony is in accord with the facts of contemporary history (Introd., IV[xi]). Only in the late priestly traditions and in what are apparently two editorial additions to the prophetic narratives (Gen. 11[28] and 15[7]) is the origin of the Hebrews traced back to Ur of the Chaldees. Evidently the ancient Babylonian Ur, over five hundred miles southeast of Haran, is the city in the mind of the later scribes; but even the place names in the late priestly list of Abraham's ancestors point to Aram rather than Babylonia (§ VI[IX]). Perhaps the fact that both Ur and Haran were devoted to the worship of the moon god Sin, and possibly the belief that Haran was founded by colonists from the older Babylonian city, are the basis of this very late Jewish tradition.

Haran, about sixty miles north of the Euphrates on one of its confluents, the modern *Belikh*, was an important city in antiquity, and is frequently mentioned on the Assyrian inscriptions. It was one of the stopping points on the great caravan route that ran from Babylonia to the eastern Mediterranean and was the trading centre for the surrounding nomadic and semi-agricultural population. It was natural that the moon, whose clear, cold light guarded the caravans across the desert and the nomads in their midnight marches, should here be worshipped. So famous was this ancient sanctuary that the moon god was known throughout northern Syria as the Baal or Lord of Haran. It is also significant that Sarah corresponds to the Babylonian *Sharritu*, the name of the goddess of Haran, the wife of the moon god worshipped at that place. Milcah, the name of Nahor's wife, also corresponds to the Babylonian *Milkatu*, who, in the mythology of Haran, was the daughter of the moon god.

VII. The Divine Promise. To interpret and appreciate the early biblical stories, it is important to adopt the point of view of the prophetic narrators. All details—the method of revelation, the size of Abraham's family, the nature of his journey, and the age in which he lived—are omitted, and attention is fixed only on the essential facts. To the patriarch came the divine call to break those bonds of land and kindred which are especially strong in the East, and to seek a new home and destiny in the great western world. With the call went the promise that he should become the father of a great nation and that the divine blessing would ever attend him, so that he and his descendants would enjoy renown and the most signal evidences of Jehovah's favor. He should be so highly blessed that his friends would share the same divine favor, while his foes would be the objects of Jehovah's wrath. Furthermore, all nations would see his God-given prosperity and crave like blessings for themselves.

VIII. The Sanctuaries Associated with Abraham. Like Noah in the earlier story, Abraham at once responded to the divine command. As he passed through the land of Canaan and came to the oak or terebinth near Shechem, he received another revelation, and the promise that his descendants would in time possess this land as their own. The sacred oak is again mentioned in Judges 9[37], where it is called *the Diviners' Oak*. As has been already noted (§ I[xii]), the early Semites believed that the deity spoke through certain trees. In Palestine to-day there are still many trees which the natives regard as sacred. Among the Canaanites this particular tree had apparently long been regarded as oracular. References in their traditions also indicate that the early Hebrews shared this ancient belief.

At the scene of the revelation Abraham reared an altar, which tradition probably identified as the site of the sanctuary at Shechem (*cf.* Josh. 24[26]). Also east of Bethel he built another altar, as a symbol of his devotion to Jehovah, and this was probably in the same way connected with the famous sanctuary at that place.

IX. Lot's Choice. Even as the first part of this brief story illustrates the fact that Abraham's eyes were fixed only on Jehovah and the future of his race, so the latter part emphasizes his fine disregard for things material. The strife between the herdsmen of Abraham and Lot is **true**

to the nomadic life of the East. The heights east of Bethel command a superb view southward over the gray limestone hills of Judah on the right and the verdant valley of the Jordan on the left. It seems probable that the early narrator believed that this fertile plain, which he likens to the garden of Eden, extended southward, including the territory later occupied by the Dead Sea. Its southernmost limit is the town of Zoar, the Zoor or Zoora of Josephus, at the southern end of the Dead Sea. In these early traditions, therefore, the cities of the Plain are probably to be thought of as lying in the centre or southern end of the deep basin which now holds the bitter, barren waters of the Dead Sea (*cf.* further § IX [iii]). Thither the choice of Lot, the traditional ancestor of the Moabites and Ammonites, carried him; while among the barren hills about Hebron the devoted servant of Jehovah dreamed of the realization of the divine promises and longed for new revelations.

X. **Historical Significance of the Stories.** The table of the nations (§ VI) has illustrated the tendency among the early Hebrews to record tribal or national history in the form of personal biography. The same method still prevails among the Arabian tribes to-day. Thus interpreted, these opening Abraham stories represent the earliest chapter in Israel's history. They state that the immediate ancestors of the Hebrews were nomads living in western Mesopotamia in the neighborhood of the ancient city of Haran. Thence the first group of immigrants moved westward, probably about 1500 or 1400 B.C., to find homes in the coastlands of the eastern Mediterranean. Some, like the Ammonites and Moabites, in time settled along the eastern side of the Jordan and Dead Sea basin. Those from whom the Hebrews were descended, however, crossed over into Canaan. Among the rocky uplands they were allowed for a time to pitch their tents and pasture their flocks, even as do the Arabs in certain parts of Palestine to-day; but they sought in vain for a permanent place of abode in the already thickly populated territory west of the Jordan.

XI. **Aim and Teachings.** The three distinct and yet related aims of the early prophetic historians are well illustrated in these opening stories. The first was to trace the outlines of Israel's history and to interpret in the light of that record the divine purpose which was being realized in it. To their inspired eyes the later victories and prosperity of their race were but the fulfilment of Jehovah's early promises. The second aim was to set before later generations in the person of their earliest ancestor a character that would inspire in his descendants the noblest ideals and aspirations. With the spirit of the true prophet,

Abraham leaves behind all that men usually cherish most and sets out on his long journey. In Canaan also he disregards his personal interests and is intent only upon knowing and doing the will of God. Self-sacrificing, courageous, obedient to the voice of God—he is supremely worthy to be the father of a prophetic nation. Blessed was the race that had such a character held up thus prominently before it!

The third aim was to illustrate concretely, and therefore the more effectively, certain universal truths which had been revealed through the experiences of the Hebrew race. Clearly they stand forth from the simple narrative: (1) God guides those who will be guided. (2) For those who will be led by him, God has in store a noble destiny. (3) God can reveal himself to those alone who seek a revelation. (4) God's revelations come along the path of duty and are confined to no place or land. (5) He that loseth his life shall find it. (6) Blessed are the peacemakers, for they shall be called the children of God. (7) Blessed are the meek, for they shall inherit the earth.

§ VIII. THE PROMISE OF A SON TO SARAH

Now Sarah was barren; she had no children; but she had an Egyptian maid-servant whose name was Hagar. And Sarah said to Abraham, Behold now, Jehovah hath denied me children; go in, I pray you, to my maid-servant; it may be that I shall obtain children by her. *1. Sarah's presentation of Hagar*

Then Abraham heeded the voice of Sarah and went in to Hagar, and she conceived. But when she saw that she had conceived, her mistress was despised in her eyes. Therefore Sarah said to Abraham, May the wrong I suffer be upon you. I myself gave my maid-servant into your bosom; and now that she sees that she has conceived, I am despised in her eyes; Jehovah judge between me and you. But Abraham said to Sarah, Behold, your maid-servant is in your power, do to her whatever seems right to you. Then Sarah ill-treated her, so that she fled from her presence. *2. Her jealousy and Hagar's flight*

And the Messenger of Jehovah found her by a spring of water in the wilderness, by the spring on the way to Shur. And he said, Hagar, Sarah's maid-servant, Whence camest thou? and whither art thou going? And she said, I am *3. Divine promise to Hagar* fleeing from the presence of my mistress Sarah. Then the Messenger of Jehovah said to her, Return to thy mistress and submit thyself to her authority. Moreover the Messenger of Jehovah said to her, I will make thy descendants so many that they cannot be numbered. The Messenger of Jehovah also said to her, Behold, thou art with child, and shalt bear a son; and thou shalt call his name Ishmael [God hears], because Jehovah hath heard of thy ill-treatment.

> He shall be like a wild-ass,
>> His hand against every man,
>> And every man's hand against him;
> And he shall dwell over against all his kinsmen.

Then she called the name of Jehovah, who had spoken to her, El-roi [Thou art a God that seeth me]; for she said, Have I seen God and am I still alive, after I have looked upon him? Therefore the well is called Beer-lahai-roi [Well of the living One who seeth me], (behold, it is between Kadesh and Bered).

4. Abraham's hospitality

Jehovah also appeared to Abraham by the oaks of Mamre, as he was sitting at the entrance of the tent in the heat of the day; and, as he lifted up his eyes and looked, there stood three men before him. And as soon as he saw them, he ran from the entrance of the tent to meet them and bowed himself to the ground, and said, My lords, if now I have found favor in your sight, do not, I pray you, pass by your servant. Let now a little water be brought, I pray you, that you may wash your feet, and rest yourselves under the tree; and let me bring a morsel of bread, that you may refresh yourselves; afterward you may pass on, since for this reason you are passing by your servant. And they replied, Do even as you have said. So Abraham hastened into the tent to Sarah, and said, Make ready quickly three measures of fine meal, knead it, and bake cakes. Abraham also ran to the herd, and took a calf, tender and good, and gave it to the servant, that he might prepare it quickly. And he took curds and milk, with the calf which he had dressed, and set before them, and he was waiting on them under the tree, while they ate.

Then they said to him, Where is thy wife? And he said, 5.Promise of a son to Abraham and Sarah There within the tent. And he said, I will certainly return to thee about a year from now, and then Sarah thy wife shall have a son. But Sarah was listening at the entrance of the tent, which was behind him. Now Sarah and Abraham were old, well advanced in years (it had ceased to be with Sarah after the manner of women). Therefore Sarah laughed to herself, saying, After I am old and worn out shall I have pleasure, my lord being old also? And Jehovah said to Abraham, Why did Sarah laugh, saying, "Shall I, even when I am old, indeed bear a child?" Is anything too wonderful for Jehovah? At the appointed time about a year hence, I will return to thee and Sarah shall have a son. Then Sarah denied, saying, I did not laugh; for she was afraid. And he said, Nay, but thou didst laugh.

I. Literary Form and Origin. Simply, graphically, and with rare fidelity to human feeling and the peculiar life of the ancient nomad, two important and closely related incidents in Abraham's domestic history are here recorded. They both deal with a theme of perennial interest —the mystery of birth and parenthood. No subject was of more vital import to every Semitic family than the birth of the son who should perpetuate its name and traditions. The story of Ishmael answered from the Hebrew point of view the question: "What was the origin of the Ishmaelites and what relation were they to the Israelites?" To their Hebrew readers the second story had a double fascination because Isaac was the bond that bound them to their ancestor Abraham. It was natural that they should think of his birth as being divinely heralded. The sudden introduction of Jehovah in connection with the promise, instead of the angelic beings, suggests perhaps that in the earlier part of the narrative the prophetic historian did not wish to represent the Deity as partaking of food.

Ovid has preserved the closest parallel (*Fast.* 5[495 ff.]). This Greek tradition states that the three gods, Zeus, Poseidon, and Hermes, were once received as guests by an old man of Tanagra, Hyrieus by name. After eating the meal which he provided for them, they desired him to ask something for himself. Since he was childless, he expressed a wish for a son. The son, whom they gave him by a miracle, was Orion.

II. Meaning of the Story of Hagar and Ishmael. The marriage customs of the East are here assumed. Even in the later Hebrew laws, barrenness was regarded as a possible basis of divorce (St. O. T., IV, Appendix 1). The husband in any case was free to take another wife. The Code of Hammurabi in one of its laws formulates the primitive usage when a wife could not bear children to her husband:

If a man has married a votary (*i.e.*, a woman consecrated to a god), and she has given a maid to her husband, who has borne children, and afterward that maid has placed herself on an equality with her mistress because she has borne children, her mistress shall not sell her. She shall place a slave-mark upon her and reckon her with the slave girls. If she has not borne children, her mistress may sell her.

This ancient law contemplates the same domestic infelicity, as arose in the household of Abraham. The patriarch's attitude in the matter is also explained and justified in the light of early Semitic custom. In the eyes of the law the slave wife was still the property of Sarah.

In fleeing from her mistress, Hagar naturally goes toward her native home. Shur is that part of the wilderness which borders on Egypt to the west (*cf.* Gen. 20¹ 25¹⁸ Ex. 15²²). Among the early Semites springs were regarded as dwelling places of the deity. The waters gushing forth from the dry, rocky earth were a never ceasing miracle. It would appear that the present tradition originally centred about the famous desert well of Beer-lahai-roi, whose name meant *well of the living one who seeth me*. The story of the revelation and promise to the traditional ancestress of the Ishmaelites made it a spot sacred even to the Hebrew inhabitants of Canaan. The place is probably to be identified with *Ain Muweileh*, a caravan station with seven wells, on the main route from Palestine to Egypt. It is about fifty miles southwest of Beersheba and twelve miles west of *Ain Kadish*.

The popular tradition also evidently aimed to explain the name Ishmael, *God hears*. The vivid, poetic description of the Ishmaelites, as represented by their tribal ancestor, is true to the character and life of the wandering Arab. They were like the wild ass, free, untamed, ever roaming from place to place. Subsisting largely by robbery, they were at enmity with all their neighbors. Out in the wilderness but on the borders of Canaan they lived, kinsmen yet foes of the Hebrews.

III. **Abraham's Divine Guests.** The account of Abraham's hospitality is one of the truest and most graphic pictures in oriental literature. The hot stillness and solitude of an eastern noonday, the patriarch seated beside his tent door, his sudden glimpse of three strangers approaching along the way, his eager and courteous reception, which makes their acceptance of his hospitality seem a favor to him rather than to them, and the haste to provide for their needs—each of these scenes stands out in clear relief. The food set before the guests is that of the nomad: thin rolls of bread, baked on the hot stones, curdled milk, the famous *leben* of the modern Arab and, as a special delicacy, a calf tender and good. To see that every want of his guests is at once supplied, Abraham himself stands by and serves them, as they sit beneath one of the wide-spreading oaks or terebinths of Mamre.

As the guests depart, the promise is given to the aged patriarch and his wife that within a year they should have an heir. In this oldest tradition the name which he bore (Isaac), is connected with the Hebrew verb *sāhăk*, to laugh, and is explained by his mother's skeptical laughter when a son is promised to her in her old age. In the parallel priestly narrative of Genesis 17[17] it is Abraham who laughs. It was thus that the popular interest in etymology and the belief in the significance of the name shaped in part these early traditions of the race.

IV. **Historical Significance of the Stories.** The story of Hagar is a chapter from early Semitic tribal history. Hagar, like Ishmael, apparently represents a nomadic people. In the inscriptions of the Assyrian king, Sennacherib, Hagaranu is the name of an Aramean tribe, living not far from Babylonia. A tribe bearing a similar name is mentioned in the south Arabian inscriptions (*cf.* also I Chr. 5[10, 19] 11[39] 27[31]).

If it could be proved that a land and people of Muçri were to be found in ancient times southwest of Canaan, it would furnish a satisfactory explanation of Hagar's origin, for *Muçri* contains the same letters as the Hebrew word for Egypt. If not, Hagar is called an Egyptian, because the Arab tribe which she represents, had been partially Egyptianized through living close to the land of the Nile. At least, in the narrative, Hagar figures as a typical daughter of the desert. Possibly, in the present narrative, Ishmael is intended to represent, as in later periods, all of Israel's nomadic neighbors to the south. It seems more probable, however, that the reference is to a definite tribe, living in early times in the wilderness south or southwest of Canaan.

Interpreted in the language of history, this tradition then would mean that the nomadic ancestors of the Hebrews early made alliances and intermarried with certain Arab tribes in the wilderness that lies between southern Palestine and Egypt. At least both recognized the same bonds of kinship and religion. This early tradition of a common origin and faith is especially significant, for in the days of Moses the Israelites received from contact with certain of these tribes that great impetus to the worship of Jehovah which is recorded in the narratives associated with Sinai (*cf.* § XXI).

The story of the promise of the birth of Isaac is rich in its illustrations of the social life and customs of the early Semitic ancestors of the Hebrews. The story, as a whole, emphasizes again concretely the supreme fact that the same divine Providence, that so signally delivered the Hebrews in many later crises was, from the earliest days, guiding the destiny of his people.

V. **Aim and Teachings.** Interest in the meaning of certain prominent names, in the origin of sacred places, of the Ishmaelites, and of their relationship to the Hebrews, and in the reason why the Hebrews were heirs to a nobler destiny undoubtedly influenced the early prophetic historians to preserve these traditions. They also add certain important touches to the growing prophetic portrait of Abraham. In a trying domestic crisis he realizes the Semitic ideal of justice and devotion to his wife. As host, in his delicate consideration for the needs and wishes of his guests, he attains to the highest standards of hospitality, whether oriental or occidental.

Each narrative also suggests its own prophetic teaching: (1) To the outcast and needy the divine voice ever comes with its message of counsel and promise. (2) The sphere of God's care and blessing was by no means limited to Israel. (3) He who generously receives strangers often entertains the messengers of the Lord. (4) Unselfish service for others always brings its sure and rich reward.

§ IX. THE DESTRUCTION OF SODOM

1. Departure of the men

Then the men rose up from there and looked off in the direction of Sodom; and Abraham went along with them to speed them on their way.

2. Jehovah's revelation to Abraham

And Jehovah said, Because the complaint concerning Sodom and Gomorrah is great, and because their sin is very heinous, I will go down and see whether they have done exactly according to the complaint which comes to me; and if not, I will know. So the men turned from there and went toward Sodom, but Abraham remained standing before Jehovah.

3. Abraham's intercession

Then Abraham drew near and said, Wilt thou consume the righteous with the wicked? Perhaps there are fifty righteous within the city, Wilt thou consume and not spare

84

the place for the fifty righteous that are in it? Be it far from thee to do after this manner, to slay the righteous with the wicked! and that the righteous should be as the wicked, far be it from thee! Shall the Judge of all the earth not do justice? And Jehovah said, If I find in Sodom fifty righteous within the city, then I will spare all the place for their sake. And Abraham answered and said, Behold now, I have presumed to speak to the Lord, even though I am but dust and ashes; perhaps there will be lacking five of the fifty righteous. Wilt thou destroy all the city for lack of five? And he said, I will not destroy it, if I find there forty-five. And he spoke to him yet again, and said, Perhaps forty will be found there. And he said, For the sake of forty I will not do it. And he said, Oh, let not my Lord be angry, but let me speak: perhaps thirty will be found there. And he said, I will not do it, if I find thirty there. And he said, Behold now, I have presumed to speak to the Lord: perhaps twenty will be found there. And he said, For the sake of twenty I will not destroy it. And he said, Oh let not the Lord be angry, but let me speak yet this once: perhaps ten will be found there. And he said I will not destroy it for the ten's sake. Then Jehovah went his way as soon as he had ceased talking with Abraham.

Then Abraham returned to his place, and the two Messengers came to Sodom in the evening as Lot was sitting in the gate of Sodom. When Lot saw them he rose up to meet them, and bowed himself with his face to the earth, and said, Now, my lords, turn aside, I pray you, into your servant's house and abide all night, and wash your feet; then you shall rise up early, and go on your way. And they said, Nay, but we will abide in the street all night. But he urged them so strongly that they turned aside to him, and entered into his house; and he made them a feast, and baked unleavened bread, and they ate.

4. Lot's reception of the men

But before they had lain down, the men of the city, both young and old, all the people from every quarter surrounded the house; and they called to Lot saying to him, Where are the men who came in to you to-night? Bring them out to us that we may know them. Then Lot went out to them at the door-way, but he shut the door after him. And he said,

5. Shamelessness of the Sodomites

I pray you, my friends, do not thus wickedly. Behold now, I have two virgin daughters; let me, I pray you, bring them out to you, and do to them as you desire, only do nothing to these men, inasmuch as they have come under the shadow of my roof. But they replied, Stand back. And they said, This one came in to sojourn, and he would set himself up as a judge; now we will treat you worse than them. And they pressed hard against Lot and drew near to break the door. But the men reached out and drew Lot to them into the house, and shut the door, and smote the men who were at the door of the house with blindness, both small and great, so that they became weary in searching for the door.

6. Deliverance of Lot Then the men said to Lot, Hast thou here any besides? Son-in-law, and thy sons, and thy daughters, and whoever thou hast in the city, bring them out of this place; for we are about to destroy this place; because great complaint concerning them hath come to Jehovah, and Jehovah hath sent us to destroy it. So Lot went out and spoke to his sons-in-law, who were to marry his daughters, and said, Up, get you out of this place; for Jehovah will destroy the city. But he seemed to his sons-in-law as one who was jesting. And when the rosy glow of morning appeared, the Messengers urged Lot, saying, Arise, take thy wife, and thy two daughters who are here, lest thou be consumed in the punishment of the city. But as he lingered, the men took hold of his hand and the hands of his wife and of his two daughters (since Jehovah was merciful to him), and brought him forth and set him outside the city. And it came to pass, when they had brought them outside, that they said, Escape for thy life; look not behind thee, neither stay thou in all the Plain; escape to the mountain lest thou be consumed. But Lot said to them, Oh, not so, my lords! Behold now, thy servant hath found favor in thy sight, and thou hast shown great mercy to me in saving my life—and I cannot escape to the mountain, lest evil overtake me, and I die—see now, this city is near to which to flee, and it is a little one. Oh, let me escape thither (is it not a little one?), and my life shall be preserved. And Jehovah said to him, I have also accepted thee concerning this thing, in that I will not overthrow the city of which thou hast spoken. Hasten, escape

thither; for I cannot do anything until thou enter there. Therefore the name of the city was called Zoar [Little]. And the sun had risen upon the earth when Lot came to Zoar.

Then Jehovah rained upon Sodom and Gomorrah brimstone and fire from Jehovah out of heaven, and he overthrew those cities, and all the Plain, with all the inhabitants of the cities, and that which grew upon the ground. But Lot's wife looked back from behind him and she became a pillar of salt. And Abraham rose up early in the morning, and looked toward Sodom and Gomorrah, toward all the region of the Plain, and beheld: and there the smoke of the land had begun to ascend as the smoke of a smelting-furnace. *7. Destruction of the cities of the Plain and fate of Lot's wife*

Then Lot went up from Zoar and dwelt in the mountain, and his two daughters with him—for he was afraid to dwell in Zoar—and lived in the cave together with his two daughters. *8. Lot's life in the cave*

And the elder bore a son, and called his name Moab. He is the father of the present Moabites. The younger also bore a son and called his name Ben-ammi. That one is the father of the present Ammonites. *9. Origin of the Moabites and Ammonites*

I. Origin of the Tradition. The scene of the story is that most striking of natural phenomena, the Dead Sea. The geological data indicate that the Jordan valley was probably once an estuary of the Red Sea, and that its salt waters in early periods washed the southern spurs of Mount Hermon. The land in the south later rose, cutting off all connection with the ocean, thus making an inland lake of which the Dead Sea alone remains. In the south, at En-gedi on the west, and in the lower Jordan valley on the north, fringes of rich tropical vegetation suggested to the ancients that the great basin between Judah and Moab was once *well watered everywhere (before Jehovah destroyed Sodom and Gomorrah), like the garden of Jehovah, as far as Zoar* (§ VII⁵). The bitter, heavy waters and the barren shores seemed to them to be convincing proof that some great destruction had overtaken the once fertile plain. The pools of petroleum, the sulphur springs and deposits at many points about the lake, and the evidence of volcanic action, probably all combined to perpetuate the present story.

In the minds of the early Hebrews and their interpreters, the prophets, the dire displeasure of Jehovah alone sufficed to explain such an overwhelming destruction. With what seemed to them convincing logic, they argued that the crimes of a people thus punished must have been unspeakably heinous. In the shameful practices of the earlier Canaanites, they found the sufficient cause.

Similar stories of the destruction of other cities by fire or water, because of inhospitality or the guilt of their inhabitants, are still current in Arabia and in many other parts of the world. The Greek story of Philemon and Baucis is the one most familiar to western students (Ovid, *Met.* VIII, 616 *ff.*).

The fate of Lot's wife was probably suggested by the peculiar geological formations still found to the southwest of the Dead Sea. From the remarkable cliffs of crystallized rock-salt, that rise to the height of six hundred feet, fragments are often detached. These pillar-like shafts frequently assume forms which suggest the outlines of the human figure. Josephus and other late Jewish writers believed that they were still able to identify the pillar of salt referred to in the story (Jos. *Ant.* II, 11⁴). Doubtless a pillar of this character, famous in ancient times, but long since wasted away by the action of the elements, was the physical basis of the strange episode. The Greek myth regarding Niobe, who was changed to stone, is probably also of similar origin.

II. Interpretation of the Story. As in the story of the tower of Babel, Jehovah is represented as coming down to investigate the guilt of the cities of the Plain. In the present form of the narrative, however, only two of the angelic beings proceed toward Sodom, while Jehovah remains behind. Abraham uses this opportunity to intercede for his kinsman, Lot. Among the early Semites the communal instinct was so strong that the suffering of the innocent with the guilty tribe or city did not seem to them unjust. Abraham, however, voicing the deeper insight of the later prophets, who have added this familiar section, pleads for the righteous few (*cf.* Ezek. 18). The appeal is not in vain. To each increasing demand upon Jehovah's justice and mercy comes the quick response. At last, however, the overwhelming consciousness of the guilt of the many silenced the patriarch's petition; but in the sequel the righteous few are nevertheless delivered. Abraham's intercessions also bring out in clear relief the heinous guilt of the wicked Sodomites. Their character is clearly illustrated by the account of their reception of the divine guests. Lot proves true to his nomadic training and traditions. Even as Abraham had received the strangers under the tree before his tent, so his nephew entertained the two guests royally in his city home. The inhabitants of Sodom, however, one and all, prove insensible to the laws of hospitality and decency. The gross degeneracy of these representative Canaanites is thus portrayed in strongest colors.

Lot places the nomadic law of hospitality even above that of parental responsibility; but the judgment falls upon the guilty before his family suffers from his mistaken sense of honor. Divine justice is vindicated and Lot's virtue is rewarded by the opportunity to escape, which is not only offered, but pressed upon him and his family by the divine messengers. He, with his wife and two daughters, flees alone and terror-stricken in the lurid light of the burning cities. The divine command is laid upon them not to look back; but again, as in the garden of Eden, a wife's curiosity proves too strong. Lot and his daughters flee on alone, leaving behind a lifeless pillar of salt.

III. **Sites of the Cities of the Plain.** The implications of the story and the identification of the pillar of salt point to the southern end of the Jordan basin, as the traditional site of the cities of the Plain. This generally accepted conclusion is still further supported by the probable site of the Moabite town of Zoar in or near the little oasis of *Ghor es-Safujeh*, at the southeastern end of the Dead Sea. This bit of green stands out in striking contrast to the general barrenness of the region, and suggests that its preservation was a special act of Providence. The meaning of its Hebrew name, *Little*, is explained by the ancient story. The same Hebrew narrative also taught that in the neighboring mountains of Moab were born to the daughters of Lot, Moab and Ammon, the traditional ancestors of the peoples living to the east of the ancient Plain of the Jordan.

IV. **Historical Significance of the Story.** The Jordan valley is still the scene of frequent earthquakes. The memory of some great upheaval, caused by a subterranean explosion of petroleum and the accompanying gases, may be the basis of this early tradition. The upheaval may have destroyed certain Canaanite cities on the southern shores of the Dead Sea. The fact that the names of the cities are remembered lends support to this conclusion. The later prophetic literature also contains many allusions to the destruction of Sodom and the neighboring cities of Gomorrah, Admah, and Zeboim (*e.g.*, Am. 4¹ Is. 1¹⁰ 3⁹ 13¹⁹ Jer. 23¹⁴ 49¹⁸ Zeph. 2⁹ Dt. 29²³). Sodom is the classic Hebrew symbol of superlative shamelessness and ignominy. The tradition vividly reflects the gross moral degeneracy of the earlier Canaanites and the impression which their customs made upon the Israelites (*cf.* also § IV¹¹).

In a form characteristic of early nomadic tradition, but far from flattering to the national vanity of their neighbors across the Jordan, the story also states the historical fact that the Moabites and Ammonites were related to the Hebrews by virtue of common origin, traditions, and customs. Contemporary records, archæology, and the later biblical references unite in confirming this fact.

V. **Aim and Teachings.** The early prophets, in common with their race and age, undoubtedly regarded the tradition as historical and retained it primarily for this reason. Like the later Judean story of the flood, to which it is in many ways closely parallel, it is one of the most dramatic illustrations of the overwhelming judgment that must inevitably overtake those who are deliberately and defiantly wicked. In the economy of the universe God himself is compelled to destroy them like worthless refuse. And yet the God who destroys is a God of infinite mercy, eager to stay the destruction, if only a leaven of good can be found. He is also just, not only to cities and nations, but to each individual. All in whom there is a gleam of promise are saved, as were Lot and his family, and given every opportunity to perform their work in the world. The one God whom the Hebrews worshipped, guided the early destinies of their polytheistic neighbors, even as he did those of his chosen people. The narrative and the stories which precede and follow also illustrate the supreme truth that the basis of the divine choice of the Hebrew race was primarily its character and aspirations, as exemplified by the lives and deeds of its traditional ancestors. A man who could plead, as did Abraham, for the life of his selfish, luxury-loving kinsman, and the shamelessly corrupt Canaanites, was the natural progenitor of a race of prophets. To those also who keep his commands the Lord ever reveals his character and purposes.

§X. BIRTH AND SACRIFICE OF ISAAC.

1. Birth of Isaac

Now Jehovah visited Sarah as he had said. And Sarah conceived and bore Abraham a son in his old age, and said, Who would have told Abraham that Sarah should give children suck? for I have borne him a son in his old age!

2. God's test of Abraham's devotion

And it came to pass after these things, that God tested Abraham, saying to him, Abraham; and he said, Here am I. And he said, Take now thy son, thine only son, Isaac, whom thou lovest, and go to the land of Moriah [Revelation of Jehovah], and offer him there as a burnt-offering on one of the mountains of which I shall tell thee.

Then Abraham rose early in the morning, and saddled his ass, and took two of his servants with him, and Isaac his son. And when he had split the wood for the burnt-offering, he arose and went to the place of which God had told him. On the third day Abraham lifted up his eyes and saw the place afar off. And Abraham said to his servants, Stay here with the ass, while I and the lad go yonder. And when we have worshipped, we will come back to you. Then Abraham took the wood of the burnt-offering, and laid it on Isaac his son; and he took in his hand the fire and the knife, and they both went on together. And Isaac spoke to Abraham his father, and said, My father! and he said, Yes, my son. And he said, Here is the fire and the wood, but where is the lamb for a burnt-offering? And Abraham said, My son, God will himself provide the lamb for a burnt-offering. So they two went on together. When they came to the place of which God had told him, Abraham built the altar there, and laid the wood in order, and bound Isaac his son, and laid him on the altar upon the wood. Then Abraham stretched forth his hand, and took the knife to slay his son. ^{omitted}

3. Abraham's obedience

But the Messenger of Jehovah called to him from heaven, saying, Abraham, Abraham! and he said, Here am I. And he said, Lay not thy hand upon the lad, neither do anything to him, for now I know that thou art one who feareth God, since thou hast not withheld thy son, thine only son, from me. Then Abraham lifted up his eyes, and looked, and behold, there was a ram caught in the thicket by his horns. So Abraham went and took the ram, and offered him up as a burnt-offering instead of his son. Abraham therefore called the name of that place Jehovah-jireh [Jehovah provides], so that it is said to-day, In the mountain of Jehovah provision will be made.

4. The divine approval

And the Messenger of Jehovah called to Abraham a second time from heaven, and said, By myself have I sworn saith Jehovah, because thou hast done this thing, and hast not withheld thy son, thine only son, that I will surely bless thee, and I will make thine offspring as numerous as the stars of the heavens and as the sand which is on the sea-shore, so that thy descendants shall possess the gates of

5. Renewal of the promises to Abraham

their enemies, and all the nations of the earth shall ask for
themselves a blessing like that of thy descendants, because
thou hast obeyed my voice.

6. Re-
turn to
Beer-
sheba

So Abraham returned to his servants, and they arose and
went together to Beersheba. And Abraham dwelt in Beersheba.

I. **The Institution of Human Sacrifice.** This ancient story reflects
the fact that the early Hebrews, like their Semitic kinsmen and neighbors, believed that the gift of their dearest possessions, and even the
sacrifice of their children or relatives, were supremely acceptable to
the Deity. Jephthah's vow (§ XXXVIII), and Saul's rash covenant
(§ XLII⁶), which almost cost the life of his son Jonathan, are the most
familiar historical illustrations of this false popular belief. The hideous
institution of human sacrifice was clearly inherited by the Hebrews
from their early Semitic ancestors. The earthen jars containing the
bones of infants, which have been found in such large quantities in the
foundations of the recently excavated Canaanite temples at Gezer and
Taanach, are grim reminders of the horrible rites which the Israelites
learned from the Palestinian peoples whom they conquered. References in the Old Testament indicate that child sacrifice was common
among the Arameans (II Kgs. 17³¹), the Moabites (II Kgs. 3²⁷), and
the Ammonites (Lev. 18²¹ 20²). Later Greek writers state that the
Carthaginians, to avert a great national calamity, sacrificed hundreds
of the children of their noblest families. The Hebrew records also
show that this horrible rite was at times practised in Judah even down
to the days immediately preceding the exile, and especially during the
reactionary reigns of Ahaz and Manasseh (II Kgs. 16³ 21⁶ 23¹⁰ Jer.
7³¹ 19⁵).

II. **Parallels to the Story.** Philo has preserved a Phœnician
tradition to the effect that an *el* or god to avert a great plague offered
his first-born son as a burnt-offering to his father Uranus. The closest
parallel to the biblical narrative is the familiar Greek story of Agamem-
non's offering of Iphigenia. In the Greek story a doe was substituted
by Artemis for the human victim. In both the Hebrew and Greek
stories the primary aim was evidently to teach that animal sacrifices
were acceptable to the Deity instead of the human offerings presented
by the more primitive and less enlightened nations.

III. **Meaning of the Biblical Story.** The account of Abraham's
sacrifice of his son is found only in the Northern Israelite prophetic

narrative. It is, however, one of the most thrilling stories found in the Old Testament. To fully appreciate Abraham's devotion to Jehovah it must be remembered that the patriarch's strongest hopes and ambitions could be realized only through his son Isaac. To Abraham in his old age, after the child had grown to be a stalwart lad, the conviction came that to show his devotion he must sacrifice to Jehovah his only son.

The scene of the sacrifice was to be the land of Moriah, which the later Jews identified with Jerusalem (II Chr. 3¹). The aged patriarch met unflinchingly this supreme test of his faith and obedience, for God's favor meant more to him than his dearest possession and even the realization of the divine promises through his descendants. Simply and dramatically and with a pathos too deep for expression, the different acts in the great tragedy of Abraham's life are described. His fatherly pity deterred him from making known to his son the true object of their mission. The lad's innocent questions only added to the patriarch's agony; but his faith in God never failed him. With calm assurance he performed each painful detail. The knife with which to slay his only son was in his uplifted hand, when there came to him a realization of the more acceptable way in which to express his devotion to his God. It was not the life of human beings that Israel's God demanded but that spirit of personal sacrifice and obedience which the patriarch supremely exemplified. Rams and sheep and oxen sufficed, as symbols of loyalty and devotion to the Deity. The old law, "Every first-born is mine," remained among Israel's statutes; but the Hebrews in time realized that this command did not require the shedding of innocent human blood.

The present story clearly represents one of the earliest protests of the enlightened prophets and lawgivers against the horrible rite of human sacrifice. The common people still believed that they could "offer the fruit of their body for the sin of their soul" (Micah 6⁷); but in this early story, as in the later prophetic teaching, the higher conscience of the nation replied:

> He hath showed thee, O man, what is good;
> And what doth Jehovah require of thee,
>> But to do justly,
>> And to love mercy,
>> And to walk humbly with thy God?

IV. **Aim and Teachings.** This story completes the early prophetic portrait of Abraham. His faith in God knows no limitation. Like the martyrs of later ages, he is ready, if it is the divine will, calmly and unflinchingly to march to the stake. His victories are victories over self, and his conquests are conquests of divine favor. By absolute obedience and trust he wins back, even in the midst of crowded, warring Canaan, that intimate relation with God and that divine favor which the first man and woman lost by their selfish, deliberate disobedience. With his eyes fixed solely on God and intent only in the future of the race, he is the first great, prophet-guide to lead men back to the true garden of Eden. Later traditions introduce less ideal elements, but in the stories of Abraham, preserved by the early prophets, we have a consistent portrait of a man after God's own heart. It is a character, however, perfected through testing and struggle. The perfection is of a simple, human type, that not only inspires but also encourages others to strive for its realization. A noble ambition, courage, unselfishness, faith and absolute obedience to the divine will are its chief elements. These are also the qualities which make true servants of God in every age and land.

§XI. SECURING A WIFE FOR ISAAC

1. Abraham's kinsmen in Aram

Now it came to pass after these things, that it was told Abraham saying, Behold, Milcah has also borne children to your brother Nahor, Uz his first-born, Buz his brother, Kemuel the father of Aram, Chesed, Hazo and Pildash, Jidlaph and Bethuel. (And Bethuel begat Rebekah.) These eight Milcah bore to Nahor, Abraham's brother. And his concubine, whose name was Reumah, also bore Tebah, Gaham, Tahash, and Maacah.

2. Instructions to his servant

When Abraham was old and far advanced in years and Jehovah had blessed him in all things, Abraham said to the eldest of his house servants, who had charge of all his affairs, Put, I pray you, your hand under my thigh, while I make you swear by Jehovah, the God of heaven and the God of earth, that you will not take a wife for my son from the daughters of the Canaanites, among whom I dwell, but that you will go to my country and to my kindred and take there a wife for my son Isaac. And the servant said to him, Perhaps the woman will not be willing to follow me to this land. Must I then bring your son back to the land from which you came? And Abraham said to him, See to it that you do not bring my son there again. Jehovah, the God of heaven, who took me from my father's house and from the land of my nativity and who talked with me and who swore to me saying, ' To thy descendants will I give this land,' may he send his Messenger before you and may you secure there a wife for my son. But if the woman is not willing to follow you, then you will be free from this oath to me; only never again bring my son back there. So the servant put his hand under his master's thigh and swore to him concerning this matter.

Then the servant took ten of his master's camels and set out, having all kinds of his master's precious things. Thus he arose and went to Aram Naharaim to the city of Nahor. And he made the camels kneel down outside the city by the well of water at eventide, the time when women go out to draw water. Then he said, O Jehovah, the God of my master Abraham, give me, I pray thee, good success to-day, and show kindness to my master Abraham. Behold I am standing by the spring of water and the daughters of men of the city are coming out to draw water. May it be that the maiden to whom I shall say, ' Pray let down your water jar that I may drink '; and she shall answer, ' Drink, and I will also water your camels,' let her be the one thou hast destined for thy servant Isaac; and by this shall I know that thou hast showed kindness to my master. _{3. The servant's journey and arrival in Aram}

Then even before he had finished speaking, behold there came out Rebekah, who was born to Bethuel the son of Milcah, the wife of Nahor, Abraham's brother, with her water jar upon her shoulder. And the maiden was very fair to look upon, a virgin whom no man had known. And she went down to the spring and filled her jar, and came up. Then the servant ran to meet her, saying, Pray let me drink a little water from your jar. And she said, Drink my lord, and hastened to let down her water jar upon her hand and let him drink. When she had finished giving him drink she said, I will draw for your camels also, until they have finished drinking. And she made haste to empty her jar into the trough and ran again to the well to draw, and drew for all his camels. Meanwhile the man was gazing at her intently, keeping silent in order to determine _{4. His meeting and conversation with Rebekah}

whether Jehovah had made his journey successful or not.
Then, as soon as the camels had finished drinking, the man
took a gold ring of a half shekel weight, and two bracelets
of ten shekels weight of gold for her arms, and said, Whose
daughter are you? tell me, I pray you. Is there room in
your father's house for us to lodge in? And she said to
him, I am the daughter of Bethuel, the son of Milcah, whom
she bore to Nahor. She also said to him, Both straw and
provender are plentiful with us and there is room to lodge
in. Then the man bowed his head and worshipped Jehovah, saying, Blessed be Jehovah, the God of my master
Abraham who hath not withdrawn his mercy and his faithfulness from my master. As for me, Jehovah hath led me
on the journey to the house of my master's kinsmen.

5. His reception at her house

Then the maiden ran and told these things to her mother's
house. Now Rebekah had a brother whose name was
Laban. And Laban ran out to the man at the spring.
And it came to pass when he saw the ring, and the bracelets
on his sister's arms, and when he heard the words of Rebekah saying, Thus the man spoke to me; that he came to
the man, who was still standing by the camels at the foun-
tain. And he said, Come in, you who are blessed of Jehovah! Why do you stand outside when I have the house
and room for the camels all ready? So he brought the
man into the house, and ungirded the camels; and gave
straw and provender for the camels, and water to wash his
feet and the feet of the men who were with him.

6. Declaration of his mission

But when food was set before him to eat, he said, I will
not eat until I have made known my errand. And Laban
said, Speak on. And he said, I am Abraham's servant.
And Jehovah hath blessed my master greatly, so that he has
become very rich. He hath given him flocks and herds,
and silver and gold, and men-servants and maid-servants,
and camels and asses. Now Sarah my master's wife bore
a son to my master when she was old, and to him he has
given all that he has. And my master made me swear
saying, ' Do not take a wife for my son from the daughters
of the Canaanites, in whose land I dwell, but you shall go
to my father's house and to my kindred and take a wife
for my son.' Then I said to my master, ' What if the

woman will not follow me.' But he said to me, 'May Jehovah, before whom I walk, send his Messenger with you and prosper your mission, and may you take for my son a wife of my kindred and of my father's house. Then you will be free from your oath to me; however, when you come to my kindred, if they do not give her to you, you shall also be free from your oath to me.' So I came to-day to the spring and said, ' O Jehovah, the God of my master Abraham, if now thou wilt prosper my mission on which I am going, behold, I am standing by the spring of water, may it be that if I shall say to the maiden who comes forth to draw, "Give me, I pray you, a little water from your jar to drink," and she shall say to me, "Drink, and I will also draw for your camels," let that one be the woman whom Jehovah hath destined for my master's son.' Even before I was through speaking to myself, behold, Rebekah came forth with her water jar on her shoulder, and went down to the spring and drew. And when I said to her, 'Pray let me drink,' she made haste, and let down her water jar from her shoulder and said, 'Drink, and I will also water your camels.' So I drank and she also watered the camels. Then I asked her, saying, 'Whose daughter are you?' And she said, ' The daughter of Bethuel, Nahor's son, whom Milcah bore to him.' Then I put the ring in her nose, and the bracelets on her arms. And I bowed my head and worshipped Jehovah, and blessed Jehovah the God of my master Abraham, who had led me in the right way to take the daughter of my master's brother for his son. Now if you are ready to deal kindly and truly with my master, tell me, and if not, tell me, that I may act accordingly.

Then Laban and Bethuel answered and said, The matter is in the hands of Jehovah. We cannot give you either an adverse or a favorable answer. Behold, Rebekah is before you; take her and go and let her be the wife of your master's son, as Jehovah hath spoken. And it came to pass that when Abraham's servant heard their words, he bowed himself to the earth before Jehovah. Then the servant brought forth jewels of silver and jewels of gold and clothing and gave them to Rebekah. He also gave to her brother

7. Consent of Rebekah's relatives

and to her mother precious things. And he and the men who were with him ate and drank, and remained all night.

8. His depart- ure and re- turn with Re- bekah When they rose up in the morning, he said, Send me away to my master; but her brother and her mother answered, Let the maiden remain with us a few days, at least ten; after that she may go. But he said to them, Hinder me not, since Jehovah hath prospered my mission. Send me away that I may go to my master. Then they said, We will call the maiden and consult her. And when they called Rebekah and said to her, Will you go with this man? she said, I will go. So they sent away Rebekah their sister, and her nurse with Abraham's servant, and his men. And they blessed Rebekah, saying to her,

> Our sister! may you become thousands and thousands!
> And may your descendants possess the gates of their
> enemies.

Then Rebekah arose with her maids and, riding upon the camels, followed the man. Thus the servant took Rebekah and went away.

9.Abra- ham's death Now Abraham had given all that he had to Isaac. And Abraham had breathed his last, dying in a good old age, old and satisfied with living, and had been gathered to his father's kin. And Isaac dwelt by Beer-lahai-roi.

10. Meeting with Isaac And Isaac had come from the direction of Beer-lahai-roi, for he dwelt in the South Country. And as Isaac was going out to meditate in the field at eventide, he lifted up his eyes and saw that there were camels coming. Rebekah too lifted up her eyes, and when she saw Isaac, she alighted from the camel. And she said to the servant, Who is this man walking in the field to meet us? And when the servant said, It is my master, she took her veil and covered herself. Then the servant told Isaac all the things that he had done. And Isaac brought her to the tent of Sarah his mother, and took Rebekah, and she became his wife; and he loved her. Thus was Isaac comforted concerning his mother, who had died at Kirjaith-arba (that is Hebron) in the land of Canaan.

LITERARY FORM OF THE STORY

I. Literary Form of the Story. This story is told with greater detail than any other in the book of Genesis. The stream of the narrative does not flow on rapidly as in the preceding stories, but slowly, even turning back upon itself, with one or two long repetitions. The story is an idyll in seven scenes, each portraying with rare grace and vividness the successive stages in the unfolding of the plot. Each individual acts his part nobly, and the narrative runs on to a happy conclusion without a discordant note. It was a story doubtless retold many times beside the camp fires, and especially at the marriage feasts in ancient Israel.

II. Abraham's Faithful Servant. The opening paragraph introduces the *dramatis personæ*. The twelve sons of Nahor represent twelve Aramean tribes living to the east and northeast of Palestine. The most attractive character in the story is Abraham's trusty slave. The English term, *household servant*, here reproduces most nearly the meaning of the Hebrew term for slave, for the interests of the master and servant are identical, and the sacred trust that the dying Abraham leaves to his aged liegeman is not betrayed.

The means by which a wife is secured for Isaac are those of the East, where the father, not the son, arranges all the marriage preliminaries. The event was of supreme importance, for the fulfilment of Jehovah's promises to the race depended upon it. The oath taken with the hand under the thigh was of the most solemn and binding nature. It was again used by Jacob when he imposed a solemn promise upon his son Joseph (§ XVIII), and it probably signified that the oath was also binding upon the descendants of the one thus swearing. It was often employed by primitive peoples, and is still in use among certain Australian tribes. The oath of Abraham's servant also reflects the pride which the Hebrews always felt in their Aramean ancestry, and their growing abhorrence, in later days, for the corrupt Canaanite civilization.

III. His Successful Mission. Laden with rich treasures to be used as the bridal dowry, the servant journeys toward western Mesopotamia, to the land lying on either side of the central Euphrates valley. As he waits at eventide outside Haran, he prays fervently that the God of his master will prosper him in the difficult mission which he has undertaken. Soon a beautiful maiden appears with a water jar upon her shoulder. At his request she gives him water to drink; then, exceeding even the oriental laws of hospitality, but in accord with the chosen sign, she waters his camels also.

Gladdened by the discovery that the beautiful maiden is the granddaughter of his master's brother, and by the unmistakable signs of divine guidance, Abraham's servant accepts the generous oriental hospitality which is offered him in response to Rebekah's report. When he and his servants and camels are all under the hospitable roof, and before he will partake of the offered food, he tells his tale and presents his suit. He also reënforces it after the oriental fashion by lavish gifts. These are given not only to the desired bride, but also to her mother and brother, who, since the father is evidently very old, stand at the head of the household. The final decision is left to Rebekah herself. She responds in a spirit worthy of the ancestress of a race destined to go forth and possess many an unknown land.

The parting blessing of her kinsmen voices the familiar hope that her descendants may be countless and triumph over their many foes.

IV. **The Return.** The form of Abraham's command to his servant suggests that the aged patriarch was on the point of death. The final scene in the story implies that Abraham had died before the servant's return, but in Genesis his death is recorded in a subsequent passage which was taken from the late priestly narrative (chap. 25). In the present text this brief, stately, expressive account of Abraham's decease has been restored to what appears to have been its original place in the prophetic history.

The vivid story reaches its climax in the picturesque meeting of Isaac and Rebekah in the wilderness at eventide. Oriental custom left no place for the expression of individual sentiment until the bride had been conducted to the tent of her future husband. By this act the eastern marriage ceremony was completed. The narrative, however, states that Isaac loved Rebekah and that she filled in the heart of the only son the place left vacant by the death of his mother.

V. **Historical Significance of the Story.** Few stories have been preserved regarding Isaac. An early prophetic narrative tells of his experiences at the court of the king of Gerar. Fearing lest the natives will kill him in order to seize his beautiful wife, he declares that Rebekah is his sister. His deception, however, is soon discovered, and he is sharply rebuked by the king of Gerar. Nevertheless, as the heir of the divine promises, prosperity still attends him. At Beersheba he makes a covenant of peace with the king of Gerar and seals it by a solemn oath. Hence to Isaac the oldest stories attribute the origin of the name Beersheba (*Well of the Oath*).

Isaac is the hero of the South Country, just as Abraham is of Hebron, and Jacob of Bethel and the sanctuaries east of the Jordan. Beer-lahai-roi, Gerar and Beersheba, to the south of Canaan, are the sites about which the Isaac stories gather, and at these sacred places they were probably first treasured. Thus tradition fixes his abode in the half nomadic, half agricultural land that lies midway between the territory of the Hebrews and of the Edomites, who regarded him as their common ancestor. From this same wilderness region came many of the tribes which later united to form the Hebrew nation.

The account of Rebekah's journey westward with her attendant servants may also be the form in which early tradition recorded the fact that later bands of Aramean immigrants followed and reënforced the first great migration represented by Abraham. The fact that her kinsmen are Aramean tribes and her descendants are two great nations, at least suggests that, although there may be an ultimate basis of individual history, the stories reflect the early movements of tribes and races.

VI. **Aim and Teachings.** The primary aim of this story was evidently to interest and entertain the audiences that gathered about the ancient story-teller. The narrative also illustrates the divine guidance of the destinies of the race. The character of Isaac is not so fully portrayed, nor is it as significant as that of either Abraham or Jacob. Isaac has his father's mildness and love of peace without the same commanding faith. He is conventionally pious, and goes out to meditate at eventide; but is stirred by no exalted ambition. To him the divine promise is renewed, yet it is not for his own sake but for that of Abraham. Isaac is a loving husband, but he is inclined to follow the line of least resistance, even though his wife is endangered by his cowardly deception. He is a true type of the average man of any age or race.

Rebekah in the story realized the oriental ideal of a wise, brave woman and wife. The portrait of the servant is of perennial value. His complete forgetfulness of self, his fidelity, his zeal and tact in carrying out the commands of his master, even though he be but a slave, and his child-like faith in God's leadership, are qualities which make men valuable members of society in every age.

§XII. JACOB AND HIS BROTHER ESAU.

Now Isaac prayed to Jehovah in behalf of his wife, because she was barren; and Jehovah heard his prayer, so that Rebekah his wife conceived. And the children struggled together within her; and she said, If it be so, why has

1. The oracle concerning the unborn twins

101

this befallen me ? Therefore she went to inquire of Jehovah. And Jehovah said to her,

> Two nations are in thy womb,
> And the two races, which spring from thee, shall sepa-
> rate from each other,
> And one people shall be stronger than the other,
> And the elder shall serve the younger.

2. Origin of the names Esau and Jacob

When her days to be delivered were fulfilled, there were
indeed twins in her womb. And the first came forth red
all over, like a hairy garment; so they called his name
Esau [Hairy]. And afterwards his brother came forth
holding fast Esau's heel with his hand; so his name was
called Jacob [Heel-holder].

3. Characteristics of the brothers

Now as the boys grew Esau became a skillful hunter, but
Jacob was a quiet man, a dweller in tents. And Isaac
loved Esau—for he had a taste for game—and Rebekah
loved Jacob.

4. Sale of the birthright

Once when Jacob was preparing a stew, Esau came in
from the field, and he was faint; therefore Esau said to
Jacob, Let me eat quickly, I pray, some of that red food,
for I am faint. (Therefore his name was called Edom
[Red]). But Jacob said, Sell me first of all your birthright.
And Esau replied, Alas! I am nearly dead, therefore of
what use is this birthright to me? And Jacob said, Swear
to me first; so he swore to him, and sold his birthright to
Jacob. Then Jacob gave Esau bread and stewed lentils,
and when he had eaten and drank, he rose up and went his
way. Thus Esau despised his birthright.

5. Isaac's request

Now it came to pass, when Isaac was so old that he could
not see, that he called Esau his eldest son, and said, Behold
I am old and know not the day of my death. Now therefore take, I pray you, your weapons, your quiver and your
bow, and go out to the field, and hunt game for me, that I
myself may bless you before I die. So Esau went to the
field to hunt game in order to bring it to him.

6. Rebekah's plot

Then Rebekah spoke to Jacob her son and said, I just
now heard your father say to your brother Esau, "Bring
me game that I may eat and bless you in the name of Je-

hovah." And Rebekah took the fine garments of Esau, her elder son, which she had with her in the house, and put them upon Jacob, her younger son, and he went to his father.

And Isaac said, Who are you, my son? And Jacob said to his father, I am Esau your first-born. I have done according as you commanded me. Arise, I pray you, and sit and eat of my game, that you yourself may bless me. And Isaac said to his son, How is it that you have found it so quickly, my son? And he said, Because Jehovah your God gave me success. And he said, Are you really my son Esau? And he said, I am. Then he said, Bring it to me, that I may eat of my son's game, in order that I myself may bless you. So he brought it to him, and he ate. He also brought him wine and he drank. 7. Jacob's deception

And his father Isaac said to him, Come near now and kiss me, my son. And as he came near and kissed him, he smelled the smell of his garment, and blessed him and said, 8. The blessing upon Jacob

> See, the smell of my son
> Is as the smell of a field which Jehovah hath blessed.
> Let peoples serve thee,
> And races bow down to thee.
>   Cursed be every one that curseth thee,
> And blessed be every one that blesseth thee.

And it came to pass, as soon as Isaac had made an end of blessing Jacob, that Esau his brother came in from his hunting, and said to his father, Let my father arise, and eat of his son's game, that you yourself may bless me. And Isaac his father said to him, Who are you? And he said, I am your son, your first-born, Esau. And Isaac trembled violently, and said, Who then is he that hunted game and brought it to me, so that I ate plentifully before you came? Verily, I have blessed him, and he shall remain blessed. When Esau heard the words of his father, he cried with a very loud and bitter cry, and said to his father, Bless me, even me also, O my father. 9. Esau's sorrow

And Esau said to himself, The days of mourning for my father are near, then will I slay my brother Jacob. But when the words of Esau her elder son were told to Rebekah, 10. Jacob's flight

JACOB AND HIS BROTHER ESAU

she sent and called Jacob her younger son, and said to him, Behold your brother Esau will avenge himself upon you by killing you. Flee to Laban my brother at Haran, until your brother's anger turn away from you.

I. Jacob's Efforts to Supplant Esau. The great prophetic teaching that Jehovah personally directed Israel's history from the first is again emphasized by the story of the birth of Jacob and Esau. Rebekah, like Sarah, was barren until Jehovah heard Isaac's prayer for offspring. The later history of the two nations, represented by Esau and Jacob, is reflected in the divine message to Rebekah. Even though the Edomites grew to be a nation and found a permanent home to the south of the Dead Sea long before the Israelites, they later became subject to their younger kinsmen.

The popular interpretation of the meaning of the two names is woven into the tradition of the birth of the two brothers. With a grim humor, peculiar to these early narratives, the long, bitter struggle between the two nations is represented as beginning at the birth of their traditional ancestors. Jacob's chief characteristic, the desire to get ahead of his rival, is revealed, even before he sees the light. Departing from their usual custom, the prophetic historians give a brief character sketch of the two brothers. Esau has the characteristics of his father; Jacob those of his mother.

According to Hebrew custom a double portion went to the first-born (cf. Dt. 21$^{15\text{-}17}$). For food to satisfy his immediate hunger the careless Esau was ready to sell his special rights as the eldest son and that rich heritage of promise which he should have passed on to his descendants. Jacob, the ambitious schemer, did not hesitate to take advantage of his brother's weakness. Neither of the brothers figures in a noble rôle.

II. Jacob's Base Deception. Jacob's character is further revealed by the means which he employs to establish his title to the birthright. In this incident he shows himself not only the favorite, but the true son of his ambitious and unscrupulous mother. Taking advantage of the infirmities of his aged father and the absence of his brother on a mission prompted by filial duty, he secures by deception the coveted paternal blessing. The blessing of a dying father was believed by the ancients to exert an important influence in the life of his descendants. The early Judean prophetic historians (whose narrative has been followed), make no effort to excuse Jacob's deliberate falsehoods. They simply record the effect of the act upon his character and later history. The sympathy of the early historians, as well as of the reader, goes out to Esau, whose sorrow, on discovering the wrong of which he is the victim, is vividly and touchingly portrayed. Jacob flees, impelled like Cain, by the fear that vengeance will fall upon his guilty head.

III. **The Underlying Tribal History.** The vividness and consistency of the early prophetic portraits of Esau and Jacob favor a personal interpretation, but there is much evidence to show that they represent more than mere individuals. The name *Jacob* has been found on the Babylonian tablets coming from the age of Hammurabi. It appears also in slightly different form, on contract tablets discovered in Cappadocia. It is likewise the name of one of the Asiatic Hyksos kings who ruled over Egypt. Thutmose III, the great conqueror of the eighteenth Egyptian dynasty, mentions a certain Jacob-el among the Palestinian cities captured by him. From these references it is clear that the name was borne by individuals; but in Palestine it was the designation of a city or tribe.

As has been already noted in the early prophetic stories, both Jacob and Esau are clearly types of the two nations which were regarded as their immediate descendants. Esau is in many ways an attractive, picturesque character. His home is out in the open air and his occupation is hunting. He is ingenuous and impulsive, but ruled by his inclinations, a child of the present, with no lofty ideal or genuine religious zeal. He is a type of the modern gypsy or tramp. The portrait is true to the character of the Edomites. Living on the borders of Canaan, they largely retained their early nomadic, roving habits, depending for existence upon the scanty products of the wilderness and the plunder which they extorted or stole from passing caravans.

The Esau stories assume the historic fact that the Edomites were established as a nation long before the Israelites. In the inscriptions telling of conquests by kings of the eighth Egyptian dynasty, Edom is the name of one of the captured cities. In the el-Amarna tablets *Udumu* or Edom figures as a city hostile to the Egyptians. In the later Assyrian inscriptions, *Udumu* is the name of both a city and a land.

The biblical narratives also proclaim that close relationship between the Edomites and Israelites, which is confirmed by similarity in language and institutions. These stories likewise reflect the close geographical and political relations, which ever linked these two peoples together, and which ultimately resulted in the conquest of the older race by the younger. These traditions evidently are intended to answer the question, Why this reversal of their earlier fortunes came about. The answer is found, as in the Noah oracle (§ IV), in the characteristics of the two races.

IV. **Significance of the Portrait of Jacob.** The deeper historical and ethical value of the Jacob stories is found in the marvellous portrait and analysis of the character and experiences of the Israelites which these narratives present. They are almost without analogy in human literature. Only the Hebrew prophets, who studied existing conditions and forces with eyes opened by the divine touch and with a thoroughness that rivals the work of the modern scientist and historian, could thus portray, so simply and yet with absolute fidelity, the strength and weaknesses of their race. For hunting and the frivolities of life Jacob has no time or inclination. In him the noble aspirations of Abraham for the future of his descendants have become a selfish passion. He ever remains beside the tents, plotting how he may win from his brother the coveted rights of the first-born. No opportunity to gain the desired prize escapes him. His fatal fault is that he is ready to employ any means to attain his ends; he even resorts to misrepresentation and actual falsehood. Cowardice, begotten by his own wrong-doing, adds to the blackness of the portrait.

Yet in contrast to Esau, who is but a drifter on the stream of life, Jacob is the more promising character. Notwithstanding his glaring faults, he has energy and ambition. His ambition is selfish and material, and yet it extends beyond himself to the prosperity and victories of his descendants.

V. **Aim and Teachings.** Of the many aims that are revealed in these stories, perhaps the chief with the prophets was to hold up before their countrymen such a clear portrait of their national character that all would see and correct their hereditary faults. As inspired interpreters of history, the prophets were also setting forth the fundamental reasons why Israel, even through failure and discipline, became at last the conquering race, with the full consciousness of a glorious destiny. The immediate teachings of the stories are obvious: (1) A man or a nation, however gifted and personally attractive, if intent only on immediate and physical enjoyment and without a spiritual ideal or ambition, is, like Esau, destined to degenerate and prove a failure. (2) Selfishness and trickery bring only injustice to others and cowardice and suffering to the wrong-doer. He who soweth the wind shall reap the whirlwind. (3) God himself cannot make a man out of an idle drifter; but he who has ambition and persistence is never impossible.

10/25 Fri

§ XIII.   JACOB'S EXPERIENCES AS A FUGITIVE

Now when Jacob set out from Beersheba, he went toward Haran. And when Jacob arrived at a certain place, he passed the night there, because the sun had set. And he took one of the stones which were there, and put it under his head, and lay down in that place to sleep. Then he dreamed and saw a ladder set up on the earth with its top reaching to heaven; and, behold, the Messengers of God were ascending and descending on it. And, behold, Jehovah stood beside him and said, I am Jehovah, the God of Abraham thy father and the God of Isaac. The land upon which thou art lying—to thee will I give it and to thy descendants. And thine offspring shall be as the dust of the earth, and thou shalt spread abroad to the west, and to the east, and to the north, and to the south, and a blessing like thine and that of thy descendants shall all the families of the earth ask for themselves. And, behold, I am with thee, and will keep thee wherever thou goest, and will bring thee again to this habitable land; for I will not leave thee until I have done that which I have promised thee. 1. Jehovah's promise to Jacob and his descendants

And when Jacob awoke from his sleep, he said, Surely Jehovah is in this place, and I knew it not. And he was filled with awe and said, How awful is this place; this is none other than the house of God [Beth-el] and this is the gate of heaven. 2. Origin of the name Bethel

So Jacob rose up early in the morning, and took the stone that he had put under his head, and set it up for a pillar, and poured oil upon the top of it. Therefore he called the name of that place Bethel [House of God], although the earlier name of the city was Luz. And Jacob made a vow saying, If God will be with me and keep me in this journey which I am making, and give me bread to eat and clothing to put on, and I come again safe and sound to my father's house, then shall Jehovah be my God and this stone which I have set up for a pillar, shall be a house of God. 3. Origin of sanctuary at Bethel

Then Jacob went on his journey, and came to the land of the children of the East. And he looked, and saw a well in the field, and there were three flocks of sheep lying down 4. Scene at the well in Haran

107

by it; for out of that well they watered the flocks; but the stone upon the mouth of the well was large. And when all the flocks were gathered here, they used to roll the stone from the mouth of the well and water the sheep, and then put the stone again in its place upon the mouth of the well.

5. Jacob's conversation with the shepherds

And Jacob said to them, My friends, whence are you? And they said, We are from Haran. Then he said to them, Do you know Laban the son of Nahor? And they said, We know him. And he said to them, Is it well with him? And they said, It is well; indeed, see Rachel his daughter coming there with the sheep. And he said, Behold, the sun is still high! it is not time for the cattle to be gathered together. Water the sheep and let them go to feed. But they said, We cannot until the flocks are gathered together and they roll the stone from the well's mouth, then we water the sheep.

6. Meeting of Jacob and Rachel

While he was yet speaking with them, Rachel came with her father's sheep; for she was a shepherdess. Now when Jacob saw Rachel the daughter of Laban, his mother's brother, and Laban's sheep, he went near and rolled the stone from the mouth of the well, and watered the flock of Laban, his mother's brother. Then Jacob kissed Rachel and wept loudly. And when Jacob told Rachel that he was a kinsman of her father, and that he was Rebekah's son, she ran and told her father.

7. Jacob's reception at her house

But as soon as Laban heard the tidings regarding Jacob, his sister's son, he ran to meet him, and embraced and kissed him, and brought him to his house. Then Jacob recounted to Laban all these things. And Laban said to him, Surely you are of my bone and of my flesh. So he remained with him about a month.

8. Agreement to serve Laban for Rachel

Then Laban said to Jacob, Because you are my kinsman should you therefore serve me for nothing? Tell me what shall be your wages? Now Laban had two daughters: the name of the elder was Leah, and the name of the younger was Rachel. And Leah had weak eyes, but Rachel was beautiful in form and feature. Therefore Jacob loved Rachel and he said, I will serve you seven years for Rachel your younger daughter. And Laban said, It is better for me to give her to you than that I should give her to another man. Stay with me. So Jacob served seven years for Rachel, and they seemed to him but a few days, because he loved her.

Then Jacob said to Laban, Give me my wife, for my days are fulfilled and let me go in unto her. Accordingly Laban gathered together all the men of the place and made a feast. And it came to pass in the evening that he took Leah his daughter and brought her to him, and Jacob went in unto her. And Laban gave Zilpah his maid-servant to his daughter Leah for a maid. When in the morning he found it was Leah, he said to Laban, What is this you have done to me? Did I not serve you for Rachel? Why then have you deceived me? And Laban said, It is not customary among us to give the younger in marriage before the elder. Remain with this one during the marriage week, then we will give to you the other also for the service which you shall render me for seven more years. Therefore Jacob did so: he remained with Leah during the marriage week. Then Laban gave him Rachel his daughter as wife. Laban also gave to Rachel his daughter Bilhah his maid-servant to be her maid. Then he went in to Rachel, but he loved Rachel more than Leah. Thus he had to serve him seven years more.

When Jehovah saw that Leah was hated, he opened her womb; Rachel, however, was barren. Accordingly Leah conceived and bore a son whom she named Reuben [Behold a son]; for she said, Jehovah hath beheld my affliction; now my husband will love me. And she conceived again and bore a son; and said, Because Jehovah hath heard that I am hated, he hath therefore given me this one also; hence she called his name Simeon [Hearing]. And she conceived again and bore a son, and said, Now this time will my husband become attached to me, because I have borne him three sons: therefore his name was called Levi [Attached]. And she conceived again, and bore a son, and said, This time will I praise Jehovah: therefore she called his name Judah [Praise]; then she ceased to bear children.

When Leah saw that she had ceased to bear children, she took Zilpah her maid-servant and gave her to Jacob as a

9. Laban's deception

10. Birth of Leah's children; Reuben, Simeon, Levi, Judah

11. By Zilpah: Gad and Asher

wife. And Zilpah Leah's maid-servant bore Jacob a son. And Leah said, Fortunate am I! therefore she called his name Gad [Fortune]. And Zilpah Leah's maid-servant bore Jacob a second son. And Leah said, Happy am I! for women are sure to call me happy; therefore she called his name Asher [Happy].

12. Rachel's children by Bilhah: Dan and Naphtali

And when Rachel saw that she bore Jacob no children, Rachel was jealous of her sister, and said to Jacob, Give me children or else I die. But Jacob's anger was aroused against Rachel, and he said, Am I in God's stead? Who hath withheld offspring from thee? And she said, Here is my maid Bilhah, go in unto her, that she may bear upon my knees and I also may obtain children by her. And so she gave him Bilhah her maid for a wife, and Jacob went in unto her. And when Bilhah conceived and bore Jacob a son, Rachel said, God hath judged me and hath also heard my voice and hath given me a son. Therefore she called his name Dan [He judged]. And Bilhah Rachel's maid conceived again, and bore Jacob a second son. And Rachel said, With superhuman wrestlings have I wrestled with my sister, and have prevailed; therefore she called his name Naphtali [Obtained by wrestling].

13. Leah's later children: Issachar and Zebulun

And God heard Leah, and she conceived and bore Jacob a fifth son. Then Leah said, God hath given me my hire, because I gave my maid to my husband; therefore she called his name Issachar [There is a hire]. And Leah conceived again, and bore a sixth son to Jacob. And Leah said, God hath endowed me with a good dowry; now will my husband dwell with me, because I have borne him six sons: and she called his name Zebulun [Dwelling]. And afterwards she bore a daughter and called her name Dinah.

14. Birth of Rachel's son, Joseph

And God remembered Rachel, and God hearkened to her, and opened her womb. So she conceived and bore a son and said, God hath taken away my reproach. And she called his name Joseph [He will add], saying, Jehovah will add to me another son.

15. The contract between Jacob and Laban

Now when Rachel had borne Joseph, Jacob said to Laban, Send me away, that I may go to my own place, and to my country. But Laban said to him, If now I have found favor in your eyes—I have divined that Jehovah hath blessed me

110

for your sake. And Jacob answered him, You know how I have served you, and what your cattle have become under my charge, for it was little which you had before I came, but now it has greatly increased, since Jehovah hath blessed you wherever I went. But now, when am I to provide for my own house as well? Then he said, What shall I give you? And Jacob said, You shall not give me anything. If you will do this thing for me, I will again feed your flock: remove from it every speckled and spotted one; then whatever is born to the flock henceforth speckled or spotted shall be mine. And Laban said, Good, let it be as you say. So he removed that day the he-goats that were striped and spotted, and all the she-goats that were striped and spotted, every one that had white on it, and gave them into the hands of his sons. Then he put the distance of a three days' journey between himself and Jacob; and Jacob fed the rest of Laban's flocks.

Now Jacob took fresh rods of white poplar, and of the almond and of the plane tree, and peeled white streaks in them, exposing the white which was in the rods. And he set the rods which he had peeled before the flocks in the watering-troughs, where the flocks came to drink (and they conceived when they came to drink), so that the flocks conceived before the rods. Therefore the flocks brought forth striped, speckled and spotted offspring. And whenever the stronger animals of the flock conceived, Jacob laid the rods in the troughs before the eyes of the flock, that they might conceive among the rods. But when the animals were weak, he put them not in; so that the weaker ones were Laban's, and the stronger Jacob's. Thus the man increased in wealth exceedingly, and had large flocks, and maid-servants and men-servants, and camels and asses.

16. Jacob's crafty trick

I. **The Divine Promise.** The late priestly narrative (Gen. 35[6a, 9–15]) and Hosea (12[4]) place the divine revelation and promises to Jacob after his return from Aram. This may have been its original position, for the promises come more naturally after he has learned in the hard school of experience the lessons which were necessary for his development. On the other hand, the representation that God appeared to him at the time of his greatest spiritual need also rings true to the teachings of the prophets. Both the Judean and Northern Israelite narratives (which have been closely blended) agree in placing the vision on Jacob's journey to Haran.

II. **The Vision at Bethel.** About ten miles north of Jerusalem, a little to the right of the great highway that leads from Hebron and Jerusalem northward to Shechem and on to Damascus, are found the ruins of the ancient sanctuary of Bethel. It is on a slight limestone elevation, strewn with rocks. Here the Hebrews revered the sacred rock on which, according to their traditions, Jacob pillowed his head, as he dreamed of the ladder leading up to the abode of God and of the divine messengers passing back and forth from earth to heaven. There the fugitive, paying the bitter penalty for his meanness and treachery, yet craving a revelation from heaven, was given anew the promise already proclaimed to Abraham (§ VII). To this was added the assurance of God's personal care and protection.

According to Hebrew tradition, it was because God (*El*) revealed himself here to Jacob that Bethel received its name and became a famous sanctuary. The belief that the spirit of the Deity resided in certain sacred stones was widely current among early peoples. Many stone circles or *gilgals* and pillars at temple sites, as, for example, those recently discovered in the ruins of Gezer, testify that the ancient inhabitants of Palestine shared the same belief. The Old Testament also refers frequently to these sacred stones or pillars that stood beside every ancient altar. At first only rude bowlders, they were in time carved into artistic pillars (*cf.* Hos. 10¹). The present story gives the accepted explanation of the sanctity of the pillar that stood beside the altar of Bethel. The reformation of Josiah in 621 B.C. made all of these high-places, with their heathen symbols and associations, illegal, but the present story evidently comes from the early period, when sacred pillars were still regarded as perfectly legitimate.

III. **The Wooing and Winning of Rachel.** The scene at the well near Haran is repeated many times in Arabia to-day, except that few sons of the desert manifest the same chivalrous zeal in serving the modern Rachels. Jacob's kisses and tears are characteristic of the emotional Oriental. Even the crafty Laban embraced and kissed the stranger; but in the heart of Jacob was stirring a love which mastered even the selfish schemer.

By his services for seven years, practically as a slave, Jacob paid the bride-price which every oriental father demands. The custom still survives in Syria. The length of the service or the amount of the bride-price is proportionate to the wealth and position of the parents. The cruel deception, of which Jacob was the victim, was a further retribution for the atrocious deceit which he had practised upon his father and brother. Laban's excuse, however, did not palliate his act. Like most of the dealings between him and Jacob, it was justified by custom but not by moral law.

IV. Jacob's Family. In connection with the account of the birth of Jacob's eleven sons the popular derivation of their names is given. Apparently the stories grew out of the meaning suggested by each name. In nearly every case the etymology is based simply on assonance and not on the real derivation. The picture which these early prophetic stories give of Jacob's home life is far from attractive. The polygamy that was forced upon him and the resulting favoritism and jealousy are but the after fruits of his own deceit and treachery. The early prophets make no attempt to conceal the hideousness of it all, for therein was taught most forcibly its obvious moral lessons.

V. His Dealings with Laban. The original story-tellers doubtless took a certain delight in the account of the shrewd dealings between Jacob and Laban. They reflect the low ethics of the desert where "a lie is the salt of a man," and successful knavery is secretly more admired than plain honesty. It is a case of Shylock *versus* Shylock, of steel cutting steel: Laban is sharp and unprincipled, but Jacob is able to surpass him in the game of wits. Laban readily agrees that Jacob's pay shall consist simply of the young sheep and goats abnormally marked. By the use of a device well known to cattle-breeders in antiquity (*cf.* Oppian, *Kynegetica*, I. 327–356), Jacob so contrives that all the strong offspring of the flock become his by legal although not by moral right. His entire life at Haran is a strange mixture of faith and selfishness, of chivalry and meanness, of true affection and jealousy, of faithful service and trickery.

VI. Historical Significance of the Stories. The marvellous simplicity of these stories deepens the impression that the hero was an individual rather than the representative of a race. A careful analysis, however, reveals much that is typical of the character and experiences of early Israel. The twelve sons of Jacob are in reality the twelve tribes which were first brought together and united under a common head in the days of Saul and David. To them Jacob was their common traditional ancestor. These stories were therefore important forces in Israel's national life, for they gave all members of the various composite tribes, that finally coalesced, the sense of blood-kinship as well as of political unity.

JACOB'S EXPERIENCES AS A FUGITIVE

The tribes whose ancestry is traced to Jacob are divided into three classes, according to the relative dates when they settled in Palestine, their importance and the purity of their descent. These classes include: (1) the descendants of the favorite wife, Rachel. These were Joseph and the youngest son, Benjamin. The two traditional sons of Joseph, Ephraim and Manasseh, were the powerful tribes of central Canaan which play the leading rôle in early Hebrew history. (2) The sons of the hated wife Leah—Reuben, Simeon, Levi, Judah, Issachar and Zebulun—tribes that stand next in importance, in purity of blood and in final geographical position to the Rachel tribes. Of these Leah tribes the first four, which found homes in the south, constitute the earlier group. (3) The four sons of the slave wives, Dan, Naphtali, Gad and Asher, the outlying tribes which contained the largest native Canaanite element, and were never very strong or closely assimilated with the other Hebrew tribes.

Thus tradition has woven into these stories the facts of later history which it also seeks to explain. The account of the shrewd dealings between Laban and Jacob doubtless reflect the bitter conflict waged for over two centuries after the days of David, in the public markets and on the battle-field, between the Arameans and the Israelites.

VII. **Aim and Teachings.** The aims of the original narratives were evidently, (1) to trace the origin of the name and sanctuary of Bethel, (2) to reassert Israel's divine destiny, (3) to emphasize the purity of its Aramean origin, and (4) to establish the popular belief that all the Hebrew tribes were of one blood. These stories were also of interest to the prophets because they illustrated certain universal and distinctly religious truths. The experiences of Jacob emphasize the supreme fact that: (1) The divine love and pity follow even the fugitive who flees, pursued by his own crimes. (2) In the most discouraging environment and in the saddest moments of life come the most glorious revelations. (3) Heaven and God himself are very near the earth, and the way of communication is close and direct. (4) Strong, pure love can evoke devoted service even from a mean man. (5) The consequences of a man's base acts pursue him wherever he may go, affecting his own fortunes and the happiness of all connected with him.

§ XIV.   JACOB'S RETURN TO CANAAN

Now Jacob heard Laban's sons say, Jacob has taken all that was our father's, and from that which was our father's he has acquired all these riches. And Jehovah said to Jacob, Return to the land of thy fathers, and to thy kindred, and I will be with thee. *1. Reasons for the departure from Aram*

Then Jacob arose and set his sons and his wives upon the camels, and drove away all his cattle. And while Laban was gone to shear his sheep, Rachel stole the household gods that were her father's. So he fled with all that he had, and set out on his way toward Mount Gilead. *2. The escape*

Then Laban took his tribesmen with him, and pursued after Jacob seven days' journey, and overtook him in Mount Gilead. Now Jacob had pitched his tent in the mountain; and Laban with his tribesmen encamped in Mount Gilead. And Laban said to Jacob, Why did you flee secretly, stealing away from me without telling me, else I might have sent you away with mirth and with songs, with tambourine and with harp. But now since you are surely going, because you long so earnestly for your father's house, why have you stolen my gods? And Jacob said to him, The one with whom you find your gods shall not live; in the presence of our kinsmen investigate for yourself what is with me and take it. Jacob, however, did not know that Rachel had stolen them. So Laban went into Jacob's tent and into Leah's, and into the tent of the two maid-servants, but he did not find them. Then he went out of Leah's tent, and entered Rachel's. Now Rachel had taken the household gods and put them in the camel's saddle and was sitting upon them, so that when Laban had searched all about the tent, he did not find them. And she said to her father, Let not my lord be angry that I cannot rise before you, for the manner of women is upon me. And he searched thoroughly, but did not find the household gods. *3. Laban's charge*

Then Jacob was angry and brought a charge against Laban; and Jacob answered and said to Laban, What is my trespass? what is my sin, that you have pursued hotly after me? Although you have searched all my goods, what *4. Jacob's counter protest* have you found of all your household possessions? Declare it here before my kinsmen and yours, that they may decide which of us two is in the right. These twenty years have I been with you; your ewes and she-goats have not cast their young, neither did I eat the rams of your flocks. That which was torn of beasts I did not bring to you; I bore the loss of it myself; from my hand you required it, whether stolen by day or stolen by night. Thus I was: in the day the drought consumed me, and by night the frost, and my sleep fled from my eyes.

5. The covenant between Laban and Jacob

Then Laban answered, Come, let us make a covenant, I and you, and let there be a witness between me and you. Therefore Jacob said to the members of his family, Gather stones. And when they had taken stones and made a heap, they ate there by the heap. And Laban called it Jegar-sahadutha [Heap of witness]; but Jacob called it Galeed [Heap of witness]. And Laban said, This heap is a witness between me and you to-day. Therefore he called it Galeed. Moreover Laban said to Jacob, Behold, this heap, which I have set between me and you, is a witness that I will not pass over this heap to you, and that you shall not pass over this heap to me, for harm. The God of Abraham and the God of Nahor (the God of their ancestors) judge between us.

6. Jacob's message to Esau

And Jacob sent messengers before him to Esau his brother to the land of Seir, the territory of Edom. And he commanded them saying, Speak thus to my lord Esau: 'Your servant Jacob says, "I have prolonged my sojourn with Laban until now, and I have oxen and asses, flocks and men-servants, and maid-servants, and I have sent to tell my lord, that I may find favor in your sight."' And the messengers returned to Jacob saying, We came to your brother Esau, even as he was coming to meet you with four hundred men.

7. His present to Esau

Then Jacob was greatly afraid and distressed. And he took from that which he had with him a present for Esau his brother: two hundred she-goats and twenty he-goats, two hundred ewes and twenty rams, thirty milch camels and their colts, forty cows and ten bulls, twenty she-asses and ten foals. And he delivered them into the hands of his servants, each drove by itself, and said to his servants, Pass over before me, and leave a space between the droves. And he commanded the foremost, saying, When Esau my brother meets you and asks you saying, 'To whom do you belong? and where are you going? and whose are these before you?' then you shall say, 'Your servant Jacob's; it is a present sent to my lord Esau; and he himself is just behind us.' Thus he commanded also the second, and the third, and all that followed the droves, saying, In this manner shall you speak to Esau, when you find him, and you shall say, 'Moreover thy servant Jacob is just behind us.' (For he said to himself, 'I will appease him with the present that goes before me, and not until then will I see his face; perhaps he will receive me.') So the present passed over before him, but he himself lodged that night in the camp.

Then he rose up that night, and took his two wives, and his two maid-servants, and his eleven children, and sent them over the ford of the Jabbok.

8. Crossing the Jabbok

Jacob was left alone, and one wrestled with him until break of day. And when he saw that he did not prevail against Jacob, he smote the hollow of his thigh and the hollow of Jacob's thigh was strained, as he wrestled with him. Then he said, Let me go, for the day is breaking. But Jacob replied, I will not let thee go except thou bless me. And he said to him, What is thy name? And he replied, Jacob. Then he said, Thy name shall be called no more Jacob, but Israel [God's struggler]; for thou hast struggled with God and with men, and hast prevailed. And Jacob asked him, saying, Tell me, I pray thee, thy name. And he said, Why is it that thou dost ask my name? So he blessed him there.

9. The long struggle and the divine blessing

But the sun rose as soon as he had passed beyond Penuel, and he limped upon his thigh. This is why to this day the Israelites do not eat the hip muscle, which is at the hollow of the thigh, for he touched the hollow of Jacob's thigh on the hip muscle.

10. Sanctity of the hip muscle

And when Jacob lifted up his eyes he saw Esau coming with four hundred men. Then he apportioned the children to Leah and to Rachel, and to the two maid-servants. And he put the maid-servants and their children in front, and Leah and her children next, and Rachel and Joseph in the rear. Then he himself passed over before them, and bowed

11. Meeting of the two brothers

117

himself to the ground seven times, until he came near to his brother. And Esau ran to meet him, and embraced him, and fell on his neck, and kissed him, and they wept. When he lifted up his eyes, and saw the women and the children, he said, Who are these with you? And he answered, The children whom God hath graciously given your servant. Then the maid-servants together with their children approached, and bowed themselves. Leah also and her children approached, and bowed themselves, and afterwards Joseph and Rachel approached, and bowed themselves.

12. Jacob's present to Esau

And Esau said, What do you mean by all this company which I met? And Jacob replied, To find favor in the sight of my lord. And Esau said, I have plenty, my brother; keep what you have. But Jacob replied, Nay, I pray you, if now I have found favor in your sight, receive my offering from my hand; for I have looked upon your face as one looks upon the face of God, and you have regarded me favorably. Take, I pray you, my gift that is brought to you, because God hath dealt graciously with me, and because I have enough. Thus he urged him importunately until he took it.

13. The peaceful parting

Then Esau said, Let us set out and go on our way, and let me go before you. But he replied to him, My lord knows that the children are tender, and that I have flocks and herds with their young; and if they overdrive them one day all the flocks will die. Let my lord, I pray you, pass over before his servant, and I will proceed leisurely according as the cattle which I am driving, and the children are able to endure, until I come to my lord at Seir. Then Esau said, Let me at least leave with you some of the people who are with me. But Jacob replied, What need is there? let me only find favor in the sight of my lord. So Esau returned that day on his way to Seir.

14. Jacob at Succoth and Shechem

But Jacob journeyed to Succoth, and built there a house for himself, and made huts for his cattle; therefore the name of the place is called Succoth [Huts]. Then Jacob came in peace to the city of Shechem in the land of Canaan, and encamped before the city. And he bought the piece of ground where he pitched his tent, from the sons of Hamor, the father of Shechem, for four hundred shekels; and he erected there an altar and called it El, God of Israel.

JACOB'S FLIGHT FROM LABAN

I. Jacob's Flight from Laban. At last Jacob found his position in Haran intolerable. His overshrewd dealings gave him no courage to face the suspicions of Laban's sons. Hence he improved the first favorable opportunity to collect his many possessions and to flee from Laban back toward Canaan. Rachel, brought up in the school of deceit, did not hesitate to steal her father's household gods, that their protection might go with the fugitives. Thus Jacob fled ignominiously from the consequences of his immediate acts to face those of his youth.

Laban quickly pursued and overtook the fugitives. Consistently with his shrewd, hard character, he suggested ironically that if they had but expressed the wish to go, he would have speeded their departure with mirth and songs! He also inquired why they had stolen his family gods. Jacob, who was ignorant of the theft, gave him full permission to search for them; but Rachel so cleverly concealed the stolen images, that Laban was unable to prove his charge.

Jacob improved this opportunity to recount his services to Laban and the hardships which he had endured. He omitted, however, all mention of his own doubtful dealings. The conclusion of their half hostile meeting was a covenant, according to which each agreed not to pass beyond a certain boundary set up between them in the territory of Gilead.

II. The Supreme Crisis of Jacob's Life. Leaving behind the fear of his father-in-law, Jacob faced the brother whom he had wronged. With his usual diplomacy, he first dispatched messengers to Esau with conciliatory greetings. Still trusting to the potency of the material possessions for which he had striven so hard, he next sent ahead a princely gift for his brother. Then stealthily by night he sent on his wives and children, while he himself remained alone in the darkness by the noisy east-Jordan stream whose name (Jabbok) meant *Struggler*. It was the supreme crisis in his life. He had struggled for flocks and herds and material honors, and in each contest had succeeded; but with the success had come haunting fear, and an inevitable sense of failure. Hitherto he had conquered men by sheer energy, persistency and superior wit; but now he struggled alone all the night through with a more than human antagonist. He came forth from the fateful struggle with bodily strength forever impaired. Yet from this contest, by virtue of his indomitable persistency, he again emerged a victor. Henceforth he was to be called not Jacob, the Supplanter, but Israel, the one who had struggled and prevailed with God. It would seem that in this strange ancient tale the early prophet aimed to portray the victory of the nobler and more spiritual impulses in Israel's complex character over the more

119

sordid, selfish tendencies. The prophetic interpretation of Hosea (12³, ⁴) is suggestive in this connection:

> In the womb Jacob supplanted his brother,
> In a man's strength he contended with God,
> He contended with the angel and prevailed,
> He wept and besought mercy of him.
> At Bethel Jehovah found him,
> And there he spoke with him.

III. The Meeting with Esau. Jacob's fears of his brother proved groundless. The meeting with Esau was in marked contrast to the bickering attendant upon his final interview with Laban. Esau manifested a generous brotherly spirit. Jacob, however, was still suspicious of the brother whom he had wronged, and so preferred to go on his way alone. At Shechem he found for a time a peaceful home, until the crimes of his sons Levi and Simeon compelled him to flee to southern Canaan. At this point the interest of the narrative in Genesis suddenly passes from Jacob to Joseph.

IV. The Historical Facts Back of the Stories. Back of the Laban stories is the memory of the later struggles between the Israelites and the Arameans. Gilead, the place of the covenant between Jacob and Laban, was the debatable territory and the scene of many battles. Doubtless tradition pointed to a certain heap of stones or sacred cairn as the scene of the treaty between the ancestors of these two related but hostile peoples.

The story of Jacob's return at the head of a large tribe probably records a third Aramean migration, reënforcing the two represented by the coming of Abraham and Rebekah. These Jacob stories also give the popular explanation of the origin of the names Penuel (Face of God) and of Succoth, and of the sanctuary at Shechem.

V. Aim and Teachings. In the portrayal of the character of Jacob, the prophets who combined these early stories clearly realized their primary aim. Though exceedingly complex, that character is remarkably consistent. Jacob's faults are those which Orientals most easily condone. Our modern western world, on the contrary, will forgive almost anything more readily than the lack of truth and honesty. Jacob's religious professions also seem but hypocrisy. Hypocrisy, however, involves a degree of spiritual enlightenment which he did not possess. Although his religion was of the bargaining type, it was genuine and the most powerful force in his life. Energy, persistency and ambition were the other qualities which enabled him at last to triumph over his glaring faults of meanness, deceit and selfishness. His life, as portrayed, vividly illustrates the constant conflict going on in every man between his baser passions and his nobler ideals. Jacob is the classic prototype of Robert Louis Stevenson's Dr. Jekyll and Mr. Hyde. His experiences show clearly how, in divine Providence, the varied fortunes, and especially the misfortunes of life, may develop the nobler impulses in the human heart, and how the meanest and most unpromising men are never beyond the pale of the divine care. It is only the base and false in man that destroy his happiness and prevent him from gaining clear visions of God's gracious purpose.

§XV. JOSEPH SOLD BY HIS BROTHERS INTO EGYPT

Joseph at the age of seventeen was a shepherd with his brothers, and he was a lad with the sons of Bilhah, and with the sons of Zilpah, his father's wives. And Joseph brought an evil report of them to their father. Now Israel loved Joseph more than all his other children, because he was the son of his old age; and he had made him a long tunic with sleeves. And when his brothers saw that their father loved him more than all his other sons, they hated him, and could not speak peacefully to him. **1. Joseph's life at home**

And Joseph had a dream, and told it to his brothers, and they hated him still more. And he said to them, Hear, I pray you, this dream which I have had; for it seemed to me that we were binding sheaves in the field, and, lo, my sheaf arose and remained standing, while your sheaves surrounded and made obeisance to my sheaf. And his brothers said to him, Will you assuredly be king over us? or will you indeed rule over us? So they hated him still more because of his dreams and his words. Then he had yet another dream, and told it to his brothers, saying, Behold, I have had another dream, and it seemed to me that the sun and the moon and eleven stars made obeisance to me. And when he told it to his father and his brothers, his father rebuked him, and said to him, What is this dream that you have had? Shall I and your mother and your brothers indeed come to bow ourselves to the earth before you? And his brothers envied him; but his father kept the thing in mind.

3. His mission to his brothers

And his brothers went to pasture his father's flocks in Shechem. Then Israel said to Joseph, Are not your brothers pasturing the flocks in Shechem? Come now I will send you to them, and he replied, Here am I. And his father said to him, Go now, see whether it is well with your brothers, and well with the flock, and bring me word again. So he sent him out from the valley of Hebron, and he came to Shechem. And a certain man found him, as he was wandering in the field, and the man asked him saying, What are you seeking? And he said, I am seeking my brothers; tell me, I pray you, where they are pasturing the flock. And the man said, They have gone from this place, for I heard them say, ' Let us go to Dothan.' So Joseph went after his brothers and found them in Dothan.

4. Seized by his brothers

And when they saw him in the distance, but before he came near to them, they conspired against him to slay him. And they said one to another, See, here comes that master-dreamer. Now come, let us slay him, and throw him into one of the cisterns, and then we will say, A fierce beast has devoured him, and we shall see what will become of his dreams. Judah, however, when he heard it, delivered him from their hands, and said, Let us not take his life. Do not shed blood; throw him into this cistern, that is in the wilderness; but do not lay hands upon him. He said this that he might deliver him from their hands to restore him to his father. Nevertheless, when Joseph came to his brothers, they stripped him of his long tunic, the tunic with sleeves that was on him. Then they took him and threw him into the cistern. And the cistern was empty, there being no water in it.

5. Carried to Egypt

Then they sat down to eat bread, and as they lifted up their eyes and looked, behold, a caravan of Ishmaelites was coming from Gilead, and their camels were loaded with spices and balsam and ladanum, on their way to carry it down to Egypt. Thereupon Judah said to his brothers, What do we gain if we kill our brother and conceal his blood? Come, let us sell him to the Ishmaelites, and let not our hand be upon him, for he is our brother, our flesh.

And his brothers listened to him. And drawing up Joseph they sold him to the Ishmaelites for twenty pieces of silver. And they brought Joseph to Egypt.

Thereupon they took Joseph's coat, and killed a he-goat, and, dipping the coat in the blood, they sent the tunic with sleeves and brought it to their father, saying, We found this; see whether it is your son's coat or not. And he recognized it and said, It is my son's coat! a fierce beast has devoured him! Joseph is without doubt torn in pieces. Then Jacob rent his garments, and put sackcloth on his loins; and he mourned for his son many days. And all his sons and all his daughters rose up to comfort him, but he refused to be comforted, saying, I shall go down to Sheol to my son, mourning. Thus his father wept for him. *6. Reported as dead*

Joseph, however, was brought down to Egypt, and Potiphar, an officer of Pharaoh's, the chief executioner, an Egyptian, bought him from the Ishmaelites, who had brought him there. *7. Sold as a slave to an Egyptian*

Now Jehovah was with Joseph so that he became a prosperous man, and was in the house of his master the Egyptian. When his master saw that Jehovah was with him, and that Jehovah always caused everything that he did to prosper in his hands, Joseph found favor in his eyes as he ministered to him, so that he made him overseer of his house, and all that he had he put into his charge. Then it came to pass from the time that he made him overseer in his house, and over all that he had, that Jehovah blessed the Egyptian's house for Joseph's sake, and the blessing of Jehovah was upon all that he had in the house and in the field. So he left all that he had to Joseph's charge, and had no knowledge of anything that he had except the bread which he ate. *8. Intrusted with the care of his master's household*

Now Joseph was handsome in form and appearance. And it came to pass after these things, that his master's wife cast her eyes upon Joseph; and she said, Lie with me. But he refused, saying to his master's wife, Behold my master has no knowledge of what is with me in the house, and he has put all that he has into my charge; he is not greater in this house than I; neither has he kept back anything from me but you, because you are his wife; how then *9. Tempted by his master's wife* can I do this great wickedness and sin against God? And although she talked thus to Joseph day after day, he did not listen to her, to lie with her or to be with her. But once about this time when he went into the house to do his work, when none of the men of the household were at home, she caught hold of his garment, saying, Lie with me; but he left his garment in her hand and fled out of the house.

10. Falsely charged with infidelity And it came to pass when she saw that he had left his garment in her hand and had fled away, she called to the men of her household, and said to them, See, he has brought a Hebrew in to us to insult us. He came to me to lie with me, and I cried with a loud voice, and it came to pass, when he heard me crying out loudly, he left his garment with me and fled out of the house. And she kept his garment by her until his master came home; then she told him the same story, saying, The Hebrew servant whom you have brought to us, came to me to insult me; but it came to pass that when I lifted up my voice and cried, he left his garment with me and fled away.

11. Imprisoned by his master Then it came to pass when his master heard the statements of his wife which she made to him, saying, After this manner your servant did to me, that he was very angry, and Joseph's master took him and put him into the prison,— the place where the king's prisoners were bound. Thus he was there in prison.

12. Trusted by his jailer But Jehovah was with Joseph and showed kindness to him, and gave him favor in the sight of the keeper of the prison, so that the keeper of the prison committed to Joseph's charge all the prisoners who were in the prison, and for whatever they did there he was responsible. The keeper of the prison did not attend to anything that was in his charge, because Jehovah was with Joseph, and whatever he did, Jehovah always caused it to prosper.

I. **General Characteristics of the Joseph Stories.** No stories are more vividly told or more closely knit together than those which gather about the name of Joseph. The dramatic interest rises and falls as the narrative runs on, but it never ceases to hold the reader's attention. The charm of the stories is found in their simple, picturesque style, in their dramatic contrasts, and in the powerful appeal which they make to universal human interests.

The reiterated promises to the race and the supernatural elements, so prominent in preceding stories, suddenly disappear. The nomad tents are also soon left behind; the background of the narrative is the highly developed civilization of Egypt. In these stories the interest is still centred in one main character, but attention is gradually turned from the traditional nomadic ancestors of the Hebrews to the opening events of their national history.

Traces are found of two slightly variant versions of these stories, the one current in the north and the other in the south. Thus, for example, in the Judean version Judah is the first-born, who seeks to save Joseph's life, and the Ishmaelites are the merchantmen who bear away the young Hebrew to Egypt. In the northern group of narratives Reuben and the Midianites take the place of Judah and the Ishmaelites. The variations are so slight, however, that they can ordinarily be disregarded and the blended prophetic narrative may be followed without confusion.

II. Joseph, the Spoiled Child. The Joseph stories are so clearly and simply told that they need little interpretation. They open with the picture of Joseph's home at Hebron. Rachel had died as Jacob journeyed southward from Shechem and Bethel. Joseph, the eldest son of the patriarch's beloved wife, was the favorite of his old age. Jacob, like many a fond and foolish father, made the fatal mistake of showing partiality within his own household. Joseph he clad in one of the long-sleeved tunics which were worn by nobles and were better adapted to a life of luxury than of hard, manual labor.

Joseph added to the jealous hatred of his brothers by reporting their misdemeanors to his father, and by telling to them those boyish dreams, which revealed his own lofty ambitions and implied that he was destined some time to rule over them.

Not suspecting the attitude of his sons, Jacob sent Joseph on a long journey northward to his brothers. He found them at Dothan, south of the plain of Esdraelon, and doubtless near the spring beside which the flocks still find excellent pasturage. Joseph's presence, however, only aroused the murderous hate of his brothers. Judah, feeling the responsibility of an eldest son, alone counselled moderation. Accordingly Joseph was seized, stripped of his tunic and cast into one of the many bottle-shaped cisterns that are still found about Dothan. Thence he was drawn out and sold as a slave for a paltry sum (about twelve dollars), to a passing caravan of Arab traders, who carried him to Egypt. There he was resold (according to the Northern Israelite version) to a certain Potiphar, whose name means in Egyptian, *He whom Ra* (the sun god) *gave*.

III. Joseph's Temptation. In the household of his new master Joseph's real character and ability were soon revealed. So faithfully did he perform his every task that he soon succeeded in winning the complete confidence of the Egyptian. In time, everything in the household was entrusted to his care. This responsibility soon brought an almost overwhelming temptation. The standards of morality are low in the East, and especially in households where there are slaves. The crime which his master's wife urged him to commit was easily overlooked by the ancient Orient. The appeal to Joseph's pride and passion was exceedingly strong. To refuse an unprincipled and determined woman meant sure disgrace and imprisonment, if not death. It was a supreme crisis in Joseph's life. His noble refusal, because he would not betray the trust imposed on him or sin against God, is one of the most significant incidents recorded in the Old Testament.

IV. The Character of Joseph and Its Significance. The prophetic historians have here presented to their readers a character very different from those of Abraham and Jacob, and yet none the less important. Abraham is the calm, far-seeing, faithful servant of God; Jacob, the clever, crafty, persistent struggler, who sees visions and ultimately wins the divine blessing, is the type of the Israelite race; Joseph represents the faithful and successful man of affairs.

Each step in the development of his character is distinctly traced. In his boyhood home Joseph was fettered by that paternal favoritism which is fittingly represented by the long-sleeved tunic. He grew up a spoiled, egotistical boy, with false ideas of life. His faults, however, were those of inexperience. If he had remained at home he would never have realized the possibilities suggested by his crude boyish dreams. The awakening at the hands of his vindictive brothers was painful but necessary. Their cruel act brought him into contact with real life and the greater world of opportunity. Amidst the new and trying circumstances he revealed the qualities that win true success in the struggle of life. Not a word of complaint escaped his lips. A faith expressed in action, not in words, upheld him. Even though it promised no personal reward, he was absolutely faithful to every trust. Armed with his strong fidelity and faith, he emerged unscathed from the most insidious temptation that could assail a youth. Unjust adversity could not crush or daunt him, for his integrity of character, his perennial cheerfulness and his spirit of helpfulness were invincible. The practical truths illustrated by Joseph's character and experience are too obvious to need formulation. For every one in the stream of life they are a constant guide and inspiration, for they show clearly how, in the face of injustice and temptation, a man may "find his life by losing it."

§XVI. JOSEPH MADE GOVERNOR OF EGYPT

Now it came to pass after these things that the cupbearer of the king of Egypt and his baker offended their lord the king of Egypt, so that Pharaoh was angry with his two officers, the chief of the cupbearers and the chief of the bakers, and imprisoned them in the house of the chief executioner, in the same prison where Joseph was confined. And the captain of the guard assigned Joseph to wait on them; and they remained in confinement for some time.

1. Assigned to two official prisoners

Meanwhile the king of Egypt's cupbearer and baker, who were confined in prison, both in the same night had a dream, each of different interpretation. Therefore when Joseph came in to them in the morning, he saw plainly that they were sad. So he asked Pharaoh's officers who were imprisoned with him in his master's house, saying, Why do you look so sad to-day? And they said to him, We have had a dream, and there is no one who can interpret it. Then Joseph said to them, Does not the interpretation of dreams belong to God? tell them to me, I pray you.

2. His offer to interpret their dreams

Then the chief cupbearer told his dream to Joseph, and said to him, In my dream I seemed to see a vine before me, and on the vine three branches, and it was as though it budded, it put out blossoms and its clusters brought forth ripe grapes. And Pharaoh's cup was in my hand, and I took the grapes and pressed them into Pharaoh's cup, and gave the cup into Pharaoh's hand. Then Joseph said to him, This is the interpretation of it: the three branches are three days; within three days shall Pharaoh lift up your head and restore you to your place, and you shall give Pharaoh's cup into his hand as you used to do when you were his cupbearer. But may you keep me in remembrance when it is well with you, and may you show kindness to me and make

3. The cupbearer's dream

127

mention of me to Pharaoh, and bring me out of this house; for I was unjustly stolen from the land of the Hebrews, and here also I have done nothing that they should put me into the dungeon.

4. The baker's dream

When the chief baker saw that the interpretation was favorable, he said to Joseph, I also saw in my dream, and, behold, three baskets of white bread were on my head, and in the uppermost basket there were all kinds of baked food for Pharaoh; and the birds were eating them out of the basket upon my head. And Joseph answered and said, This is its interpretation: the three baskets are three days; within three days Pharaoh will take off your head, and hang you on a tree, and the birds shall eat your flesh from off you.

5. Their fulfilment

And it came to pass the third day, which was Pharaoh's birthday, that he made a feast for all his servants. Then he lifted up the head of the chief cupbearer and the head of the chief baker among his servants. And he restored the chief cupbearer to his office so that he again gave the cup into Pharaoh's hand. The chief baker, however, he hanged, as Joseph had interpreted to them. Yet the chief cupbearer did not remember Joseph, but forgot him.

6. Pharaoh's dreams

Now it came to pass after two full years, that Pharaoh had a dream in which he seemed to be standing by the Nile and to see coming up from the Nile seven cows, sleek and fat, which had been feeding in the reed grass. Then he seemed to see seven other cows coming up after them out of the Nile, bad-looking and lean, and standing by the other cows on the bank of the Nile. And the bad-looking cows ate the seven sleek, fat cows. Then Pharaoh awoke. Afterward he slept and had a second dream, and he seemed to see seven good ears of grain growing on one stalk. Also he seemed to see seven ears, thin and blasted by the east wind, springing up after them. And the thin ears swallowed up the seven plump, full ears. Then Pharaoh awoke, and, behold, it was a dream.

7. Failure of his wise men to interpret them

And it came to pass in the morning that his spirit was troubled, and he sent and called all the sacred scribes and wise men of Egypt; and Pharaoh told them his dreams, but there was no one who could interpret them to Pharaoh.

JOSEPH MADE GOVERNOR OF EGYPT

Then the chief cupbearer spoke to Pharaoh saying, My sins I now recall: Pharaoh was very angry with his servants, and imprisoned me and the chief baker in the house of the chief executioner; and we both had a dream the same night, each having a dream of different interpretation. And there with us was a Hebrew youth, a servant of the chief executioner; and we told him and he interpreted to us our dreams, to each man differently according to his dream. And exactly as he interpreted our dreams to us so they came to pass: me they restored to my office, and him they hanged. *8. The cupbearer's testimony*

Then Pharaoh sent and called Joseph, and they brought him hastily out of the dungeon; and he shaved himself and changed his clothes and came to Pharaoh. And Pharaoh said to Joseph I have had a dream, and there is no one who can interpret it. Now I have heard it said of you that when you hear a dream, you can interpret it. And Joseph answered Pharaoh, saying, Not I; God alone will give Pharaoh a favorable answer. *9. Joseph before Pharaoh*

Then Pharaoh said to Joseph, In my dream as I was standing on the bank of the Nile, I saw seven cows, fat and sleek which had been feeding in the reed grass. Then I seemed to see coming up after them seven more cows, thin, bad-looking and lean, worse than I ever saw in all the land of Egypt; and the lean and bad-looking cows ate the first seven fat cows; and when they had eaten them up, one could not tell that they had eaten them, for they were still as bad-looking as at the beginning. Then I awoke. Again I dreamed and seemed to see coming up on one stalk seven ears, full and good; and then seven ears, withered, thin, blasted with the east wind, sprang up after them; and the thin ears swallowed up the seven good ears. And I have told it to the magicians, but there is no one who can inform me regarding it. *10. Repetition of Pharaoh's dreams*

Then Joseph said to Pharaoh, What Pharaoh has dreamed signifies the same thing; what God is about to do he hath declared to Pharaoh. The seven good cows are seven years, and the seven good ears are seven years. It is one and the same dream. And the seven lean and ugly cows that came up after them are seven years, and also the seven empty ears *11. Joseph's interpretation of them* blasted with the east wind shall be seven years of famine. That is why I said to Pharaoh, What God is about to do he hath showed to Pharaoh. Behold, there are coming seven years of great plenty throughout the land of Egypt, and there shall be after them seven years of famine, so that all the plenty shall be forgotten in the land of Egypt; and the famine shall consume the land; and the plenty shall not be known in the land by reason of that famine which follows; for it shall be very severe. As for the fact that the dream came twice to Pharaoh, it is because the thing is established by God, and God will shortly bring it to pass. Now therefore let Pharaoh choose a man discreet and wise, and set him over the land of Egypt. Let Pharaoh take action and appoint overseers over the land and take up the fifth part of the produce of Egypt in the seven plenteous years. And let them gather all the food of these good years that come, and lay up grain under the authority of Pharaoh for food in the cities, and let them keep it. And the food shall be a provision for the land against the seven years of famine which shall be in the land of Egypt, that the land may not perish because of the famine.

12. Pharaoh's reward And the plan pleased Pharaoh and all his servants. And Pharaoh said to his servants, Can we find one like this, a man in whom is the spirit of God? And Pharaoh said to Joseph, See, I have appointed you over all the land of Egypt. And Pharaoh took off his signet ring from his finger and put it upon Joseph's finger, and clothed him in garments of fine linen, and put a gold chain about his neck, and made him ride in the second chariot which he had. Then they cried before him, Bow the knee! Thus he set him over all the land of Egypt. Pharaoh also said to Joseph, I am Pharaoh, but without your consent shall no man lift up his hand or his foot in all the land of Egypt. Pharaoh also called Joseph's name Zaphenath-paneah, and gave him as a wife Asenath, the daughter of Potiphera, priest of On.

13. His provisions for the famine And Joseph went out over all the land of Egypt, and gathered up all the food of the seven full years, which were in the land of Egypt, and stored the food in the cities, putting in each city the products of the fields about it.

And the seven years of famine began to come, just as Joseph had said. And when all the land of Egypt was famished, the people cried to Pharaoh for bread, and Pharaoh said to all the Egyptians, Go to Joseph; and what he tells you do. And when the famine was upon all the earth, Joseph opened all the storehouses and sold to the Egyptians. But the famine was severe in the land of Egypt. ^{14. The seven years of famine}

And there was no bread in all the land, since the famine was very severe, so that the land of Egypt languished because of the famine. And Joseph gathered in all the money that was found in the land of Egypt, for the grain which they bought; and Joseph brought the money into Pharaoh's house. ^{15. Pharaoh's tribute: all the money of Egypt}

And when the money was all spent in the land of Egypt, all the Egyptians came to Joseph, and said, Give us bread; for why should we die before your eyes, because our money fails? Then Joseph said, Give your cattle, and I will give you grain for your cattle, if money has failed. So they brought their cattle to Joseph, and Joseph gave them bread in exchange for the horses, the flocks of sheep, and herds of cattle and the asses. Thus for that year he sustained them with bread in exchange for all their cattle. ^{16. All the herds}

And when that year was ended, they came to him the second year, and said to him, We do not hide it from my lord, now that our money is all spent; and even the herds of cattle are my lord's; there is nothing left to give to my lord but our bodies and our lands. Why should we perish before your eyes, both we and our land? take possession of us and our land in return for bread, and we and our land will become possessions of Pharaoh; and give us seed, that we may live, and not die, so that the land may not become desolate. So Joseph bought all the land of Egypt for Pharaoh; for the Egyptians sold every man his field, because the famine was severe upon them. Thus the land became Pharaoh's. And as for the people, he reduced them to servitude from one end of Egypt even to the other. Only the land of the priests he did not buy, because the priests had a definite allowance from Pharaoh, and ate their portion which Pharaoh gave them; hence they did not sell their land. ^{17. All the land except that of the priests}

18. Establishment of a permanent tax

Then Joseph said to the people, Behold, I have bought you and your land to-day for Pharaoh. Here is seed for you, and you shall sow the land. And at the ingatherings you shall give a fifth to Pharaoh, and four parts shall be your own, for seed for the field, and for your food, and for those of your households, and for food for your little ones. And they said, You have saved our lives; let us find favor in the sight of my lord, and we will be Pharaoh's servants. Thus Joseph made it a statute concerning the land of Egypt to this day, that Pharaoh should have the fifth; only the land of the priests did not come into the possession of Pharaoh.

I. Dramatic Contrasts in the Story of Joseph. Nothing more dramatic can be imagined than the sudden and striking contrasts in Joseph's experiences. The pampered favorite of his father suddenly finds himself a slave in Egypt. The trusted head of his master's household is in a moment cast into a dungeon with little hope of release. From this same dungeon he is now raised to a position of highest honor and responsibility in the most powerful and brilliant empire of the age. This marvellous transformation takes place not through a miracle, but because the great need found the man, and the man had been fitted by his varied experiences to meet the need. Joseph's destiny turned upon his attitude toward his fellow-prisoners and the opportunities for helpfulness which they offered. Apparently like himself the royal cupbearer and baker were victims of oriental injustice.

The ancients believed universally that the gods spoke to them through dreams. According to the Egyptian inscriptions the kings were often guided in determining their policy by intimations conveyed to them in dreams. Among Orientals the intuitions are highly developed, and it is not impossible that in some cases their intuitions were reflected in their dreams. The dreams of Joseph's fellow-prisoners were each suggestive. It required, however, a keen-sighted, courageous man like Joseph to discern and declare their meaning.

II. The Prisoner Raised to High Authority. The good deed done and the interpretation fulfilled, two years more of discouraging, yet patient waiting passed before the dungeon door opened. In the light of Egyptian religious belief, Pharaoh's dream was especially significant. Cows were sacred to the cow-headed goddess Hathor, and to Isis who seems to have sometimes symbolized the land fertilized by the Nile. Fat, sleek cows, as well as full ears of grain, also suggested plenty. Joseph, however, is the only one in all the land who could clearly and convincingly interpret the meaning of Pharaoh's strange dreams. More important still, he was able to outline a wise and definite policy to be pursued. None of the varied and painful experiences that had come to the young Hebrew, who in his youth had also dreamed dreams, were in vain. Pharaoh and his counsellors recognized the man of the hour and were not slow to act. All the honors that an oriental despot could confer were at once heaped upon Joseph. The Egyptian name given to him appears to mean *Nourisher of the land, Giver of Life* or *God spake and he came into life.* Asenath, the name of his wife, means, *Belonging to the goddess Neith.*

With these honors came responsibility. Joseph first wisely provided for the needs of the people. At the same time he showed his loyalty to his master by adding greatly to Pharaoh's wealth and authority. To-day we would condemn Joseph's policy as unjust and tyrannical. The ancient East, however, thought little of the rights of the masses. The early Hebrew story-tellers record the incident simply as further proof of Joseph's fidelity.

Under the first twelve Egyptian dynasties the land was almost entirely owned by the nobles. The change in land tenure here ascribed to Joseph appears to have been brought about by Aahmose I, the founder of the eighteenth dynasty, who freed Egypt from the rule of the invading Hyksos. The priests in the earlier period were supported by the offerings and revenues which came from the temple lands. In later times, at least, the kings made liberal gifts and concessions to different temples, with the result that the priests held a large part of the total wealth of Egypt.

III. **Aim and Teachings.** Again the primary aim of these stories is realized in the vivid portrayal of the experiences and character of Joseph. His patience and cheerfulness in the most unfair and adverse circumstances, his eagerness to seize every opportunity for service, his unique organizing and executive ability, and his fidelity to his masters are vividly illustrated. Chief among the many teachings of these stories are: (1) The trials which come to each individual are essential for the development of his character and ability. (2) Therefore, "Those whom the Lord loveth he chasteneth." (3) "All things work together for good to those who love God." (4) The only successful way to forget one's own burdens is to help bear another's. (5) Men forget, but God never forgets his faithful servants. (6) He alone who improves the small opportunities will not miss the great chance of life.

(7) "Whosoever would become great among you shall be your minister, and whosoever would be first among you shall be your servant." (8) Trained ability is essential to success and the highest honor.

§XVII.   JOSEPH AND HIS BROTHERS

1. Journey of Joseph's brothers to Egypt

Now when Jacob saw that there was grain for sale in Egypt, Jacob said to his sons, Why do you stand looking at each other? And he said, Behold, I have heard that there is grain for sale in Egypt; go down there and buy for us from thence, that we may live and not die. So Joseph's ten brothers went down to buy grain from Egypt. But Benjamin, Joseph's own brother, Jacob did not send with his brothers; for he said, Lest harm befall him. Thus the sons of Israel came among others to buy grain; for the famine was in the land of Canaan.

2. His first interview with them

Now Joseph was the governor over the land; he it was who sold to all the people of the land. Therefore Joseph's brothers came and bowed themselves before him with their faces to the earth. And when Joseph saw his brothers he knew them, but he acted as a stranger towards them and talked harshly to them, and said, Whence do you come? And they said, From the land of Canaan to buy food. Thus Joseph knew his brothers, but they did not know him. Then Joseph remembered the dreams which he had had about them and said to them, You are spies come to see the defenselessness of the land. And they said to him, Nay, my lord, but your servants have come to buy food. We are all one man's sons; we are honest men; your servants are not spies. But he said to them, Nay, to see the defenselessness of the land you have come. They replied, We your servants are twelve brothers, the sons of one man in the land of Canaan; and, behold, the youngest is to-day with our father, and one is no more. And Joseph said to them, It is just as I said to you, 'You are spies.' By this you shall be proved: as sure as Pharaoh lives you shall not go from here unless your youngest brother comes hither. Send one of you, and let him bring your brother, while you remain in confinement, that your words may be proved, whether

134

or not there be truth in you. Or else, as sure as Pharaoh lives, you are indeed spies. And he put them all together into prison for three days.

Then Joseph said to them the third day, This do, and live; for I likewise fear God. If you are true men, let one of your brothers remain bound in your prison-house; but you go, carry grain for the needs of your households, and bring your youngest brother to me. So shall your words be verified, and you shall not die. And they did so. And they said to each other, Truly we are guilty in regard to our brother, in that when we saw the distress of his soul, while he was beseeching us for pity, we would not hear; therefore this distress has come upon us. But Reuben also answered them, saying, Did I not say to you, 'Do not sin against the boy,' but you would not listen? therefore now also his blood is required. And they did not know that Joseph understood them, for he had spoken to them through an interpreter. He, however, turned himself about from them and wept; then he returned to them, and spoke to them and took Simeon from among them, and bound him before their eyes. Then Joseph commanded to fill their vessels with grain, and to restore every man's money into his sack, and to give them provision for the way. And thus it was done to them.

So they loaded their asses with their grain, and departed. And when they came to Jacob their father in the land of Canaan, they told him all that had befallen them, saying, The man who is lord in that land spoke harshly to us, and put us in prison as though we were spying out the country. And we said to him, We are honest men; we are not spies; we are twelve brothers, sons of our father; one is no more and the youngest is to-day with our father in the land of Canaan. And the man who is lord in that land said to us, By this shall I know that you are honest men: leave one of your brothers with me, and take the grain for the needs of your households, and go your way; bring your youngest brother to me, then shall I know that you are not spies, but that you are honest men; so will I give up your brother to you and you shall be free to go about in the land.

3. The second interview

4. Return of the brothers and their report to Jacob

135

5. Discovery of the money in their sacks

But as they were emptying their sacks, they found that every man's purse of money was in his sack; and when they and their father saw their purses of money, they were afraid. And their hearts failed them and they turned trembling to one another, saying, What is this that God hath done to us? And Jacob their father said to them, You bereave me of my children: Joseph is no more and Simeon is no more, and you would take Benjamin also; all these things have befallen me. But Reuben said to his father, You may put my two sons to death, if I do not bring him to you. Put him in my charge and I will bring him back to you. Then Jacob said, God Almighty give you mercy before the man, that he may release to you your other brother and Benjamin. But I—if I be bereaved of my children, I am bereaved.

6. The need of grain

And the famine was severe in the land. And when they had eaten up the grain which they had brought from Egypt, their father said to them, Go again, buy us a little food. And Judah said to him, The man protested strongly to us saying, 'You shall not see my face unless your brother is with you.' If you will send our brother with us, we will go down and buy you food, but if you will not send him, we will not go down; for the man said to us, ' You shall not see my face unless your brother is with you.' And Israel said, Why did you bring evil upon me by telling the man you had another brother? And they said, The man asked particularly about us and our kindred, saying, ' Is your father yet alive? have you another brother?' So we informed him according to the tenor of these questions. How were we to know that he would say, 'Bring your brother down?' But he said, My son shall not go down with you; for his brother is dead and he only is left. If harm befall him on the way by which you go, then you will bring down my gray hairs with sorrow to Sheol.

7. Judah's proposal

Judah, however, said to Israel his father, Send the lad with me, and we will arise and go that we may live, and not die, both we and you and also our little ones. I will be surety for him; from my hand you may require him; if I do not bring him to you and set him before you, then let me bear the blame forever; for if we had not lingered, surely we would now have returned the second time. Therefore their father said to them, If it must be so, then do this: take some of the products of the land in your vessels, and carry down a present to the man: a little balsam and a little grape syrup and ladanum, pistacia nuts, and almonds. Take also twice as much money in your hands, and the money, that was returned in the mouth of your sacks, carry back with you; perhaps it was a mistake. Take also your brother, and arise, go again to the man. So the men took this present with twice as much money in their hands, and Benjamin, and rose up, and went down to Egypt, and stood before Joseph.

Now when Joseph saw Benjamin with them, he said to the steward of his house, Bring the men into the house, and slay, and make ready, for these men will dine with me at noon. And the man did as Joseph said, and brought the men to Joseph's house. The men, however, were afraid, because they were brought to Joseph's house, and they said, Because of the money that was returned in our grain-sacks at the first are we brought in, that he may seek occasion against us, and fall upon us, and take us for bondmen, together with our asses. And when they came near to the steward of Joseph's house, they spoke to him at the door of the house, and said, Oh, my lord, we simply came down the first time to buy food; and it came to pass, when we reached the place, where we were to pass the night, that we opened our sacks, and, behold, every man's money was in the mouth of his sack, our money in full weight; and we have brought it back with us. And we have brought down other money in our hands to buy food; we do not know who put our money into our sacks. And he said, Peace be to you, fear not; your God and the God of your father hath given you treasure in your sacks; I had your money. Then he brought Simeon out to them. And the man brought the men into Joseph's house, and gave them water that they might wash their feet, and he gave their asses fodder. Then they made ready the present in anticipation of Joseph's coming at noon, for they had heard that they were to eat there.

Now when Joseph came to the house, they brought in to him the present which was in their hands, and bowed down before him to the earth. And he asked them regarding their welfare and said, Is your father well, the old man of

8. Their reception at Joseph's house

9. Joseph's royal hospitality toward them

137

whom you spoke? Is he yet alive? And they said, Your servant, our father, is well, he is yet alive. And they bowed their heads, and made obeisance. And Joseph lifted up his eyes and saw Benjamin his brother, his mother's son, and said, Is this your youngest brother, of whom you spoke to me? And he said, God be gracious to you, my son. And he made haste; for his heart yearned toward his brother; and he sought a place to weep; and he went into his room and wept there. Then he bathed his face and came out and controlled himself, and said, Bring on food. And they brought on food for him by himself, and for them by themselves, and for the Egyptians who ate with him, by themselves, because the Egyptians might not eat with the Hebrews; for that is an abomination to the Egyptians. And they sat before him, the first-born according to his birthright, and the youngest according to his youth; and the men looked at each other in astonishment. And he took portions from before him for them; But Benjamin's portions were five times as much as any of theirs. And they drank and were merry with him.

10. Concealment of his cup in Benjamin's sack

Then he commanded the steward of his house, saying, Fill the men's grain-sacks with food as much as they can carry, and put my cup, the silver cup, in the mouth of the sack of the youngest. And he did according to the word that Joseph had spoken.

11. Command to pursue and recover the cup

When the morning dawned, the men were sent away, together with their asses. They had gone out of the city, but were still not far away, when Joseph ordered his steward, Rise, pursue the men; and when you overtake them, say to them, ' Why have you repaid evil for good? Why have you stolen my silver cup? Is not this that in which my lord is accustomed to drink, and by which he divines? you have done wrong in so doing.'

12. Its discovery in Benjamin's sack

So he overtook them and said these words to them. And they said to him, Why does my lord speak such words as these? Far be it from your servants that they should do such a thing! Behold, the money which we found in our sacks' mouths, we brought back to you from the land of Canaan; how then should we steal from your lord's house silver or gold? That one of your servants with whom it

is found shall die, and we will also be my lord's bondmen.
And he said, Now then let it be according to your words;
he with whom it is found shall be my bondman; but you
shall be blameless. Then they hastily took down every
man his sack to the ground, and every man opened his
grain-sack. And he searched, beginning with the oldest, and finishing with the youngest; and the cup was
found in Benjamin's grain-sack. Then they rent their
clothes and every man loaded his ass and returned to the
city.

So Judah and his brothers came back to Joseph's house; **13. The brothers before Joseph**
and he was yet there; and they fell before him on the ground.
And Joseph said to them, What deed is this that you have
done? did you not know that a man like me could divine
with certainty? And Judah said, What shall we say to
my lord? what shall we speak? or how shall we clear ourselves? God hath found out the iniquity of your servants;
behold, we are my lord's bondmen, both we and he also in
whose hand the cup is found. But he said, Far be it from
me that I should do so! the man in whose hand the cup is
found shall be my bondman; but you yourselves go up in
peace to your father.

Then Judah came close to him, and said, Oh, my lord, **14. Judah's appeal to Joseph**
let your servant, I pray you, speak a word in my lord's ears,
and do not let your anger be kindled against your servant;
for you are as Pharaoh. My lord asked his servants saying, 'Have you a father, or a brother?' And we said to
my lord, 'We have a father, an old man, and a child of his
old age, a little one; and as his brother is dead, he alone is
left of his mother; and his father loves him.' And you said
to your servants, ' Bring him down to me, that I may set
my eyes upon him.' But we said to my lord, ' The lad
cannot leave his father; for if he should leave his father,
his father would die.' Then you said to your servants,
' Unless your youngest brother comes down with you, you
shall not see my face again.' And when we went up to
your servant, my father, we told him the words of my lord.
And our father said, 'Go again, buy us a little food.' But
we said, ' We cannot go down. If our youngest brother
is with us, then we will go down; for we may not see the

man's face unless our youngest brother is with us.' And your servant, my father, said to us, 'You know that my wife bore me two sons; and one went from me, and I said, "Surely he is torn in pieces"; and I have not seen him since; now if you take this one also from me, and harm befall him, you will bring down my gray hairs with sorrow to Sheol.' And now if I come to your servant, my father, without having with us the lad in whose life his life is bound up, then when he sees that there is no lad, he will die; and your servants will bring down the gray hairs of your servant, our father, with sorrow to the grave. For your servant became surety for the lad to my father, when I said, ' If I do not bring him to you, then I shall bear the blame before my father forever.' Now therefore let your servant, I pray you, remain instead of the lad as a bondman to my lord, but let the lad go up with his brothers. For how shall I go up to my father, if the lad is not with me?—lest I should see the sorrow that would come upon my father.

15. Joseph's declaration of his identity

Now Joseph could not control himself before all those who were standing by him and he cried out, Cause every man to go out from me. Now there stood no man with him while Joseph made himself known to his brothers. But he wept so loudly that the Egyptians heard and Pharaoh's household heard. Then Joseph said to his brothers, I am Joseph. Is my father yet alive? And his brothers could not answer him, so dismayed were they to see him. Then Joseph said to his brothers, Come near to me, I pray you. And they came near. And he said, I am Joseph your brother, whom you sold into Egypt. But now be not troubled, nor angry with yourselves that you sold me hither, for God sent me before you to preserve life. For now the famine has already been two years in the land. And there are yet five years in which there shall be neither plowing nor harvest. And God sent me before you to give you a remnant on the earth, to effect for you a great deliverance. So now it is not you that sent me here but God. And he hath made me a father to Pharaoh and lord of all his house and ruler over all the land of Egypt.

Hasten and go up to my father and say to him, Thus saith your son Joseph, God has made me lord of all Egypt, come down without delay. You shall dwell in the land of Goshen, and you shall be near me, and your flocks and your herds and all that you have, and there will I provide for you, for there are yet five years of famine, lest you be brought to poverty, together with your household and all that you have. And behold, your eyes see, and the eyes of my brother Benjamin, that it is my mouth that is speaking to you. And you shall tell my father of all my glory in Egypt and of all that you have seen, and you must quickly bring my father down hither. And he fell upon his brother Benjamin's neck and wept, and Benjamin wept upon his neck. And he kissed all his brothers, and wept upon them; and afterwards his brothers talked with him.

16. Command to bring his father and kinsmen to Egypt

And the report was heard in Pharaoh's house, that Joseph's brothers were come; and it pleased Pharaoh and his servants; therefore Pharaoh said to Joseph, Say to your brothers, ' This do, load your beasts and go and enter the land of Canaan, and take your father and your households, and come to me, and I will give you the best of the land of Egypt, that you may eat the fat of the land.' And he commanded them, This do, take wagons out of the land of Egypt for your little ones and for your wives, and bring your father and come. Also do not pay any attention to your household goods, for the best of all the land of Egypt is yours. And the sons of Israel did so.

17. Pharaoh's command

I. **Literary Beauty of the Story.** In the account of Joseph's meeting with his brothers these stories reach their climax. In literary charm and depth of feeling they are unsurpassed. They also reveal the noblest qualities in Joseph's character. A pathos runs through them all which tugs strongly at the heart-strings. Every scene is suffused with pent-up emotion. The anxiety of the brothers, the pathetic fears of the fond, aged father, the elder brother's noble sense of responsibility, and the burning affection of Joseph react and blend in a marvellous series of pictures. The impassioned address of Judah (14) is also one of the strongest appeals in all literature. The story is a closely knit literary unit; to be fully appreciated it must be read and studied as a whole.

JOSEPH'S TEST OF HIS BROTHERS

II. **Joseph's Test of his Brothers.** The story is so simply and fully told that it almost interprets itself. The background is the ancient oriental world in which the law of revenge was still the dominant principle in public codes and private ethics. The brother, who had been shamefully treated and pitilessly sold as a slave, now had his opportunity to avenge his wrongs. Joseph's outward acts in the earlier part of the narrative suggest that this was his purpose; but the sequel reveals his real aim and the true greatness of his character.

Experience had made Joseph a keen student of human nature. His knowledge of his brothers was limited to his boyhood experience. If their characters had not changed, to show them the many favors which it was in his power to bestow, would be but to cast pearls before swine. For their own sake it was necessary, that they should know his power and recognize his authority. The different tests to which he subjected them have these definite aims in view. Early in the story the narrator reveals to the reader the affectionate heart concealed behind the rude exterior. Joseph, however, held his own natural feelings in check until he could be sure of his brothers' contrition, and until he knew that the opportune moment had arrived.

III. **The Crucial Test of Joseph's Character.** When he was assured that he could trust them, Joseph's love for his father and for his brothers, who had so flagrantly wronged him, swept away all barriers. The scene which followed is one of the most dramatic in the Old Testament. All personal resentment was forgotten by Joseph in his zeal to help his kinsmen, and the divine quality of forgiveness found expression in the noblest words and deeds. For the honored and successful governor of Egypt to acknowledge as his own brothers the rude Canaanite nomads, who had given him every reason for repudiating them, called for the highest loyalty and devotion. Many men resist the temptations of youth, and attain positions of eminence, and then fail to pay the debt which they owe to their humble kinsmen who have helped them to success. With Joseph the debt, if any, was small. There was also no absolute necessity of revealing his identity, much less of inviting his uncouth kinsmen to the land of Egypt. His action, therefore, reveals a simple nobility of character rarely equalled in the past or present.

IV. **Teachings of the Story.** Many vital truths are illustrated by this marvellous story. The chief perhaps are: (1) Every man who does wrong is confronted by the consequence of his act at the most unexpected and painful crises of his life. (2) Forgiveness and love are

142

invincible. (3) God is ever overruling evil for good. (4) The severest tests of character come at the most unexpected moments and in the most unexpected forms. (5) A man's loyalty to his humble kinsmen in the hour of his own success is the surest evidence of his nobility.

§XVIII. JOSEPH'S LOYALTY TO HIS KINSMEN

Now when the sons of Israel told him all the words which Joseph had said to them, Israel said, It is enough: Joseph my son is yet alive. I will go and see him before I die. *1. Israel's decision*

Then Israel set out on his journey with all that he had. And he sent Judah before him to Joseph, that he might show him the way to Goshen. Now when they came into the province of Goshen, Joseph made ready his chariot, and went up to Goshen to meet Israel his father. And as he presented himself to him, he fell on his neck, and wept on his neck a long time. Then Israel said to Joseph, Now let me die, since I have seen your face, that you are yet alive. And Joseph said to his brothers, and to his father's house, I will go up and tell Pharaoh and say to him, My brothers and my father's house, who were in the land of Canaan, have come to me. Now the men are shepherds, for they have been keepers of cattle; and they have brought their flocks and cattle and all that they have. And when Pharaoh shall call you, and shall say, ' What is your occupation?' then say, ' Your servants have been keepers of cattle from our youth even until now, both we and our fathers,' that you may dwell in the province of Goshen; for every shepherd is an abomination to the Egyptians. *2. Joseph's reception of his kinsmen*

Then Joseph went in and told Pharaoh, and said, My father and my brothers with their sheep and cattle and all that they possess have come from the land of Canaan; and, behold, they are in the province of Goshen. And from among his brothers he took five men, and presented them to Pharaoh. And Pharaoh said to his brothers, What is your occupation? And they said to Pharaoh, Your servants are shepherds, both we and our fathers. They also said to Pharaoh, We have come to sojourn in the land, because there is no pasture for your servants' *3. Pharaoh's provision for their needs* flocks, since the famine is severe in the land of Canaan. Now therefore we pray, let your servants dwell in the province of Goshen. And Pharaoh spoke to Joseph, saying, In the province of Goshen let them dwell; and if you know any capable men among them, you may put them in charge of my cattle. So Joseph provided food for his father and his brothers and all his father's household according to the number of the little children. And Israel dwelt in the land of Egypt and in the province of Goshen.

4. Israel's instructions regarding his burial

Now when the time drew near that Israel must die, he called his son Joseph and said to him, If now I have found favor in your sight, put, I pray you, your hand under my thigh, and show kindness and faithfulness to me; do not bury me, I pray you, in Egypt; but when I lie down to sleep with my fathers, you shall carry me out of Egypt, and bury me in their burying-place. And Joseph replied, I will surely do as you have said. Then he said, Give me your oath: so Joseph gave him his oath. And Israel bowed himself toward the head of the bed.

5. His blessing upon Joseph's sons

Then Israel strengthened himself and sat up on the bed, and said, Bring, I pray you, your two sons to me, and I will bless them. Now the eyes of Israel were dim with age, so that he could not see. And Joseph took them both, — Ephraim in his right hand toward Israel's left hand, and Manasseh in his left hand toward Israel's right hand, and brought them near to him. Then Israel stretched out his right hand and laid it upon the head of Ephraim, who was the younger, and his left hand upon the head of Manasseh, crossing his hands intentionally; for Manasseh was the first-born. And he blessed them, saying, The God before whom my fathers Abraham and Isaac walked, the God who hath been my shepherd all my life long unto this day, the Messenger, who hath redeemed me from all evil, bless the lads; and let my name be perpetuated by them, and the name of my fathers Abraham and Isaac; and let them grow into a multitude in the midst of the earth. But when Joseph saw that his father laid his right hand upon the head of Ephraim, it displeased him, and he seized his father's hand to remove it from Ephraim's head to Manasseh's head. And Joseph said to his father; Not so, my father; this one is the first-born; put your right hand upon his head. But his father refused and said, I know, my son, I know, he also shall become a people, and he also shall be great; nevertheless his younger brother shall be greater than he, and his descendants shall become a multitude of nations.

Then Israel drew his feet up into the bed, and was gathered unto his people. And Joseph fell upon his father's face and wept upon him and kissed him.

6. His death

Then Joseph commanded his servants the physicians to embalm his father. So the physicians embalmed Israel, and they devoted forty days to it; for thus long the days of embalming last; and the Egyptians wept for him seventy days.

7. The embalming of Israel

And when the days of weeping for him were past, Joseph spoke to the house of Pharaoh, saying, If now I have found favor in your sight, speak, I pray you, in the ears of Pharaoh, saying, 'My father made me take oath, saying, " Lo, I am dying; in my grave which I have digged for myself in the land of Canaan, there you shall bury me." ' Now therefore let me go up, I pray you, and bury my father; after that I will return. And Pharaoh said, Go up and bury your father, as he made you take oath.

8. Pharaoh's permission to bury him in Canaan

So Joseph went up to bury his father; and with him went up all the servants of Pharaoh, the elders of his house, and all the elders of the land of Egypt, and all the house of Joseph, and his brothers, and his father's house. Only their little ones and their sheep and cattle they left in the province of Goshen. And there went up with him both chariots and horsemen, so that it was a very great company. And when they came to Goren-ha-Atad [Threshing-floor of the thorn bush] which is beyond Jordan, there they held a very great and solemn lamentation; and Joseph made a mourning for his father seven days. And when the inhabitants of the land, the Canaanites, saw the mourning in Goren-ha-Atad, they said, This is a solemn mourning which the Egyptians are holding. Therefore its name was called Abel-Mizraim [Mourning of the Egyptians]; it is beyond the Jordan. Then Joseph returned to Egypt after he had buried his father, together with his brothers and all who went up with him to bury his father.

9. The public burial and mourning

10. Joseph's assurances to his brothers

Now when Joseph's brothers saw that their father was dead, they said, What if Joseph should hate us, and should requite us all the evil which we did to him! So they sent a message to Joseph, saying, Your father commanded before he died saying, ' Thus shall you say to Joseph, "O forgive, now, the wickedness and sin of your brothers, in that they have treated you basely." ' So now, we pray, forgive the wickedness of the servants of your father's God. And Joseph began to weep, as they were speaking to him. And his brothers also went and fell down before him and said, Here, take us as your slaves. But Joseph said to them, Do not be afraid; for am I in the place of God? You meant evil against me, but God meant it for good, in order to accomplish that which is being done this day,—the saving of the lives of many people. Now therefore do not be afraid; I will provide food for you and your little ones. Thus he comforted them and spoke reassuringly to them.

11. His long and prosperous life

So Joseph dwelt in Egypt together with his father's house. And Joseph lived a hundred and ten years. And Joseph saw Ephraim's great-grandchildren; the children also of Machir, the son of Manasseh, were borne upon Joseph's knees.

12. Instructions regarding his burial

Then Joseph said to his brothers, I am about to die; but God will surely visit you and bring you up from this land to the land which he confirmed by an oath to Abraham, Isaac and Jacob. Joseph then took an oath of the children of Israel, saying, When God visits you, as he surely will, then you shall carry up my bones from here. So Joseph died being a hundred and ten years old; and they embalmed him, and he was put in a coffin in Egypt.

I. **Joseph's Provision for His Kinsmen.** The opening paragraphs of this section record one of the noblest scenes in the Joseph stories. In the eyes of the Egyptians shepherds were regarded with scorn and hatred. Although, doubtless, well aware of this strong antipathy, Joseph was not content until he had introduced his aged father and shepherd brothers to Pharaoh and his court.

According to the earliest narrative, his kinsmen were assigned to the territory of Goshen. This evidently included the fertile, low-lying lands extending eastward from the Delta of the Nile to the Isthmus of Suez and the desert. The agricultural resources of this region were not developed until the reign of Ramses II. In the days of Joseph these level plains were evidently still given up to flocks and herds. The land of Goshen, therefore, furnished an ideal home for these men from the wilderness. There they could still retain their tribal organization, their nomadic habits and, to a great extent, their independence. Through this territory ran the great caravan route from Egypt, back through the wilderness to Palestine, so that the Hebrews were able to keep in close touch with their kinsmen in Canaan and the South Country.

An interesting parallel to the biblical story is found in an inscription of Merneptah, which comes from the latter part of the thirteenth century B.C. It tells of certain Shasu or Bedouin tribes coming from Aduma or Edom, which were allowed to pass "the fortress of king Merneptah in Thuku (Succoth) to the pools of King Merneptah, which are in Thuku, that they might obtain food for themselves and for their cattle in the field of the Pharaoh, who is the gracious sun in every land."

II. **Israel's Dying Blessing.** The intense interest which the Hebrews always felt in a father's dying blessing again finds expression in the patriarchal stories. A later editor has introduced in connection with the story of the death of Israel, a group of tribal songs cast in the form of oracles. As will be seen later (§ XXXV), in their final form they probably come from the days of the united kingdom under David. In the original Judean narrative, Israel's blessing is bestowed primarily upon the two sons of Joseph, Ephraim and Manasseh. These represent the two great tribes of central Israel. Of these two, Ephraim was the more important, although the tribe of Manasseh was apparently the first to secure a permanent home (east of the Jordan), and was, therefore, regarded as the older. The later superiority of the tribe of Ephraim is recognized in the account of the patriarch's blessing. Not upon the head of the older, Manasseh, but upon the head of Ephraim the younger, rested the right hand of Israel. In the writings of the northern prophet Hosea, Ephraim also represents Northern Israel as a whole, even as Judah stands for Southern Israel. The blessing itself is similar to that found on the lips of the earlier patriarchs: it promises political power and great increase in numbers.

Thus, in a ripe old age, refined and softened by the struggles of his earlier years, the aged patriarch died surrounded by his sorrowing sons. Tradition adds that, followed by his children and the mourning Egyptians, his body was borne back in solemn procession and buried in the land of Canaan.

Joseph continued, after the death of his father, to treat his conscience-stricken brothers with the same noble generosity, assuring them by word and deed of his complete forgiveness. To Joseph were granted the three superlative beatitudes: honor and respect, long life and loyal offspring. After his death, his body was embalmed and, according to the Northern Israelite narrative and in keeping with the solemn oath of his brothers, was later borne back by the returning Israelites, when they left Egypt and set their faces toward Canaan.

III. The Various Elements in the Joseph Stories. No careful reader can fail to recognize the presence of a large ideal element in the Joseph stories. The aim of the prophetic story-tellers was evidently to portray a perfect type of the successful man of affairs. No history or literature contains a more vivid illustration of the qualities essential to success. Honesty, perseverance, cheerfulness in adversity, fidelity and eagerness to improve every opportunity are invincible in any age. According to the standards of Joseph's day, these qualities were crowned by the highest conceivable rewards. Nothing that oriental imagination could suggest was wanting to fill the cup of Joseph to overflowing. Yet throughout, the portrait is true to life and especially to the life of the ancient East.

As has already been indicated, the origin of certain Egyptian institutions, as for example, the agrarian laws, are also attributed to Joseph. The story of his temptation is strikingly similar to the Egyptian "Tale of the Two Brothers," current probably long before the days of Joseph. The tendency to combine traditions, originally distinct, was perhaps at work here as elsewhere in the patriarchal stories; but back of the narratives as a whole, there is clearly a substantial basis of historic fact.

IV. Archæological Exactness of the Joseph Stories. The historical character of the Joseph stories is strongly attested by their remarkable archæological exactness. Where there was every opportunity for error, they are almost without exception faithful to their peculiar setting. No ancient civilization was more distinct and unique than that of Egypt. Highly developed, self-satisfied, and shut in by natural barriers, Egypt lived apart almost as a hermit nation. Her customs, her language and her system of writing were shared by no other peoples of antiquity, and yet at every point the narrator reveals a thorough familiarity with Egyptian life. Not only was he acquainted with Egypt's peculiar system of taxation and with its current literature, but he also introduces several Egyptian names and words. Peculiar Egyptian customs are also reflected in the stories, as for example, the giving of the much-prized golden collar, which was bestowed upon a public servant for distinguished achievement. Thus, according to a well-known inscription, Aahmes, a famous admiral, received it for his prowess and courage in an important battle. Even the references to the famine may be paralleled by passages from contemporary Egyptian inscriptions. The number of years which Joseph lived—one hundred and ten —was in itself a realization of a characteristic Egyptian ideal. In this way, for example, the virtue of the ancient Egyptian sage, Ptah-hotep, was rewarded.

V. The Josephs of Egyptian History. The court of Egypt, especially under the rulers of the eighteenth dynasty, offered, even to those of humble origin, rare opportunities of attaining prominence and authority. Relations with Asia were very close, and the later rulers of this dynasty not only made treaties with Asiatic kings but also entered into marriage with their daughters. A large number of Semitic words, as well as ideas and customs, gained admission at this time into the land of the Nile. During the reign of Amenhotep III, and especially that of his son, the great reforming king, Amenhotep IV, several Semites, whose names are recorded, rose to positions of great authority. Thus, for example, according to the contemporary el-Amarna tablets, a certain Dudu was one of the trusted officials of Amenhotep IV. He is addressed by one of the governors of Egypt as, "my lord, my father." Even more interesting and significant are the references to another Semite, Yanhamu, who had control of the magazines of corn in the land of Jarmutu, which probably included the east Delta. He also directed the Egyptian rule in Palestine. The Egyptian governors of Palestine frequently refer to him in terms which suggest that his authority was second only to that of the Pharaoh himself. Rib-addi of Gebal, to secure a favorable settlement of certain of his grievances, asks the king of Egypt to say to Yanhamu, "Behold, Rib-addi is in thy power and anything which happens to him touches thee." In another letter he asks the king to command Yanhamu to take the field at once with troops. The governor of Gaza and Joppa also speaks of having been brought, while still young, to the Egyptian court by the same Yanhamu.

While Yanhamu may not be identical with the original Joseph of the Hebrew tradition, the analogy is exceedingly suggestive. In the light of all these facts the most satisfactory explanation of the Joseph stories is that they record, doubtless in a somewhat idealized form, the experiences of a young Semite, who by his personal ability attained to a position of great authority and honor in the land of Egypt.

VI. The Age at Which Joseph Lived. The older Egyptologists were inclined to find the background of the Joseph story in the days of the Hyksos conquest. Then Semitic rulers controlled the land of the Nile. To maintain their precarious position in the presence of a large and hostile population they would naturally encourage Asiatic immigration, and would show especial favors to men of Semitic origin. The Joseph stories, however, imply that not a foreign, but a native Egyptian king then ruled on the throne. The favors which came to Joseph were also won not by the sword, but by the ability and services of the hero. Furthermore, the evidence of the ancient inscriptions suggests that the ancestors of the Hebrews were not found in the land of Palestine in the days of the Hyksos conquest, but that they first began to appear as nomadic immigrants in the later days of the eighteenth dynasty, and at a date not earlier than 1500 B.C. In view of these facts and of the policy and characteristics of the later kings of the eighteenth dynasty it seems far more probable that Amenhotep III or IV was the Pharaoh at whose court the young Hebrew won signal distinction. The same period furnishes a most satisfactory background for the migration of certain Hebrew tribes toward eastern Egypt. This conclusion is also substantiated by the chronology of the oldest Hebrew narratives, which assign only about one hundred and fifty years to the sojourn of the Hebrews in Egypt (cf. § XIX[vi]). Thus, if the exodus be dated about 1200, Joseph's date would be near the middle of the fourteenth century B.C., when the rule of the eighteenth Egyptian dynasty was drawing to a close.

VII. The Primary Value of the Patriarchal Stories. The literary, historical and archæological value of the Joseph stories, and of the patriarchal narratives which precede, is obvious; but that which gives these ancient tribal stories their abiding interest and authority is the work of the later prophetic historians. These interpreters of the divine presence in human life emphasize in this concrete way the great truth that, before the dawn of Hebrew history, Jehovah was guiding the destinies of his chosen people. The individual men and races are but the actors in the great drama which illustrates the eternal laws of life and reveals God's active participation in the affairs of men. If it should be proved that the patriarchs were but the creations of the prophetic story-teller's art, Abraham, Jacob and Joseph would still live to inspire and guide men in resisting that which is evil and in choosing that which is good.

THE BONDAGE AND DELIVERANCE FROM EGYPT

§ XIX. THE OPPRESSION OF THE HEBREWS IN EGYPT

Now Joseph died and all his brothers and all that generation. And the Israelites became numerous and powerful. Then there arose a new king over Egypt, who knew not Joseph. And he said to his people, See, the Israelite people are becoming more numerous and powerful than we; come, let us deal subtly with them, lest they become so numerous that, if a war arise, they will join our enemies, and fight against us, and go out of the land. *1. Rapid increase of the Israelites*

Therefore the Egyptians set over them taskmasters to impose tasks upon them. And they built for Pharaoh store-cities, Pithom and Ramses. But the more the Egyptians afflicted them, the more numerous they became and the more they spread abroad so that the Egyptians became apprehensive of the Israelites. Therefore they made their lives bitter with hard service in mortar and in brick, but the people became very numerous and powerful. *2. Measures to prevent their increase*

And the king of Egypt spoke to the Hebrew midwives, of whom the name of one was Shiphrah, and the name of the other Puah; and he said, When you perform the office of midwife for the Hebrew women, and see them upon the birth-stool; if it be a son, then you shall kill him; but if it be a daughter, she shall live. But the midwives feared God, and did not do as the king of Egypt commanded them, but saved the male-children alive. Therefore the king of Egypt called for the midwives, and said to them, Why have you done thus and saved the male-children alive? The midwives answered Pharaoh, Because the Hebrew women are not as the Egyptian women; for they are vigorous; before the midwife comes to them, they are already delivered. *3. Slaughter of the male-children*

151

Therefore God dealt well with the midwives. And it came to pass, because the midwives feared God, that he built up their families. Then Pharaoh commanded all his people saying, Every son that is born to the Hebrews you shall cast into the river, but every daughter you shall save alive.

I. The Stories Regarding the Bondage and Exodus. The book of Exodus marks the transition from early tribal stories to the real history of the Hebrews. The book itself is divided at the second verse of the nineteenth chapter into two distinct parts. The latter part consists of laws and detailed directions regarding the building of the tabernacle, but the first half continues the history of Genesis. The same three great strands of narrative run through these first eighteen chapters, and, as in Genesis, they are so closely combined that they make one consecutive history. The late priestly material is comparatively unimportant. The main narrative is the early Judean, supplemented by extracts from the Northern Israelite prophetic stories. Each of these prophetic histories has its marked peculiarities. Thus, for example, in the Judean the Hebrews are settled in Goshen, an Egyptian province east of the Delta and bordering on Arabia. There they retain their flocks and tribal organization and soon become very numerous. The northern history, on the contrary, represents them as living among the Egyptians, and so few that two midwives suffice for the needs of the Hebrew mothers.

In general, however, the two prophetic narratives closely agree. Both pass over the oppression very briefly and focus attention on Moses, the great prophetic character of the period. No definite dates are given in these early histories. Not even the names of the Pharaohs of the oppression and of the exodus are remembered. As in Genesis, the personality of the great leaders, the significance of Israel's varied experiences, and the religious import of the different stories chiefly concern the prophetic writers. While the narrative contains much valuable historical data, it is more than a mere record, it is a religious philosophy of history.

In the text adopted (in § XIX) the two prophetic versions of the oppression have been combined. The northern account has been placed at the end, since it contains the natural introduction to the birth of Moses.

II. The Serf Class in Egypt. Changes in dynasties, with corresponding changes in policy, were frequent in Egypt. The victorious foreign campaigns conducted by the kings of the eighteenth dynasty

(Introd. III^v) brought back many captives to swell the large serf class in Egypt. The policy of the later kings also called for vast levies of forced labor. The result was that the serfs so far outnumbered the free Egyptians that there was abundant ground for the fears suggested in the biblical narrative. Doubtless the painful memories of the Hyksos invaders also led the Egyptians to look with hatred and fear upon the Asiatic shepherds, settled on their eastern borders. Throughout most of its history, Egypt's conquerors came from the east. In case of war these foreign Semitic settlers would naturally join with the foe.

III. The Discovery of Pithom. As a result of the excavations of the Egypt Exploration Fund in 1883, Pithom has been identified with certain ruins in the Wady Tumilat, not far from the eastern terminus of the modern railway which runs from Cairo to the Suez Canal. It lay, therefore, within the biblical land of Goshen. Naville, who excavated at this point, found several inscriptions apparently bearing the Egyptian name of the city, *P-atum, House of the god Atum.* In later Egyptian geographical lists *P-atum* appears as the name of a local province.

The excavations disclosed a great square brick wall with the ruins of a temple and store-chambers inside. These large store-houses or granaries were peculiar to these ruins. They were large structures containing many rectangular chambers of various sizes, surrounded by walls, two or three yards in thickness, made of crude bricks. The chambers were not connected. From contemporary inscriptions it appears that they were filled with grain from the top and were emptied in the same way, or through a door at the side.

The excavations have also shown that the city was founded by the great builder, Ramses II. During the first twenty years of his reign, he developed and colonized for the first time the territory lying east of the Delta. This was the region known to the biblical writers as the land of Goshen or Rameses. An Egyptian papyrus also states that one of the chief cities founded by him in this territory and evidently not far from Pithom was "the house of Ramses," with a royal residence and temples. A later poet speaks of it as being situated between Egypt and Syria. From this it may be inferred that it was one of the fortified cities that guarded the Asiatic frontier.

IV. The Pharaoh of the Oppression. In the light of these facts there is little doubt that Ramses II, who reigned from about 1292 to 1225 B.C., was the Pharaoh of the oppression. All that is stated in the biblical narratives is in perfect harmony with the character and policy of that energetic, splendor-loving, tyrannical king, who filled all Egypt with huge statues of himself and memorials of his vast building enterprises.

V. The Absence of References to the Hebrews in Egypt. The fact that the Egyptian inscriptions contain no reference to the Hebrews in Egypt has led certain scholars to question whether or not the Israelites were ever in the land of the Nile. The one contemporary allusion to Israelites is found in the recently discovered triumphal stele of Merneptah, son of the great Ramses II (*cf.* vii). The Israelites there referred to are clearly living in the land of Palestine. In the face of this definite contemporary testimony, it is necessary to weigh carefully the comparative evidence. That certain Israelite tribes were for a time found in the land of Egypt is attested by the following considerations: (1) Nearly all the earliest Old Testament writers allude to it as a well-established incident in their national history. Their unanimous and independent testimony is best explained by a common basis of historical fact. (2) It is improbable and practically inconceivable that a story, so humiliating to the pride of the Hebrews, would have been invented in a later period when Egypt was their ally, as in the days of Solomon, or when it was but a weak and waning power. (3) There is fundamental agreement between the earliest biblical narratives and the contemporary inscriptions regarding the attitude of the Egyptians toward the foreigners in their midst. (4) In the light of Egyptian usage it is not strange that there is no reference to the Israelite serfs in the land of Egypt. Under the nineteenth dynasty, as a result of the many successful campaigns and the building policy of the reigning Pharaohs, an exceedingly large serf class was found in the land of the Nile. These aliens are designated, not according to their racial origin, but as a distinct class. Therefore, if any reference was made to the Israelites, it would have been by this general designation.

VI. Duration of the Sojourn. While there is little doubt that there were Hebrews in the land of Egypt, it is evident that the biblical narratives must be interpreted in the light of contemporary records and conditions. The different sources are not in agreement regarding many details. The early Judean narrative is silent regarding the duration of the sojourn. In Genesis 15^{16}, which belongs to the Northern Israelite history, it is stated that the Hebrews were to return to Palestine in the fourth generation. This implies a period of between one hundred and one hundred and fifty years. The same duration is suggested by the priestly writer in Numbers 26$^{57-59}$. The late priestly writer of Exodus

6^{16-20} states that Moses was of the fourth generation from Levi, which would give the same relative period of one hundred and fifty years. On the other hand, a late editor, in Genesis 15^{13}, predicts that the period of foreign sojourn was to last exactly four hundred years. Another compiler, in Exodus 12^{40}, affirms that the time the Israelites dwelt in Egypt was four hundred and thirty years. With this passage definitely in mind, the author of Galatians 3^{17} assigns four hundred and thirty years to the period from Abraham to Sinai. Josephus and the translators of the Samaritan and Greek versions, give the duration of the sojourn as two hundred and fifteen years, which is evidently a compromise between the shorter and the longer periods suggested by the earlier writers.

With these conflicting biblical data the final decision must turn upon the testimony of the contemporary Egyptian records. If Amenhotep IV was, as seems very probable, the Pharaoh who raised the young Syrian, known to the Hebrews by the name of Joseph, to a position of commanding authority, the beginning of the Hebrew sojourn in Egypt would fall under the rule of that king (who reigned from 1375 to 1358 B.C.). Accepting Ramses II (who reigned from 1292 to 1225 B.C.) as the Pharaoh of the oppression, and dating the exodus about 1200 (cf. §XXII^{IV}), the duration of the sojourn would be about one hundred and fifty years. It is significant that this conclusion is in substantial agreement with the earliest Hebrew records. On the other hand, if Joseph's Pharaoh be identified with one of the Hyksos, who were expelled about 1580 B.C., the total period of the sojourn would be about four hundred or four hundred and thirty years. Josephus even went so far as to identify the Hebrews with the Hyksos. The longer period assigned by the latest biblical writers is probably the result of a similar identification. Either of these periods would give a sufficient time for the increase in the numbers of the Israelites suggested by the earlier traditions; but the shorter period on the whole accords best with the facts of Egyptian and Hebrew history.

VII. The Hebrew Tribes in Egypt. Although inferred in the Joseph stories, it is by no means certain that all the Hebrew tribes went down to Egypt. References in the record of the campaigns of Seti I and Ramses II to a state called *Asaru* or *Aseru*, situated in western Galilee, would seem to indicate that the Northern Israelite tribe, which bore the corresponding name *Asher*, was already settled in Palestine. The reference in the account which his son Merneptah gives of the victorious campaign in Palestine, leaves no doubt that at that time a considerable portion of the people, which later crystallized into the Hebrew nation, was to be found in Canaan. The reference is as follows:

> Plundered is Canaan with every evil;
> Askalon is carried into captivity;
> Gezer is taken;
> Yenoam is annihilated,
> Israel is desolated, her seed is not,
> Palestine has become a widow for Egypt.
> All lands are united, they are pacified.
> Every one who is turbulent has been bound by King Merneptah.

The earliest Hebrew records also indicate that several of the Arab tribes, which later coalesced into the tribe of Judah, had at an early time secured a foothold in southern Palestine.

In the light of these facts it seems probable that only a part of the twelve Hebrew tribes went to Egypt. The prophetic narratives themselves suggest that these were the Joseph tribes of Ephraim and Manasseh, and possibly the ancestors of certain other clans that ultimately found their home in central and southern Canaan.

The earlier narratives do not agree regarding the number of Hebrews found in the land of Egypt. The fact that, according to the Northern Israelite version, two midwives sufficed to meet the needs of the mothers in Israel implies that the Israelites at that time were to be numbered by hundreds rather than by thousands (*cf.* § XXIII[ii]).

VIII. **The Effects of the Egyptian Sojourn.** In addition to their rapid and important increase in numbers, the Hebrews clearly profited in many ways by their sojourn in Egypt. Although they appear to have largely retained their nomadic habits and traditions, and to have maintained their connection with the neighboring tribes of Palestine and the desert, they must have been influenced by the civilization of Egypt. That influence appears to have been material rather than religious. Living near the eastern frontier, they had ample opportunity to study the Egyptian methods of warfare and military equipment. To a certain degree they would also acquire a knowledge of the Egyptian arts of agriculture. Under the rule of the great Ramses II they were strongly affected, even though against their wills, by the highly organized social and political system which then bound together all the peoples in the land of the Nile.

The influence, which appears to have left the deepest and lasting impression upon them, was, however, their reaction against the customs and religious ideas of their hated oppressors. The oppression itself also tended to bind together by the common bond of suffering the various clans who later, under the leadership of Moses, sought freedom and deliverance in the wilderness. Their suffering and need thus prepared the way for the work of Moses and the birth of the Hebrew nation.

§ XX. MOSES'S CHILDHOOD AND TRAINING

Now a man of the house of Levi had married a daughter of Levi. And the woman conceived, and bore a son; and when she saw that he was a beautiful child, she hid him for three months. But when she could no longer hide him, she took for him an ark of papyrus reeds, and daubed it with bitumen and pitch, and after she had put the child in it, she placed it in the reeds by the bank of the Nile. And his sister stood at a distance to learn what would be done to him. *1. Moses's birth and concealment*

Now the daughter of Pharaoh came down to bathe in the Nile, and while her maids were walking along beside the Nile, she saw the ark among the reeds, and sent her waiting-maid to bring it. And when she opened it and saw the child, behold, the baby-boy was crying. And she had pity on him and said, This is one of the Hebrews' children. Then his sister said to Pharaoh's daughter, Shall I go and call a nurse of the Hebrew women, that she may nurse the child for you? And Pharaoh's daughter said to her, Go. So the maiden went and called the child's mother. And Pharaoh's daughter said to her, Take this child away and nurse it for me, and I will give you wages. Then the woman took the child and nursed it. But when the child had grown up, she brought him to Pharaoh's daughter, and he became her son. And she called his name Moses, for she said, I drew him out of the water. *2. Adoption by Pharaoh's daughter*

Now it came to pass in those days, when Moses had grown up, that he went out to his kinsmen and saw their tasks; and he beheld an Egyptian smiting a Hebrew, one of his kinsmen. And he looked this way and that, and when he saw that there was no one in sight, he smote the Egyptian, and hid him in the sand. *3. Moses's murder of an Egyptian*

And he went out on the following day and saw two men of the Hebrews striving together; and he said to the one who was doing the wrong, Why do you smite your fellow-workman? But he replied, Who made you a prince and a judge over us? do you intend to kill me as you killed the Egyptian? Then Moses was afraid and said, Surely the thing is known. When, therefore, Pharaoh heard this thing, he sought to kill Moses. But Moses fled from the presence of Pharaoh and took up his abode in the land of Midian.

Now he was sitting down by a well. And the priest of Midian had seven daughters; and they came and drew water, and filled the troughs to water their father's flock. But the shepherds came and drove them away; then Moses stood up and helped them and watered their flock. And when they came to Reuel their father, he said, How is it that you have come so early to-day? And they said, An Egyptian delivered us from the shepherds, and besides, he drew water for us, and watered the flock. Then he said to his daughters, And where is he? why have you left the man? Call him that he may eat bread with us. And Moses was content to dwell with the man; and he gave Moses Zipporah his daughter. And she bore a son, and she called his name Gershom [An alien resident there]; for he said, I have been an alien resident in a foreign land.

I. **The Moses Stories.** With the second chapter of Exodus the narrative ceases to be a record of national experiences and again becomes a personal biography. Moses, however, stands as the representative of his age. Simply and with superlative dramatic power the narrative records the different stages in the training of the prophet. Poetic and prophetic imagination may have supplied the details in these wonderful stories; but the narratives themselves are in perfect harmony with conditions of the age. Stories regarding the birth of a great hero usually spring last into existence. The exquisite story of the birth of Moses was apparently not known to the earliest historians, for it is found only in the Northern Israelite group of narratives; but it is in harmony with the other facts in Moses's life.

II. **Moses's Birth and Early Training.** The prophetic tradition associates Moses with the tribe of Levi, which figures in later history as the tribe especially devoted to the care of the sanctuaries and of Jehovah's oracles. A very late priestly tradition also adds that Moses was the fourth in the line from Levi, the son of a certain Amram and Jochebed.

The modern reader shares the fear of the mother, the keen interest of the watching sister, and the sense of relief and joy when the Hebrew baby is received into the palace of the Pharaohs and entrusted to the tender care of his own mother. Although the Old Testament histories do not record the fact, the statement in Acts 7²² that Moses was instructed in all the wisdom of the Egyptians is in perfect accord with the implications of the story. Opportunity was thus given for the future prophet to become intimately acquainted with the policy and character of the reigning house of Egypt and to note the oppression of his people and to estimate intelligently the possibilities of their deliverance. Moses's life in the Egyptian court also gave him that training and knowledge which were essential to his work as the leader of an infant nation.

III. The Great Crisis in Moses's Life. The great crisis in Moses's life came to him unexpectedly. The event proved, however, that he was not unprepared to meet it. The temptation to luxury and to a false view of life, which were strong in the court of the Egyptians, had not dulled his sense of justice and loyalty to his race or his power to act. Judged by the laws of Egypt, his slaying of the Egyptian taskmaster was a crime. Measured by the universal laws which must govern men or nations at great critical moments in their history, when the issue is clear between intrenched injustice and the rights of classes or of the individual, Moses's act was akin to that of the great patriots of the past and the present who have taken the sword to deliver their people from the hands of tyrants. His act may be condemned as hasty. In its immediate results it was as fruitless, as is every hasty and intemperate attempt to right a wrong by violence. It was significant, however, because it allied Moses definitely with his kinsmen. It also marked an important step in the making of the prophet. The great need, which is the first essential in the call of a prophet, had been clearly revealed to him, and he had responded to the call. Henceforth he was committed to the greater task of freeing his kinsmen from that oppression which had aroused his youthful wrath. With him it was a question of further training in knowledge and method. These came in the new field of experience which opened to him as he fled a fugitive out into the wilderness.

IV. The Origin of the Jehovah Religion. Although it is not definitely stated, it is probable that he followed the great highway which runs from the Isthmus of Suez to the eastern arm of the Red Sea. He fled back to those nomad tribes on the border of Edom, which appear to have shared with his ancestors the worship of the same God. This conclusion is confirmed by the readiness with which he was received, even as Jacob of the patriarchal stories, by the Midianite chieftain, who soon adopted him as a member of his own family. In the early Judean narrative, this father-in-law of Moses bears the name of.Hobab or Reuel, but in Northern Israelite stories he is known by the more familiar name of Jethro. The Midianites were a nomadic people who appeared sometimes to the southeast and sometimes to the east of Palestine. In general, however, they ranged up and down east of Edom and the eastern arm of the Red Sea. In the subsequent narratives Jethro is still further identified as a Kenite. In the earliest Hebrew traditions the Kenites figure as worshippers of Jehovah, the God of the Hebrews. The clear implication of these early narratives is that Moses worshipped the God of these local Midianite tribes, and from that God received the message which made him the prophetic leader of his people.

From these facts the conclusion has been drawn by recent writers that Moses for the first time there learned of the new God, whom he worshipped and later proclaimed as the true God and deliverer of his kinsmen in Egypt. It has been urged that the religion of the Hebrews was unique, primarily because at the exodus they were delivered by this newly revealed God, and then that the debt of gratitude which they therefore felt was the basis of their national faith. While this inference is not impossible, it is only a conjecture, and not altogether satisfactory. At this early period the different tribes in southwestern Arabia, and especially to the south of Canaan, appear to have been closely bound together by tradition, custom and religious belief. This fact is definitely and repeatedly stated in the patriarchal stories. It is also difficult to conceive of a group of clans, like the Hebrews in Egypt, suddenly adopting the worship of a hitherto unknown god. It seems more probable, therefore, that Moses only appealed to the faith of his clansmen, which had perhaps been dimmed by the long and painful contact with the dominating civilization of Egypt. If this is true, Moses's experiences in Midian, as the subsequent stories imply, meant simply that revival of his own faith in the God of his race, which was essential to his great prophetic work.

V. Influence of the Wilderness Life upon Moses. The wilderness, with its barren wastes, its solitude, its rocky heights, its sense of dependence, ever intensified by the paucity of food and water, was well

160

fitted to develop the religious instincts of the youthful fugitive. The close communication between Midian and the land of Egypt also enabled him to keep in constant touch with the needs of his kinsmen. In the quiet of the wilderness the great need, the divine message and the man to deliver it came together, and thus a prophet was born.

VI. **Aim and Teachings of the Stories.** The primary aim of these stories is historical and biographical; but the truths which they illustrate find their basis in universal human experience. Even if tradition has contributed certain details to these fascinating narratives, they remain absolutely true to life. They reveal the working of the divine Providence which overrules for good the most cruel and despotic plans of men. (1) The seemingly trivial accidents of life are important factors in the realizing of God's purpose in the lives of men and nations. (2) The blow struck hastily and in anger, even in behalf of a righteous cause, is usually futile. (3) The recognition of a crying public need is the first element in a prophet's call. (4) Long and special training is required for every great service. (5) Opportunities for training come to each man whose spirit is right. (6) These opportunities lie along the ordinary paths of life.

§ XXI. MOSES'S CALL TO DELIVER THE HEBREWS

Early Judean Prophetic	Northern Israelite	Late Priestly History	
Now it came to pass in the course of those many days that the king of Egypt died. Then the Messenger of Jehovah appeared to [Moses] in a flame of fire out of the midst of a thorn bush; and he looked and behold the thorn bush burned with fire without being consumed. Then Moses said, I will turn aside	Now Moses was keeping the flock of Jethro, his father-in-law, the priest of Midian. And he led the flock to the back of the wilderness, and came to the mountain of God, to Horeb. Then God called to him, saying,	Now the Israelites sighed by reason of the forced labor, and they cried, and their cry came up to God because of the forced labor. And God heard their groaning, and God remembered his covenant with Abraham, with Isaac and with Jacob. And God looked upon the Israelites, and God knew. Therefore God	1. The divine revelation to Moses

now, and see this great sight, why the thorn bush is not burned. And when Jehovah saw that he turned aside to see, he said from the midst of the thorn bush, Draw not nigh hither; put off thy sandals from off thy feet, for the place whereon thou standest is holy ground.

Moses, Moses. And he said, Here am I. And he said, I am the God of thy father, the God of Abraham, the God of Isaac, and the God of Jacob. And Moses hid his face; for he was afraid to look upon God.

spoke to Moses and said to him, I am Jehovah; and I appeared to Abraham, to Isaac and to Jacob, as El-Shaddai [God Almighty]; but by my name Jehovah I did not reveal myself to them. And I have also established my covenant with them, to give them the land of Canaan, the land in which they sojourned.

2. Moses's commission

And Jehovah said, I have surely seen the affliction of my people that are in Egypt, and have heard their cry of anguish, because of their taskmasters, for I know their sorrows; and I am come down to deliver them out of the power of the Egyptians, and to bring them up out of that land to a land, beautiful and broad, to a land flowing with milk and honey; Go and gather the elders of Israel together and say to them, Jehovah, the God of your fathers, the God of Abraham, Isaac and Jacob, hath appeared to

Then God said, Now, behold, the cry of anguish of the Israelites has come to me; moreover I have seen how sorely the Egyptians oppress them. Come now, therefore, and I will send thee to Pharaoh, that thou mayest bring forth my people the Israelites out of Egypt. But Moses said to

And moreover I have heard the groaning of the Israelites, whom the Egyptians keep in bondage; and I have remembered my covenant. Therefore say to the Israelites, 'I am Jehovah, and I will bring you out from under the burdens of the Egyptians, and I will deliver you from their forced labor, and I will redeem you with an outstretched arm, and with me, saying, I have surely visited you, and seen that which is done to you in Egypt; and I have said I will bring you up out of the affliction of Egypt to a land flowing with milk and honey. And they shall hearken to thy voice; and thou shalt come, together with the elders of Israel, to the king of Egypt, and ye shall say to him, 'Jehovah, the God of the Hebrews hath appeared to us; and now let us go, we pray thee, three days' journey into the wilderness, that we may sacrifice to Jehovah our God.'

God, Who am I, that I should go to Pharaoh, and should bring the Israelites out of Egypt? And he said, I will surely be with thee; and this shall be the sign to thee, that I have sent thee: when thou shalt have brought forth the people out of Egypt, ye shall worship God upon this mountain.

mighty judgments, and I will take you for my people, and I will be to you a God; and ye shall know that I am Jehovah your God, who bringeth you out from under the burdens of the Egyptians. And I will bring you to the land which I sware to give to Abraham, to Isaac and to Jacob; and I will give it to you as a heritage, I am Jehovah.'

Then Moses answered and said, But, behold, they will not believe me, nor hearken to my voice; for they will say, 'Jehovah hath not appeared to you.' And Jehovah said to him, What is that in thy hand? And he said, A staff. And he said, Cast it on the ground. And he cast it on the ground and it became a serpent; and Moses fled from before it. Then Jehovah said to Moses, Put forth thy hand and take it by the tail (and he put

Then Moses said to God, Behold, if I go to the Israelites and say to them, 'The God of your fathers hath sent me to you,' and they ask me, 'What is his name?' what shall I answer them? Then God said to Moses, I

Then Moses spoke thus to the Israelites; but they hearkened not to Moses for lack of courage, and because of the hard forced labor. Therefore Jehovah commanded Moses, saying, Go in, speak to Pharaoh king of Egypt, that he let the Israelites go out of his land. But

3. His hesitation and the divine assurance

forth his hand and laid hold of it, and it became a staff in his hand), that they may believe that Jehovah, the God of their fathers, the God of Abraham, the God of Isaac, and the God of Jacob, hath appeared to thee. And Jehovah said furthermore to him, Put now thy hand into thy bosom. And he put his hand into his bosom; and when he took it out, behold, his hand was leprous, as white as snow. And he said, Put thy hand into thy bosom again. (And he put his hand into his bosom again; and when he took it out of his bosom, behold, it had become again as his other flesh). And then, if they will not believe thee, nor hearken to the testimony of the first sign, they will believe the testimony of the other. But if they will not believe even these two signs, nor hearken to thy testimony, thou shalt take of the water of the Nile, and pour it upon the dry land; and the water which thou takest out of the Nile shall become blood upon the dry land. But Moses said to Jehovah, Oh, Lord, I am not eloquent, neither before nor since

AM THAT I AM; and he said, Thus shalt thou say to the Israelites, 'I AM hath sent me to you.' And God also said to Moses, Thus shalt thou say to the Israelites, 'Jehovah, the God of your fathers, the God of Abraham, the God of Isaac, and the God of Jacob, hath sent me to you'; this is my name forever, and by this shall I be remembered from generation to generation. But I know that the king of Egypt will not give you leave to go, unless compelled by a mighty pow-

Moses spoke before Jehovah, saying, Behold, the Israelites have not hearkened to me; how then shall Pharaoh hear me, who am not skilled in speaking? Then Jehovah said to Moses, See, I have made thee as a god to Pharaoh; and Aaron thy brother shall be thy prophet. Thou shalt speak all that I command thee; and Aaron thy brother shall speak to Pharaoh, that he let the Israelites go out of his land. But I will harden Pharaoh's heart, and make my signs and my wonders many in the land of Egypt. Nevertheless Pharaoh will not hearken to you. Then I will lay my hand upon Egypt and bring forth my hosts, my people thou hast spoken to thy servant; for I am slow of speech, and slow of utterance. Then Jehovah said to him, Who hath given a man a mouth? or who maketh one dumb, or deaf, or seeing, or blind? is it not I, Jehovah? Now therefore go, and I will be with thy mouth, and teach thee what thou shalt speak. er. Therefore I will put forth my hand and smite Egypt with all my wonders which I will do in its midst; and after that he will let you go. the Israelites, out of the land of Egypt by great judgments. And the Egyptians shall know that I am Jehovah, when I stretch forth my hand upon Egypt, and bring out the Israelites from among them.

So Moses went and gathered together all the elders of the Israelites, and spoke all the words which Jehovah had spoken to him, and did the signs in the sight of the people. And the people believed; and when they heard that Jehovah had visited the Israelites, and that he had seen their affliction, they bowed low their heads in worship. *4. Delivery of Jehovah's message to the people*

Then Moses came to Pharaoh and said, The God of the Hebrews hath met with me; let us go, we pray, three days' journey into the wilderness that we may sacrifice to Jehovah our God; lest he fall upon us with pestilence or with the sword. But Pharaoh said, Behold, the people of the land are now many, and would you make them rest from their tasks? And the same day Pharaoh commanded the taskmasters who were over the people, saying, You shall no longer give the people straw to make brick, as heretofore; let them go and gather straw for themselves. But the fixed number of bricks which they have been making heretofore, you shall lay upon them; you shall not diminish it at all, for they are idle; that is why they cry aloud, saying, 'Let us go and sacrifice to our God.' Let heavier work be laid upon the men, that they may labor therein and that they may not regard lying words. *5. Pharaoh's defiant refusal to let the Hebrews depart*

Therefore the taskmasters of the people went out, and spoke to the people, saying, Thus saith Pharaoh, I will no longer give you straw. Go yourselves, get straw wherever you can find it; but none of your work shall be diminished. *6. The added oppression*

So the people were scattered abroad throughout all the land of Egypt to gather stubble for straw. And the taskmasters were urgent, saying, You must complete your daily work, just as when there was straw. And the overseers of the Israelites, whom Pharaoh's taskmasters had set over them, were beaten, and asked, Why have you not completed to-day, as yesterday, your prescribed task in making brick?

7. Complaints of the overseers Then the overseers of the Israelites came and complained to Pharaoh, saying, Why do you deal thus with your servants? There is no straw given to your servants, and yet they are saying to us, ' Make bricks,' and now your servants are being beaten; and you wrong your people. But he said, You are lazy, you are lazy; therefore you say, ' Let us go and sacrifice to Jehovah.' Go at once to work, for no straw shall be given to you, yet you must deliver the required number of bricks. And the overseers of the Israelites saw that they were in an evil plight, when it was said, You shall not diminish anything from your daily total of bricks. And they met Moses and Aaron, who had stationed themselves there to meet them as they came forth from Pharaoh, and they said to them, Let Jehovah regard and pronounce judgment; because you have made us odious in the eyes of Pharaoh and in the eyes of his courtiers, in that you have put a sword in their hand to slay us.

8. Moses's protest Then Moses turned again to Jehovah, and said, Lord, Why hast thou brought calamity upon this people? why is it that thou hast sent me? For since I came to Pharaoh to speak in thy name, he has dealt ill with this people; and thou hast not delivered thy people at all.

9. Jehovah's reassurance And Jehovah answered Moses, Now thou shalt see what I will do to Pharaoh; for, compelled by a mighty power, he shall assuredly let them go, yea, compelled by a mighty power, he shall drive them out of his land.

I. The Three Different Accounts of Moses's Call and Commission. In the Old Testament, as in the Gospel narratives, the more important events are recorded in three and sometimes four different versions. Regarding Moses's call there are three distinct accounts and each is important. Back of them all lies a deep spiritual experience, which determined not only the course of Moses's life but that of Hebrew history.

In conveying to their readers a definite impression of the nature of that inner experience, it was inevitable that each group of narrators should employ different literary figures. The task was comparable to that of the early Judean prophet, who in the third chapter of Genesis has pictured the struggle in the mind of the woman between appetite, æsthetic sense, curiosity and the love of knowledge on the one hand, and love and gratitude and obedience on the other. Each group of narrators, with marvellous skill, has succeeded in bringing out, in form intelligible to their readers, the essential facts. Regarding these facts they are also in fundamental agreement.

II. The Earliest Version. The divine call, according to the early Judean narrative, came to Moses from a flaming thorn bush. The story reflects the primitive belief that the Deity sometimes spoke through trees (*cf.* § I[xii]). The essential fact, which the ancient Hebrew story clearly sets forth, is that out of the midst of the wild life of the wilderness there came to the mind of Moses a vivid conception of Jehovah's transcendent holiness and majesty, of the needs of the oppressed Hebrews, of the possibility of their deliverance, and of his own obligation to return and lead them forth.

This version of the call of Moses is in many ways strikingly similar to that of the youthful Isaiah, recorded in the sixth chapter of his prophecy. Both felt the crying needs of their race, and the necessity that some one arise and proclaim the divine truth that alone promised deliverance. Both were also profoundly impressed by the majesty of the Almighty who thus spoke to them. Their call represented that unique moment in their experience, when the voices of duty calling to them from every side became the mighty challenge from God himself, to which they responded, "Here, Lord, send me."

III. The Later Prophetic and Priestly Versions. The early Northern Israelite narrators state that Moses led the flock of Jethro, his father-in-law, which he was guarding, to the back of the wilderness and came to the mountain of God. On that sacred mount, which probably stood out in striking contrast to the rolling, rocky wilderness, God spoke directly to the heart of the future prophet and received the desired response. The memories of the way in which that God had revealed himself in the life and experience of his ancestors rose clearly before the mind of Moses. Awe overwhelmed him in the presence of the Almighty, but above all there came to him the anguished cry of his countrymen, sorely oppressed by the Egyptians, and the personal call to deliver them from the hand of Pharaoh. With this call there came the divine assurance that in the strength of the God of the sacred mountain they should be led forth to worship him at that holy spot.

The late priestly narrators give the needs of the oppressed Hebrews the same central place in the call of their prophetic deliverer. They likewise emphasize God's revelation of himself in the past history of the race, and formulate in their characteristic legal language the assurance that by the divine hand the Hebrews shall be delivered from their cruel oppression, and that Moses is called to be the agent of that deliverance.

IV. The Divine Assurance. Moses's hesitation in accepting the divine call is also brought out in each of the three versions. In the early Judean, his faith is strengthened by two miraculous signs which, in turn, are to be used as credentials, as he presents himself before the elders of his race. The chief reason for his hesitation is that he is not gifted in the art of public address. This excuse is answered by the divine assurance that Jehovah himself, who created the life of man, will be with his mouth and teach him what he shall speak.

In the Northern Israelite version the revelation of the sacred name, *Jehovah* or *Yahweh*, is recorded for the first time. The popular meaning "I am that I am," interpreted in the light of Jehovah's work as creator and leader of his people, is made the earnest of the promised deliverance. Thus Moses's fear that his mission will be fruitless is dispelled by the divine assurance, based on the character of God, as already revealed in the life of man.

The late priestly narrators, interested in the history of their traditional father Aaron, meet Moses's objection that he is not a gifted speaker by providing that Aaron shall be his spokesman. In the classic passage, which illustrates the Hebrew conception of the true character of the prophet, Aaron is appointed as Moses's prophet, that is, one who, like the prophets of Jehovah, shall first learn the will and message of the one he represents, and then, in form adapted to the intelligence of the people, proclaim it to them clearly and authoritatively.

V. The Underlying Facts. The later events of Hebrew history point definitely to a personality and work like that of Moses. His work is, in turn, explained only by some deep spiritual experience which turned his activity into the channels of national leadership. Early Hebrew history, therefore, as a whole, confirms the testimony of these variant traditions that in some mysterious way the divine call came to Moses and that in response to it he became a prophet. These variant narratives also suggest the different factors that entered into that call:

THE UNDERLYING FACTS

the pitiable oppression of his kinsmen and the need of an enlightened leader, who would bind them together and champion their cause, even in the presence of the tyrannical Pharaoh. The background—the wilderness with its solitude, with its life emphasizing the constant need of divine care and protection, the manifestations of the power of God in Nature, and the holy mountain with its historic associations—all these prepared the ear of the prophet to hear God's still small voice. Moses's hesitation, like that of Jeremiah, reveals his high sense of responsibility. His full appreciation of the greatness of the task and his faith in God's power and ability to realize his divine purposes in human history are the unfailing marks of a true prophet.

§ XXII. THE EGYPTIAN PLAGUES

Then Jehovah said to Moses, Pharaoh's heart is stubborn; he refuseth to let the people go. But thou shalt say to him, 'Jehovah, the God of the Hebrews, hath sent me to thee to say, "Let my people go that they may worship me in the wilderness; but hitherto thou hast not hearkened. Thus saith Jehovah, In this thou shalt know that I am Jehovah; behold, I will smite, and the fish that are in the Nile shall die, and the Nile shall become foul, so the Egyptians shall loathe to drink the water from the Nile."' *1. Jehovah's warning to Pharaoh*

Thereupon Jehovah smote the Nile, and the fish that were in the Nile died, and the Nile became foul, so that the Egyptians could not drink the water from the Nile. And all the Egyptians dug round about the Nile for water to drink; for they could not drink the water of the Nile. *2. Defilement of the Nile*

When seven full days had passed after Jehovah had smitten the Nile, Jehovah commanded Moses, Go in to Pharaoh, and say to him, 'Thus saith Jehovah, "Let my people go that they may worship me. And if thou refuse to let them go, then I will smite all thy territory with frogs; and the Nile shall swarm with frogs which shall go up and come into thy house, and into thy bedchamber, and upon thy bed, and into the house of thy courtiers, and upon thy people, and into thine ovens and kneading troughs; and the frogs shall come up even upon thee and thy people and all thy courtiers."' Thereupon Jehovah smote the land of Egypt with frogs. *3. Swarms of frogs*

169

4. Pharaoh's request Then Pharaoh called for Moses and said, Make supplication to Jehovah, that he may take away the frogs from me, and my people; then I will let the people go, that they may sacrifice to Jehovah. And Moses said to Pharaoh, Will you graciously inform me at what time I shall make supplication in your behalf and in behalf of your courtiers and people, that the frogs be destroyed from your palaces and be left only in the Nile? And he answered, To-morrow. Then Moses said, Be it as you say; that you may know that there is none like Jehovah our God. The frogs shall depart from you, and from your palaces, from your courtiers and people, they shall be left only in the Nile.

5. His perfidy Then when Moses had gone out from Pharaoh, he cried to Jehovah in regard to the frogs which he had brought upon Pharaoh. And Jehovah did according to the word of Moses; and the frogs died out of the houses, out of the courts, and out of the fields. And they gathered them together into innumerable heaps; and the land was filled with a vile odor. But when Pharaoh saw that a respite had come, he hardened his heart.

6. Swarms of gad-flies Then Jehovah said to Moses, Rise up early in the morning, and stand before Pharaoh, just as he goes out to the water, and say to him, 'Thus saith Jehovah, "Let my people go that they may worship me. For if thou wilt not let my people go, then I will send swarms of gad-flies upon thee, thy courtiers, and thy people, and into thy palaces, so that the houses of the Egyptians shall be full of swarms of gad-flies, as well as the ground whereon they are. And I will set apart in that day the land of Goshen, in which my people dwell, so that no swarms of gad-flies shall be there, in order that thou mayest know that I am Jehovah in the midst of the earth. And I will put a division between my people and thy people; by to-morrow shall this sign be." ' And Jehovah did so; and there came troublesome swarms of gad-flies into the palace of Pharaoh; and in all Egypt the land was ruined because of the swarms of gad-flies.

7. Pharaoh's consent and request Then Pharaoh called Moses, and said, Go, sacrifice to your God here in this land. But Moses said, It is not advisable so to do; for we shall sacrifice to Jehovah our God that which the Egyptians abhor; if now we sacrifice before their eyes that which the Egyptians abhor, will they not stone us? We wish to go three days' journey in the wilderness and sacrifice to our God, as he shall command us. And Pharaoh said, I will let you go, that you may sacrifice to Jehovah your God in the wilderness; only you shall not go very far away. Make supplication in my behalf. And Moses said, I am now going out from you, and I will make supplication to Jehovah that the swarms of gad-flies may depart from Pharaoh, from his courtiers and people to-morrow; only let not Pharaoh again deal deceitfully by refusing to let the people go to sacrifice to Jehovah.

So Moses went out from Pharaoh and made supplication to Jehovah. And Jehovah did according to the word of Moses; and he removed the swarms of gad-flies from Pharaoh, from his courtiers and people, until not one was left. But Pharaoh was stubborn in heart this time also, and he did not let the people go.

8. His repeated perfidy

Then Jehovah said to Moses, Go in to Pharaoh and tell him, 'Thus saith Jehovah the God of the Hebrews, "Let my people go that they may worship me. For if thou refuse to let them go and still holdest them, then will the hand of Jehovah be upon thy cattle which are in the field, upon the horses, the asses, the camels, the herds and the flocks, in the form of a very severe pest. But Jehovah will make a distinction between the cattle of Israel and the cattle of Egypt, and nothing shall die of all that belongs to the Israelites."' Accordingly Jehovah appointed a set time, saying, To-morrow Jehovah shall do this in the land. And Jehovah did that thing on the morrow: and all the cattle of Egypt died; but of the cattle of the Israelites none died. Then Pharaoh sent and found that not even one of the cattle of the Israelites was dead. But the heart of Pharaoh was stubborn and he did not let the people go.

9. Death of the cattle of the Egyptians

Then Jehovah said to Moses, Rise up early in the morning, and stand before Pharaoh, and say to him, 'Thus saith Jehovah, the God of the Hebrews, "Let my people go, that they may worship me. Dost thou still exalt thyself against my people, in that thou wilt not let them go? Then to-morrow about this time I will send down a very heavy fall of hail, such as hath not been in Egypt since the day it was

10. Destructive hail

founded, even until the present."' So Jehovah sent thunder and hail; and fire ran down upon the earth; and Jehovah rained hail upon the land of Egypt. And the hail was very severe, such as had not been in all the land of Egypt since it became a nation. And the hail smote all the vegetation of the field, and shattered every tree of the field. Only in the province of Goshen, where the Israelites were, was there no hail.

11.Pharaoh's continued perfidy

Then Pharaoh sent, and called for Moses, and said to him, I have sinned this time; Jehovah is in the right and I and my people are in the wrong. Make supplication to Jehovah —for there has been more than enough of these mighty thunderings and hail. I will let you go, and you shall stay no longer. Then Moses said to him, As soon as I am gone out of the city, I will spread out my hands in prayer to Jehovah; the thunders shall cease, and there shall be no more hail, that thou mayest know that the land is Jehovah's. But as for you and your courtiers, I know that even then you will not fear Jehovah. So Moses went out of the city from Pharaoh, and spread out his hands to Jehovah. Then the thunders and hail ceased, and the rain was no longer poured upon the earth. But when Pharaoh saw that the rain and the hail and the thunders had ceased, he sinned yet again and was stubborn in heart, he together with his courtiers.

12. Jehovah's warning

Then Jehovah said to Moses, Go in to Pharaoh. So Moses went in to Pharaoh, and said to him, Thus saith Jehovah, the God of the Hebrews, 'How long wilt thou refuse to humble thyself before me? let my people go that they may worship me. For if thou refuse to let my people go, to-morrow I will bring locusts into thy territory, and they shall cover the surface of the earth, so that one shall not be able to see the earth, and they shall eat the residue of that which is escaped, which remaineth to you from the hail, and shall eat every tree which groweth for you out of the field; and thy palaces shall be filled, and the houses of all thy courtiers, and of all the Egyptians; neither thy fathers nor thy fathers' fathers have seen the like, since the day that they were upon the earth to this day.' Then he turned and went out from Pharaoh.

Thereupon Pharaoh's courtiers said to him, How long is this man to be a snare to us? Let the men go that they may worship Jehovah their God. Do you not know that Egypt is being destroyed? So Moses was brought again to Pharaoh, and he said to him, Go worship Jehovah, your God; but who are they that shall go? And Moses said, We will go with our young, and with our old men, with our sons and with our daughters, with our flocks, and with our herds will we go; for we must hold a feast to Jehovah. And he said to them, May Jehovah then be with you. If I let you go together with your little ones, beware, for evil is before you. Nay, rather, you men go and worship Jehovah, for that is what you desire. Then they were driven out from Pharaoh's presence. 13. Partial consent of Pharaoh and his courtiers

And Jehovah caused an east wind to blow over the land all that day, and all the night; and when it was morning the east wind had brought the locusts, and they settled down in all the territory of Egypt, exceedingly many; before them there were never so many locusts as they, neither after them shall there ever be so many. For they covered the surface of the whole land, so that the land looked dark, and nothing green was left, either tree or herb of the field, throughout all the land of Egypt. 14. Devastation of the land by locusts

Then Pharaoh called for Moses in haste, and said, I have sinned against Jehovah your God, and against you. Now therefore forgive, I pray thee, my sin only this once, and make supplication to Jehovah your God, that he may at least take away from me this deadly plague. So he went out from Pharaoh and made supplication to Jehovah. And Jehovah caused to blow from the opposite direction an exceeding strong west wind, which took up the locusts and cast them into the Red Sea; not a single locust was left in all the territory of Egypt. 15. Pharaoh's request

Then Pharaoh called Moses, and said, Go, worship Jehovah, only let your flocks and your herds remain behind; let your little ones also go with you. But Moses said, You must also give us sacrifices and burnt-offerings, that we may sacrifice to Jehovah our God. Our cattle also must go with us; not a hoof shall be left behind; for we must take these to offer to Jehovah our God; and we do not know what 16. Moses's final interview with Pharaoh we must offer to Jehovah, until we come thither. Thereupon Pharaoh said to him, Begone from me, beware, never see my face again; for in the day you see my face you shall die. And Moses said, You have spoken truly, I shall never see your face again.

17. The final warning

But Moses said, Thus saith Jehovah, 'About midnight I will go throughout the midst of Egypt; and all the first-born in the land of Egypt shall die, from the first-born of Pharaoh who sitteth upon his throne, even to the first-born of the maid-servant, that is behind the mill. And there shall be a great wail of lamentation throughout all the land of Egypt, the like of which has never been, and shall never be again.' But against none of the Israelites shall a dog move his tongue, against neither man nor beast; that you may know that Jehovah doth make a distinction between the Egyptians and Israel. And all these your courtiers shall come down to me, and prostrate themselves before me, saying, 'Go forth, together with all the people that follow you'; and after that I will go out. Thereupon he went out from Pharaoh in hot anger.

18. Directions regarding the departure

Then Moses called all the elders of Israel, and said to them, Draw out and take lambs from the herds and kill. And you shall take a bunch of hyssop, and dip it in the blood that is in the basin, and strike the lintel and the two door-posts with the blood that is in the basin; but, as regards yourselves, none of you shall go out of the door of his house. For Jehovah will pass through to smite the Egyptians; and when he seeth the blood upon the lintel, and on the two door-posts, Jehovah will pass over the door, and will not suffer the Destroyer to come into your houses to smite you. Then the people bowed low their heads in worship.

19. Death of the first-born of the Egyptians

And it came to pass at midnight, that Jehovah smote all the first-born in the land of Egypt, from the first-born of Pharaoh who sat on his throne to the first-born of the captive that was in the prison. Then Pharaoh rose up in the night, together with all his courtiers and the Egyptians, and there arose a great wail in Egypt for there was not a house where there was not one dead. And he called Moses and Aaron by night and said, Arise, go forth from the midst of my people, together with the Israelites; go, worship Jehovah as you have requested. Also take with you your sheep and your cattle, as you have requested, and go and ask a blessing for me. And the Egyptians urged the people strenuously, that they might send them quickly out of the land, for they said to themselves, Else we shall be dead. Therefore the people took their dough before it was leavened, their kneading troughs being bound up in their clothes upon their shoulders.

I. The Different Groups of Plague Stories. In the remarkable treaty, which Ramses II concluded early in his reign with the Hittites who held northern Syria (Introd. III[vi]), provision was made for coöperation in punishing delinquent subjects and in the extradition of political fugitives and immigrants, so that it was almost impossible to escape from the power of the Pharaoh. The problem of why the Israelite serfs were ever allowed to depart from Egypt was evidently in the minds of the later Hebrew narrators. All the traditions are agreed that the Egyptians did not consent until a series of remarkable calamities had broken their spirit and weakened their resources. Regarding the nature of these calamities each group of narrators had its characteristic version. In the late priestly narratives the plagues are all of a miraculous origin and character. They are, in fact, not so much plagues as wonders, performed in the presence of Pharaoh by Aaron's magical staff, to prove his superiority over the Egyptian magicians. In the Northern Israelite narratives Moses himself wields the staff which calls forth the plague. In the early Judean narratives (*cf.* above) Jehovah sends the plagues after Moses has each time warned Pharaoh of the coming calamity. In these oldest records the plagues are not miracles, but simply natural phenomena characteristic of Egypt. Their magnitude and severity alone are unprecedented. Fortunately, this oldest history has been quoted fully, only two or three paragraphs having been lost. Separated from the later versions, it furnishes a closely connected account of seven distinct plagues.

II. The Oldest Account of the Plagues. Each plague is introduced by the same formulas and scenes. Each succeeding plague is more severe than the preceding, until the divine judgment reaches its culmination in the death of the first-born. They also appear to stand in a certain logical and chronological order. The defilement of the waters of the Nile may well have occurred in July or August, when the river is at its height. The second plague would fall most naturally in September, when frogs are most common in Egypt. Their rapid increase would naturally follow from the defilement of the waters. In the hot climate of Egypt the huge heaps of decaying frogs would inevitably breed great swarms of flies in the following months of October and November. The flies would in turn spread abroad the disease germs which attacked the animals and flocks in the pest-ridden region of the Nile. In the land of Egypt the plague of hail would be possible only in the rainy month of January. The great swarms of locusts, which may have obscured the sun, causing the local darkness described in the Northern Israelite narratives, came most naturally in the early spring just before the Passover, with which the last plague was associated.

III. The Egyptian Background of the Plagues. Owing to the presence of vegetable matter or minute organisms washed down by the Nile when it rises in June, the water is first colored green and then later turns to a dull reddish tinge. Many early travellers have commented on the unwholesomeness of the water at this stage. To-day, as in the past, the Nile is the only source of water supply in lower Egypt. Any unusual natural or local cause, which would corrupt the water of this sacred river, would bring in its train the plagues which immediately follow each other in the biblical stories. Early writers report repeated plagues of frogs in different parts of the ancient world. Gnats and stinging flies of various kinds are perennial plagues in the land of the Nile. Cattle plagues are also common. One was reported in 1842, which destroyed forty thousand oxen. In the late priestly account the plague attacked men as well as animals. The Hebrews, living apart in the land of Goshen, were in a different zone and would naturally escape those plagues which appear, according to the earliest records, to have been confined to the lower Nile valley.

Thunder storms, with lightning and hail, although very rare in Egypt, are not unknown during the rainy months. One observer saw hail storms but three times in twelve years. Lepsius states that "in December, 1843, there was a terrific storm with hail which made the day dark as night." The statement in the Northern Israelite version that the plague came "when the barley was in the ear and the flax was in the bloom" fixes the date about the middle of January.

Although the locust plagues are more common in Palestine, travellers in Egypt have observed great swarms of these insects, which often obscure the light of the sun and destroy all vegetation in their path.

From ancient times Egypt has been the home of many kinds of pestilence. Its hot climate and dense population favor the propagation and spread of contagious diseases. The preceding plagues had prepared the way for the sudden and terrible pestilence which spared neither young nor old, strong nor weak, cutting off the flower (the first-born) of every Egyptian home. Again, however, the Hebrews, living apart from the afflicted district, escaped the dread scourge.

IV. Historical Facts Underlying the Plague Stories. The contemporary Egyptian records contain no direct references to the biblical plagues. Merneptah, in his old age, succeeded his father Ramses II. For ten years at least, until 1215 B.C., he maintained the Egyptian rule in Palestine. He also succeeded in repelling the Libyan hordes which came from the northwest, and died peacefully and was buried with his ancestors at Thebes.

After the death of Merneptah, however, a series of calamities overtook Egypt, which are probably the basis of the Hebrew plague stories. Rival pretenders contended for the throne and civil war broke out in many parts of the empire. By the close of the thirteenth century complete anarchy prevailed. The local nobles and chiefs improved the opportunity to proclaim their independence or to make war upon each other. The land was deluged with blood. A later king (Ramses III) states that, "Every man was thrown out of his right; they had no chief ruler for many years until later times. The land of Egypt was in the hands of the nobles and rulers of towns; each slew his neighbor, great and small" (*Harris Papyrus*, IV, 398). Famine with all its misery and horrors followed.

At this time also a certain Syrian proclaimed himself king. "He made the entire land tributary to him; he united his companions and plundered their possessions. They made the gods like men and no offerings were presented at the temples" (*Harris Papyrus*). While no one would attempt to identify this Syrian with Moses, the narrative reveals a state of affairs in Egypt, which made it very easy for the Hebrews on the eastern borders to break away from their hateful bondage. The Libyans and other foreign invaders also improved this opportunity to invade and plunder Egypt. In the hot, unsanitary climate of the Nile, the anarchy and bloodshed and famine that prevailed may well have given rise to a series of plagues culminating in a terrible pestilence, as recorded in the oldest Hebrew traditions. Although differing in details, the oldest biblical narratives and the contemporary records are therefore in fundamental agreement.

V. The Significance of the National Calamities. The Egyptian king, who finally succeeded in restoring order, implies in the account of his work that the preceding disasters were due to the disfavor of the gods. With true insight Israel's prophetic historians saw in these same events the hand of Jehovah preparing the way for the deliverance of his people. As the traditions were handed down, each succeeding generation expressed this truth in more definite and concrete terms, until the stories have assumed their present form. Underlying these stories is the great truth that there is no chance in God's universe. The seemingly important and unimportant events in human history all conserve his divine purpose. No human power—the will of kings nor the might of empires—can hinder the realization of that purpose. Those who resist it are broken, but those who, like the Israelites, act in accord with the divine will are trained for service and led on to a noble destiny.

VI. **The Traditional Origin of the Passover.** Both the early and the late Hebrew traditions agree in tracing the origin of the feast of the Passover to the great deliverance from Egypt. Moses's original request of Pharaoh was that the Hebrews might go out three days' journey into the wilderness to sacrifice to their God. The object was evidently to celebrate the spring festival which had long been an established institution among the Semitic ancestors of the Hebrews. At this ancient feast all members of a clan or tribe came together to renew the covenant with their tribal god. A lamb was sacrificed and its flesh eaten amidst feasting and rejoicing (*cf.* St. O.T., IV, p. 258). It was a time of joy and thanksgiving. In associating it with the great deliverance from Egypt, the later Hebrew prophets and priests gave it a new meaning, and yet at the same time emphasized the original content of the old Semitic feast. Even as the ancient Teutonic and Roman festivals were transformed into Christmas, so the old Semitic feast of thanksgiving became the Hebrew Passover. It remained preëminently the festival of the family or clan. The paschal lamb symbolized the renewal of the covenant with Jehovah. The blood sprinkled on the door-posts and lintels, the dish of bitter herbs, the girded loins, the sandals on the feet, and the staff in hand all recalled the great deliverance. The songs and prayers appropriately voiced the gratitude of the race for this and the subsequent proofs of Jehovah's tender love and care.

§ XXIII. THE EXODUS

Now the Israelites went forth from Egypt, about six **1. The departure from Egypt** hundred thousand men on foot, not including children. And a mixed multitude went up also with them; and flocks and herds, even very great possessions. And they baked unleavened cakes of the dough which they had brought forth out of Egypt; for it was not leavened, because they had been driven out of Egypt, and could not wait, neither had they prepared for themselves any food for the way.

And Jehovah went before them by day in a pillar of cloud, **2. Jehovah's guidance** to show them the way, and by night in a pillar of fire, to give them light; that they might march by day and by night; the pillar of cloud by day and the pillar of fire by night did not depart from before the people.

When the king of Egypt was told that the people had fled, **3. Pharaoh's pursuit of the Israelites** the feeling of Pharaoh and his courtiers toward the people was changed, and they said, What is this we have done, that we have let Israel go from serving us? And he made ready his chariot, and took his people with him, and all the chariots of Egypt.

And when Pharaoh drew near, the Israelites lifted up **4. Terror of the Israelites** their eyes and saw the Egyptians marching after them; and they were exceedingly afraid, and they said to Moses, Was it because there were no graves in Egypt, that you have taken us away to die in the wilderness? Why have you dealt thus with us, in bringing us forth out of Egypt? Is not this what we told you in Egypt, when we said, 'Let us alone, that we may serve the Egyptians? For it was better for us to serve the Egyptians than that we should die in the wilderness.' And Moses said to the people, Fear not, stand still and see the deliverance which Jehovah will accomplish for you to-day; for as surely as you now see the Egyptians, you shall never see them again forever. Jehovah will fight for you, and you are to keep still.

Then the pillar of cloud changed its position from before **5. The great deliverance** them and stood behind them. And the cloud lighted up the night; yet throughout the entire night the one army did not come near the other. And Jehovah caused the sea to go back by a strong east wind all that night, and made the bed of the sea dry. And it came to pass in the watch before the dawn, that Jehovah looked forth through the pillar of fire and of cloud upon the host of the Egyptians, and he bound their chariot wheels, so that they proceeded with difficulty. Then the Egyptians said, Let us flee from before Israel; for Jehovah fighteth for them against the Egyptians. But the sea returned to its ordinary level towards morning, while the Egyptians were flying before it. And Jehovah overthrew the Egyptians in the midst of the sea, so that not one of them remained. Thus Jehovah saved Israel that day out of the power of the Egyptians; and Israel saw the Egyptians dead upon the sea-shore.

6. Song of thanksgiving

Then Moses and the Israelites sang this song to Jehovah, using these words:

> I will sing to Jehovah for he is greatly exalted;
> Horse and his rider hath he thrown into the sea.
> Jehovah is my strength and my song,
> For to me hath he brought deliverance;
> This is my God, him I praise,
> My fathers' God, him I extol.

7. Jehovah's might as a warrior

> Jehovah is indeed a warrior, Jehovah is his name:
> The chariots of Pharaoh and his host hath he cast into the sea;
> And the best of his captains have sunk down in the Red Sea;
> The floods cover them, they have gone down into the depths like a stone.
> Thy right hand, O Jehovah, is glorious in power,
> Thy right hand, O Jehovah, shattereth the foe.
> Through the greatness of thy majesty thou overthrowest thine opposers.
> Thou sendest forth thy wrath, it consumeth them like stubble.

8. His overthrow of the Egyptians

> By the wrath of thy nostrils were the waters piled up,
> The surging waters stood upright as a heap.
> The floods were congealed in the midst of the sea.

The foe said, ' I will pursue, yea, I will overtake,
I will divide spoil, on them shall my desire be satisfied,
I will draw my sword, my hand shall destroy them.'
Thou didst blow with thy breath, the sea covered him,
Down in the mighty waters they sank like lead.

I. The Triple Tradition of the Exodus. As in the case of each important event in early Hebrew history, there are three distinct accounts of the deliverance from Egypt. These have been closely blended into a continuous narrative, but the task of separating them is not difficult. The early Judean prophetic and the late priestly versions are each complete. The Northern Israelite account has been quoted only in part, but can be supplemented in the light of Joshua's address found in Joshua 24. These three distinct versions illustrate well the transformation through which the story passed, when transmitted from generation to generation through different groups of teachers. In the earliest account the narrative is circumstantial and in harmony with conditions pictured in the contemporary Egyptian inscriptions. The instrument of deliverance, the east wind which blows back the waters, is in perfect keeping with the means used by Jehovah to accomplish his purposes, in the present as in the past. The late priestly version, however, which comes from those exilic teachers who were more profoundly impressed by God's transcendent power than by the actual ways in which he accomplishes his ends, magnifies the supernatural element.

II. The Number of the Hebrews. In the early Judean narrative it is stated that the Hebrew refugees included six hundred thousand men, not counting children. This number is repeated in Exodus 12³⁷, which belongs to the same source. Possibly the Hebrew text originally read and should be translated, *six hundred clans*. Inasmuch as definite numbers are rarely given in this early source, it is also possible that the present statement was added by some later compiler. Certainly it is not supported by the evidence which comes from the subsequent stories. As has already been noted, the Northern Israelite narrative of Exodus 1¹⁵⁻¹⁹ suggests that they numbered hundreds rather than thousands. Even in the days of Deborah, when they had absorbed many other desert and Canaanite tribes, only about forty thousand warriors rallied on the battle-field. In the days of David the census of the larger northern tribes reveals but eight hundred thousand fighting men. The stories of the deliverance, the wilderness wanderings and the conquest, all indicate that not more than a few thousand He-

181

brews were included in that nucleus of the later nation which escaped from the land of bondage.

III. **Their Probable Route.** The late priestly narrative states that the Hebrews rallied at Succoth (Egyptian *Thuku*, *cf.* § XVIII[i]), which may be identical with the Pithom of the earliest records. Two routes lay before them. One ran to the north, then turned to the northeast along the shore of the Mediterranean. This was known as the "Way of the Philistines" and led directly to the land of Palestine. It was, however, more exposed to Egyptian attack, and advance was barred on the borders of Palestine by the Philistines, who were a strongly intrenched, energetic people. Escape along this route, therefore, was almost impossible. The Hebrews evidently chose the so-called, "Way of the Red Sea," the highway which ran straight out into the desert along the caravan route which ultimately led to Elath and central Arabia. A journey of fifteen or twenty miles along the valley, which extended eastward toward the desert, brought them to the frontier fortresses which guarded the eastern entrance to the land of Egypt. From the reign of Merneptah comes a list, prepared by an officer of one of the frontier garrisons which guarded the caravan route, of those who passed by on this great artery of communication between Asia and the land of the Nile. It would seem that this frontier fortress was built near either the western arm of the Red Sea or the series of shallow lakes which marked its northern extension. It is also probable that a frontier wall ran from the fortress and connected with these lakes, compelling all who entered or departed from the land of Egypt to pass through its gates.

IV. **The Method of Travel in the Wilderness.** The early Judean narrative gives a vivid picture of the way in which the Hebrews marched. The underlying historical facts are suggested by the way in which caravans still journey through the wilderness. The leader who goes in front often bears aloft, on the end of a long pole, a brazier filled with smoking coals from which rises a column of smoke. In the clear light of the desert, this column of smoke can be seen by the different members of the caravan, even though they lag many miles behind. Thus it is possible to determine at all times the position of the leader and the direction in which the caravan is moving. By night these glowing coals, held on high, accomplish the same end and make possible the long midnight journeys, which are often required in order to reach the distant springs. In the inimitable language of the early story-tellers, the fundamental truth that Jehovah through his prophet was ever leading them by day and by night on to their destiny is forcibly set forth.

V. The Great Deliverance. Soon after the news of the flight of the Hebrew serfs is brought to the Egyptian authorities, a detachment of cavalry is in hot pursuit. As the Hebrews approach the border fortress they evidently find its gates closed and their way of escape cut off. In the light of the Egyptian records and the topography of the region the situation can readily be imagined: before them, the fortress with walls which extended out into the shallow waters of the Sea of Reeds; behind them, the pursuing Egyptians; and in their own ranks fear and distrust of the prophet, who had held up before them in the name of Jehovah the definite promise of deliverance. Escape seems impossible to all save the undaunted leader, whose trust is fixed in the God who had revealed himself on the sacred mount.

The more familiar late priestly narrative pictures Moses, as simply stretching out his hand over the sea, and then leading his followers through the divided waters, which stand as a wall on either side. The older and simpler narrative, however, suggests the historical facts. In the time of their direst need the God, who controlled the forces of Nature, sent forth a strong east wind, which drove back the shallow waters of the Sea of Reeds, making it possible for his people to escape around the guarding walls across the bed of the sea and out into the freedom of the desert. The Egyptians, pursuing with their heavy chariots, were caught and overwhelmed in the returning waters.

VI. Similar Natural Phenomena. Many analogies to the phenomenon here recorded might be cited from modern records. As is well known, the Russians, in 1738, entered and captured the Crimea through a passage made by the wind through the Putrid Sea. The closest analogy, however, is recorded by Major-General Tulloch, who states that the shallow waters of Lake Menzaleh, which lies a short distance north of the scene of the deliverance of the Hebrews, were driven back seven miles by a strong wind, leaving the bottom of the lake dry (*Journal of the Victorian Institute*, Vol. XXVIII, p. 267, and Vol. XXVI, p. 12). A recent illustration of the power of wind over water, especially when reenforced by the tide, is found in the Galveston disaster of 1900.

VII. The Song of Thanksgiving. The prophetic narrators have quoted two lines of the refrain, and possibly certain other stanzas of the song which the grateful Hebrews sang after the signal deliverance. The later poets, familiar with the present composite narrative, have extended this refrain into a noble and commemorative ode, which recalls the different scenes in that great crisis which revealed so clearly God's power and love for his people.

VIII. Significance of the Great Deliverance. The fact that God used natural means "his wonders to perform" makes the deliverance none the less significant. It simply illustrates the truth that there is no chance in his universe. Not so much the method, but the opportuneness of the deliverance clearly revealed the divine hand. At the moment of their supreme need, he showed not only his power but his eagerness to deliver his people. The great deliverance confirmed the authority of Moses and made it possible to impress profoundly his personality and teaching upon the character and consciousness of his race. It also established a basis for that covenant which they conceived of as existing between them and the God, who had thus signally saved them. All Hebrew literature abounds in references to this event. Amos and Hosea appeal to it as the supreme reason why Israel should be loyal to its God. In the laws of Deuteronomy, generosity toward the slave, kindness and justice toward the resident alien, and charity toward the poor and needy, are all urged "because thou wast a slave in the land of Egypt and Jehovah thy God redeemed thee."

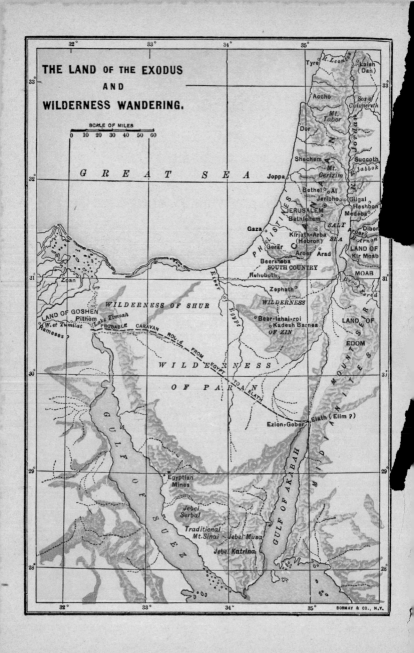

THE LAND OF THE EXODUS
AND
WILDERNESS WANDERING.

SCALE OF MILES
0 10 20 30 40 50 60

G R E A T   S E A

Joppa

Tyre R. Leont
Laish (Dan)
Accho
Sea of Chinnereth
Mt. Tabor
Dor
Shechem
Mt. Gerizim
Succoth
Jabbok
Bethel Ai
Jericho Gilgal
Heshbon
JERUSALEM Medeba
Bethlehem
Gaza
Kirjath-Arba (Hebron)
Gerar
Aroer Arad
Beersheba
SOUTH COUNTRY
Rehoboth
SALT SEA
Dibon
R. Arnon
LAND OF Kir Moab
MOAB
Zoan
WILDERNESS OF SHUR
LAND OF GOSHEN
Pithom
W. et Tumilat
Lake Timsah
Rameses ?
PROBABLE CARAVAN ROUTE FROM EGYPT TO ELATH
Zephath
WILDERNESS
Beer-lahai-roi
Kadesh Barnea
OF ZIN
Brook Jered
LAND OF EDOM
W I L D E R N E S S
O F   P A R A N
Ezion-Geber Elath (Elim ?)
GULF OF SUEZ
GULF OF AKABAH
M I D I A N I T E S
MOUNTAINS
Egyptian Mines
Jebel Serbal
Traditional Mt. Sinai Jebel Musa
Jebel Katrina

BORMAY & CO., N.Y.

THE HEBREWS IN THE WILDERNESS AND EAST OF THE JORDAN

§ XXIV. THE REVELATION AND COVENANT AT SINAI

Then Moses led Israel onward from the Red Sea, and they went out into the wilderness of Shur and marched three days into the wilderness, without finding water. Then they came to Marah, but could not drink the water of Marah because it was bitter. Hence its name was called Marah [Bitterness]. Therefore the people murmured against Moses, saying, What shall we drink? And he cried to Jehovah, and Jehovah showed him a tree, and he cast it into the waters, and the waters were made sweet. *1. Experiences at Marah*

And they came to Elim where there were twelve springs of water, and seventy palm-trees, and they encamped there by the waters. *2. At Elim*

Then they journeyed from Elim, and they came to the wilderness of Sinai and encamped in the wilderness. *3. March to Sinai*

Then Jehovah said to Moses, I will come down in the sight of all the people upon Mount Sinai. And thou shalt set bounds for the people all about, with the command, ' Take heed to yourselves that ye go not up on the mountain nor even approach its base; whoever toucheth the mountain shall surely be put to death; nothing shall touch it without being stoned to death or shot through; whether it be beast or man; he shall not live.' *4. The divine directions*

And Mount Sinai was wholly enveloped in smoke, because Jehovah came down upon it in fire; and the smoke of it ascended like the smoke of a furnace, and the whole mountain quaked violently. And when Jehovah came down upon Mount Sinai to the top of the mountain, he called Moses to the top of the mountain; and Moses went up. *5. The advent of Jehovah*

185

And Jehovah said to Moses, Go down, warn the people solemnly lest they press forward to see Jehovah, and many of them perish. And let the priests also, who come near Jehovah, sanctify themselves lest Jehovah break forth upon them. So Moses went down to the people and told them.

6. The two tablets of stone

Then Jehovah said to Moses, Hew out two stone tablets, and be ready by morning, and come up in the morning to Mount Sinai, and present thyself there to me on the top of the mountain. And no one shall come up with thee; neither let any one be seen in any part of the mountain, nor let the flocks and herds feed before that mountain. So he hewed out two stone tablets; and Moses rose early in the morning, and went up to Mount Sinai, as Jehovah had commanded him, and took in his hand two stone tablets. And Moses stood with him there and called on the name of Jehovah.

7. The terms of the early covenant

And Jehovah said, Behold, I make a covenant. Observe that which I command thee to-day:

THOU SHALT WORSHIP NO OTHER GOD.

THOU SHALT MAKE THEE NO MOLTEN GODS.

THE FEAST OF UNLEAVENED BREAD SHALT THOU OBSERVE.

EVERY FIRST-BORN IS MINE.

SIX DAYS SHALT THOU TOIL, BUT ON THE SEVENTH THOU SHALT REST.

THOU SHALT OBSERVE THE FEAST OF WEEKS AND INGATHERING AT THE END OF THE YEAR.

THOU SHALT NOT OFFER THE BLOOD OF MY SACRIFICE WITH LEAVEN.

THE FAT OF MY FEAST SHALL NOT BE LEFT UNTIL MORNING.

THE BEST OF THE FIRST-FRUITS OF THY LAND SHALT THOU BRING TO THE HOUSE OF JEHOVAH THY GOD.

THOU SHALT NOT SEETHE A KID IN ITS MOTHER'S MILK.

8. Recording the ten words

Then Jehovah said to Moses, Write these words; for in accordance with these words have I made a covenant with thee and with Israel. And he was there with Jehovah forty days and forty nights; he neither ate bread nor drank water.

And he wrote upon the tablets the words of the covenant, the ten words [Decalogue].

Then Moses came and called for the elders of the people, and set before them all these words which Jehovah commanded him. And all the people answered together, and said, All that Jehovah hath spoken we will do. And Moses reported the words of the people to Jehovah.

And Jehovah said to Moses, Come up to Jehovah, together with Aaron, and Nadab, and Abihu, and seventy of the elders of Israel, and worship afar off; and Moses alone shall come near to Jehovah; but they shall not come near; neither shall the people go up with him. So Moses went up together with Aaron, Nadab, and Abihu, and seventy of the elders of Israel, and they saw the God of Israel; and under his feet it was like a pavement of sapphire stone, and like the very sky for clearness. And against the nobles of the Israelites he did not stretch out his hand; so they beheld God and ate and drank.

9. Acceptance of the ten words

10. The sacrificial meal

I. The Records of the Revelation and Covenant at Sinai. Sinai, the sacred mountain of God, was regarded by succeeding generations as the spot where the covenant between Israel and Jehovah was established and where all of Israel's laws were promulgated. The further removed from the days of Moses, the more firmly did each succeeding generation cherish this tradition. Each new code, although it incorporated new principles and laws adapted to new conditions, was attributed to Moses. In time all of these codes naturally found a place in the growing body of legislation that was connected with Mount Sinai.

The earliest prophetic narratives suggest the historical basis of this later expanded tradition. In slightly different form, they each picture the revelation at Sinai and preserve that primitive decalogue, which appears to have been the basis of the original covenant between Jehovah and his people.

II. The March Through the Desert. The earliest narrative implies that the Hebrews, on leaving Egypt, marched directly across the desert. After three days' journey they found one of the brackish springs, which characterize that desert region. A little later they come to Elim, with its twelve springs of water and grove of palm-trees. The only satisfactory identification of this fertile spot is at the head of the north-

187

eastern arm of the Red Sea. As the name suggests, it is probably to be identified with the biblical Elath, the important port which connected the trade of Canaan and Edom with Arabia, India and Africa. It was also at the end of the caravan route which led directly across the desert from Egypt (*cf*. map opp. p. 185). It was a journey of about two hundred miles, and could be comfortably made by a caravan in about a week. That Moses would lead his fugitive followers along he same direct highway to the land of Midian, as he himself had followed years before, was to be expected. In this way it would be possible most quickly to escape beyond the rule and pursuit of the Egyptians into a friendly asylum among kindred peoples. His aim was, doubtless, also to lead them to the sacred mountain of Jehovah, where he, a short time before, had received his divine call to lead forth his people from the bondage of Egypt.

III. **The Situation of Mount Sinai.** The course of the march of the Israelites turns in part upon the identification of Mount Sinai. The tradition, which identifies it with one of the imposing peaks in the southern part of the Sinaitic peninsula, cannot be traced earlier than the third or fourth century of the Christian era. It comes from those centuries in which the process of identifying biblical sites advanced most rapidly. It was an age in which conjecture and zeal to fix the background of every important event were regnant, with the result that nine out of every ten of these identifications have been shown by modern excavation and research to be incorrect.

All the Old Testament references to Sinai indicate clearly that the mountain was in the vicinity of Edom and probably one of the many imposing peaks to the southwest of Mount Seir. In the ancient song of Deborah, Judges 5, Sinai is associated with Mount Seir and the land of Edom (§ XXXVI[6]). In the early poem, found in Deuteronomy 33, the parallelism is equally significant.

> "Jehovah came from Sinai,
> And beamed forth from Seir,
> And shone forth from Mount Paran."

Elijah's journey (recorded in I Kings 19[3-8]) from Beersheba to Mount Horeb would have been possible if the mountain of God had been one of the southwestern spurs of Mount Seir, but practically impossible, if at the southern end of the Sinaitic peninsula. In the light of the Egyptian inscriptions and the recent excavations conducted by Professor Petrie (*cf. Researches in Sinai*), it is evident that there were important quarries and mines guarded by Egyptian garrisons on the eastern side of the peninsula. It is highly improbable, therefore, that the Hebrews would have journeyed along a caravan route thus guarded by Egyptian soldiers. Even if they had succeeded in reaching the traditional Mount Sinai, they would not have escaped Egyptian pursuit. The statement that Moses, when he received his call, arrived at the sacred mountain with the flock of Jethro, his father-in-law, after a journey of only three days, indicates that it was not far from the land of Midian. The implication that Mount Sinai was the mountain at which the Midianites worshipped the same God as the Israelites, clearly points to a northern rather than a southern site, for at this period the Midianites were found only to the south and east of Mount Seir. Mount Sinai also appears to have been near Kadesh (only fifty miles south of Beer-sheba, *cf.* map, opp. p. 185) the centre of the Hebrew life in the wilderness. Thus, with remarkable unity, all the early evidence points to one of the southwestern spurs of Mount Seir as the sacred mountain of Jehovah.

IV. **Nature of the Revelation at Sinai.** The Old Testament contains three distinct accounts of the divine revelation at Sinai. In the late priestly, the cloud is represented as covering the mountain and *the appearance of the glory of Jehovah* is like a devouring fire on the top of the mountain. Into this cloud Moses ascends and there receives the law. In the Northern Israelite version a thick cloud likewise envelopes the mountain, which is designated as *Horeb* or simply *the mountain.* When, at God's command, the people approach, they are so terrified by the thunder and the lightnings that they request Moses to receive for them the divine message. In the early Judean version the people are forbidden to approach Mount Sinai, which is enveloped with smoke and quakes violently. Moses himself alone ascends to receive the divine message.

The three narratives, therefore, agree in the statement that a bright cloud, lighted up by flames of fire, shrouded the mountain. The Northern Israelite version implies that a raging thunder storm revealed to the waiting people below the presence of their God. The picture in the early Judean and late priestly narratives perhaps suggests an active volcano. Either phenomenon, so majestic and awe-inspiring, was calculated to make a profound impression upon the consciousness and memory of a primitive people, accustomed to the dry, almost rainless tracts of Egypt and the desert. Thus it is that, in language peculiar to itself, each tradition records the fact that the Deity made his presence powerfully felt at this initial stage in the life of his people.

V. Meaning of the Covenant in Ancient Semitic Life. The well-authenticated tradition that a covenant was established between Jehovah and his people at Sinai is in harmony with the peculiar customs of the ancient nomadic East. To-day, as in the past, a covenant is the strongest bond that can bind together men or tribes. In certain parts of Arabia, as in the ancient East, a covenant is established between two individuals, when they have drunk their mingled blood. Such a solemn covenant carries with it an obligation on the part of each to protect the other, even at the cost of life. Henceforth they owe to each other the same duties, as do those who are descended from common ancestors. Thus it was that tribes in ancient times made alliances with each other. The ancient Semites also conceived of their deities as dwelling in certain definite abodes and capable of entering into solemn covenants with men and tribes. This prevalent Semitic conception clearly underlies the Hebrew tradition of the covenant at Sinai.

VI. The Giving of the Law at Sinai. In welding into a nation the scattered fugitives from Egypt and the kindred tribes of Midian, it was natural that Moses should employ the well-established Semitic institution of the covenant. That he did so is confirmed by combined testimony of the earliest records. Sinai would naturally be chosen as the scene of this covenant, for it was a covenant binding together those tribes, which regarded the sacred mountain as Jehovah's abode. Both of the earlier prophetic narratives record a solemn sacrificial feast, which symbolized the establishment of this covenant. According to the Northern Israelite version, oxen were sacrificed and the blood was sprinkled upon the people, as in the later Hebrew ritual. The essential element, however, in the covenant was not the symbolism but the terms of agreement to which each of the contracting parties subscribed. Jehovah's promises to deliver and protect his people had already been proclaimed by Moses and fulfilled in the marvellous deliverance from Egypt. The oldest traditions state that the obligations assumed by the people were formulated in ten brief commands. According to the early Judean narrative in Exodus 34, these commands were inscribed by Moses on two stone tablets which he had prepared by divine command. In the later versions of the story, Jehovah himself is represented as having inscribed with his own finger these ten words on two tablets which he gave to Moses.

VII. The Original Decalogue. In the present order of the narratives in Exodus, two distinct decalogues are given, the familiar one in Exodus 20 and the more distinctly ceremonial decalogue in Exodus 34. The implication of the narratives, however, is that the same decalogue was promulgated in both cases, and there is no suggestion that its original form was changed in the second account of the giving of the law.

In the light of the variations between the two decalogues, two distinct questions arise: Which was the older and original of these decalogues? and, What is the explanation of their present position and order? The contents of the decalogue given in Exodus 34 at once suggest that it is the older of the two. It demands absolute loyalty to Jehovah. This loyalty is to be expressed, however, in the observation of the ancient festivals, in the sacrificial gifts from the flocks and herds and field, and in conformity to the requirements of the early ritual. It contains in outline that ancient, popular definition of religion, which prevailed among the Hebrews, until the great ethical prophets, like Amos, Hosea and Isaiah placed the emphasis on spirit and deeds. It is, therefore, in harmony with the point of view of Moses's age. Furthermore, its language is that of the early Judean narrative. In its original form it was apparently the immediate sequel of the account of the divine revelation in Exodus 19. Practically all of its regulations are repeated in slightly different form in the corresponding Northern Israelite laws found in Exodus 20^{22}-23^{19}. Thus the two oldest prophetic narratives testify that this ceremonial decalogue was a common heritage coming from the earliest period of Hebrew history. It is also significant that each of its regulations is repeated in the Old Testament at least three, and some of them six or seven times. It would seem, therefore, to represent the foundation of Israel's legal system. Moreover, these distinct yet converging oldest lines of evidence all point to Moses as the great prophetic leader, who first formulated in this simple direct form the duties of the new-born nation.

VIII. The Duty of Loyalty to Jehovah. The first command demands the entire loyalty of the Hebrews to Jehovah. The denial of the existence of other gods is left to a later age; but within the ranks of that bond of Arab tribes known as Israel, the first command leaves no place for the worship of other desert deities. Henceforth Israel's strength lay in the fact that it was a people which acknowledged one rather than many gods.

The second command does not forbid the worship of those family gods and graven images which appear to have been found in the home of every early Israelite (as for example, that of David, I Sam. 19, *cf.* also § XXXIV). Isaiah and Jeremiah first openly denounced this time-honored practice. The ancient command is rather a protest against the molten gods of heathen nations, such as the Egyptians, the Babylonians and the Phœnicians. It is, therefore, but a further application of the great principle laid down in the first command. It may also be a result of that strong reaction against the polytheism and idolatry of the Egyptians, which is traceable in the early Hebrew religion.

The third command enforces the obligation to observe the ancient Semitic spring festival; although the fact that it is called the feast of unleavened bread may reveal later Canaanite influence. The fourth and ninth commands specify the tribute which each member of the nation should bring to his Divine King as evidence of loyalty and devotion. They but reiterate the more or less clearly defined customs already in vogue throughout the Semitic world.

IX. **The Seventh Day of Rest.** The law of the sabbath presents many problems. The life of the nomad with his flocks and herds gives little opportunity for rest from labor. It is only on the agricultural stage that the command to rest on the seventh day could be fully carried out; yet it seems probable that the institution of the sabbath was already in existence in the days of Moses; for the most satisfactory explanation of its origin connects it with the primitive worship of the moon.

The moon god was especially worshipped at the cities of Ur and Haran, which the Hebrews regarded as the home of their ancestors. Recent archæological discoveries also indicate that the moon god was revered throughout Arabia. This worship was natural among a people who regarded the sun, with its hot, burning rays, as hostile, and the moon, with its cold, clear light, as friendly. Even to a modern observer no object in the heavens is as impressive as the moon with its changing phases. To the ancient nomads, as they pastured their flocks or made their long journeys by night through the desert, the moon was a never-ceasing miracle. Its four distinct phases—the crescent moon, at its first appearance in the west, the half moon, when the circle was clearly divided between light and darkness, the full moon, with its rounded orb, and the gibbous moon, with its peculiar form—each made its profound impression upon early man, who saw in the wonderful and unusual the highest revelation of the Deity. Many early peoples held sacred each of the four days at which the moon entered its different quarters. Among the Hebrews the new moon and the sabbath were closely connected.

Both of these sacred days were apparently observed by the same ceremonies and the same rest from labor. As Strabo states, rest from labor was demanded by the ancients on all sacred days. If the sabbath, therefore, was originally a sacred day, observed at the beginning of each new phase of the moon, there is every reason to believe that it was already an established institution among the Midianites and the ancestors of the Hebrews. It was natural that the sabbath law should also have found a place in the decalogue coming from the days of Moses. The emphasis upon rest perhaps reflects that nobler social and philanthropic interpretation of the sabbath, which was first clearly formulated by the later prophets and reasserted by Jesus, when he declared that "the sabbath is for man and not man for the sabbath."

X. **Ceremonial Laws.** The sixth command requires the observation of the ancient Semitic feast of the ingathering at the end of the year. The seventh, eighth, and tenth demand the careful observation of certain ceremonial rites, the origin of which goes back to such a primitive stage in the history of religion that it is difficult to determine the original motive. Possibly leaven was not to be used in connection with the sacrificial blood because it represented corruption. Since the fat and the blood were the parts especially sacred to the Deity, the law that the fat should not be left until the morning was probably to guard against the possibility of decay and to insure its being offered by fire to Jehovah.

XI. **The History of the Oldest Decalogue.** The tradition that this decalogue was written on two tablets of stone is found in both of the early prophetic histories. Possibly these tablets with the ten words were first set up in the temple of Solomon that their contents might be read and thus impressed upon the consciences of the people. The brief decalogue form suggests, however, that the ten words were originally intended to be written not on stone, but upon the popular memory. The simplest explanation of their decalogue and pentad form is that they originally consisted of two groups of five short commands or words, each of which was to be remembered in connection with a finger of the two hands. Ten clearly defined decalogues are found in Exodus 20-23, and the parallel passages in Deuteronomy (*cf.* §§ LIX, LX). Others are included in the so-called "Holiness Code" of Leviticus 17-26. The decalogue would appear to have been the form in which, from earliest times, Israel's popular laws were cast. This simple but effective method of impressing vital truths upon untrained minds is well worthy of the inspired genius of a great prophetic leader like Moses.

§ XXV. MAN'S INDIVIDUAL DUTIES TO GOD AND MAN

God also spoke all these words:
1. THOU SHALT HAVE NO OTHER GODS BEFORE ME.
2. THOU SHALT NOT MAKE FOR THYSELF ANY GRAVEN IMAGE.
3. THOU SHALT NOT TAKE THE NAME OF THE LORD THY GOD IN VAIN.
4. REMEMBER THE SABBATH DAY TO KEEP IT HOLY.
5. HONOR THY FATHER AND THY MOTHER.
6. THOU SHALT NOT KILL.
7. THOU SHALT NOT COMMIT ADULTERY.
8. THOU SHALT NOT STEAL.
9. THOU SHALT NOT BEAR FALSE WITNESS.
10. THOU SHALT NOT COVET.

I. **Character of the Prophetic Decalogue.** The laws considered in the preceding section define the obligations of the nation Israel to Jehovah. If they had stood alone in Exodus 20–34, no one would have failed to recognize in them the ten words originally promulgated by Moses. The decalogue, however, now most closely associated with Moses and the covenant at Sinai, contains the familiar ten words of Exodus 20. Its superior ethical value is incontestible. It represents "the corn," if not "the full corn in the ear," while the decalogue of Exodus 34 is but "the blade." It defines religion in the terms of life and deed, as well as worship. The noble standards maintained by Amos and Isaiah are here formulated in short, forcible commands. This prophetic decalogue certainly represents one of the high water-marks of Old Testament legislation. It fully merits the commanding position at the head of the Old Testament laws and its unique place in the hearts of Jews and Christians.

II. **Its Literary History.** A careful examination of the context of Exodus 19–34 reveals much editorial revision. In view of the transcendent importance of Sinai and Moses in the thought of later generations, such revision was almost inevitable. In their present setting the presence of two distinct decalogues, written on tablets of stone, is explained by the story of the apostasy of the Israelites in con-

194

nection with the golden calf. The evidence, however, is strong that the story of the golden calf is one of the later additions to Exodus, and that it was not found in the early Judean history. The earlier prophets, and even Elijah and Elisha, make no protest against the calves or bulls, overlaid with gold, which Jeroboam I set up in the national sanctuaries at Bethel and Dan (*cf.* § LXI). The obvious protest, which the story of the golden calf contains, clearly comes from the more enlightened age, when prophets like Amos and Hosea had begun to look askance at the practices which flourished at the popular shrines. A later compiler has found or made a place for the ancient decalogue of Exodus 34 in the light of the statement that Moses, at the sight of the golden calf, destroyed the first two tablets. The compiler fails, however, to explain why the two versions differ so widely in theme and content. When the late material has been removed, the original decalogue in Exodus 34 appears as the immediate sequel of the Judean account of the revelation at Sinai. Similarly the sequel of the Northern Israelite version of the revelation is not the decalogue in the first part of Exodus 20, but the closing verses of that chapter and the laws which follow. It would seem, therefore, that a later compiler made the words, "Moses spoke and God answered him" (at the close of chapter 19), the occasion for introducing the nobler ethical decalogue of Exodus 20.

III. **The Parallel Version in Deuteronomy 5.** This decalogue is found again in a very different setting in Deuteronomy 5. It is attributed to Moses, but the occasion is not the establishment of the covenant at Sinai but his farewell address on the plains of Moab. In the sabbath command the older term *observe* is used in the Deuteronomic version rather than *remember*, suggesting that the Deuteronomic version is the older of the two. Otherwise the original ten brief words in Exodus 20 and Deuteronomy 5 are identical. Each version has, however, been supplemented by many explanatory and hortatory notes. Those in Deuteronomy 5 agree in part and differ in part from those in Exodus 20, showing that each version has passed through different hands. Thus, for example, to the exhortation in Exodus 20 to "honor thy father and thy mother that thy days may be long," the version in Deuteronomy adds, "and that it may go well with thee."

IV. **The Real Character of the Decalogue in Exodus 20.** As has been already noted, the decalogue in Exodus 34 defines the religious and ceremonial obligations of the nation to Jehovah. The ten words in Exodus 20 (Deuteronomy 5) define the obligations of the individual to God, to his parents and to other members of society. The two are not antithetic but rather supplement each other. While the decalogue of Exodus 34 was in all probability the basis of the original covenant at Sinai, the ten words of Exodus 20 may also represent the personal obligations which Moses impressed upon each individual Israelite.

V. Date and Authorship of the Decalogue in Exodus 20. The date and authorship of the noblest of the decalogues can never be definitely determined. Because of its high ethical standards and its close relationship with the teachings of the later prophets, it has been assigned by many modern scholars to the eighth or seventh century B.C. The law against making graven images embodies a principle first clearly proclaimed in the seventh century before Christ. These wooden images apparently survived in the homes of the Hebrews long after the public idols were torn down. They correspond to the sacred pictures and images of the Virgin and saints that are still tolerated by certain Christian churches. Even such a spiritual prophet as Hosea continued in the eighth century to regard them as legitimate (Hos. 3⁴). In its earliest form the second command, like the first, may have been a duplicate of the corresponding law in the older decalogue, and have read *molten* instead of *graven* image.

The command not to covet reveals a highly developed moral sense; but otherwise there is no law in this decalogue, which might not in its extant form have come from Moses. Most of the principles which underlie it were already in force in the days of Hammurabi, although the great prophets of Israel were the first to make them the basis of religion. Although the settings of the different versions of this prophetic decalogue are late, the prominence which is given to it indicates that it is much older than its present literary settings. In the light of all these facts there is a strong probability that the traditions, which trace its origin back to Moses, are substantially historical; at least, it is more than probable that, as the judge and prophet of the Israelite tribes in the wilderness, he laid down and enforced the principles which are incorporated in these ten words.

VI. Meaning of the Different Commands. The laws fall into two groups. The first pentad defines the duties of the individual to his divine and human parents. The meaning of most of the commands is clear. Originally the first may have simply demanded that Jehovah be given the first place in the faith and worship of Israel. Later prophets, like Elijah, and Isaiah, interpreted it as excluding all other cults. The second command was made very explicit by later commentators. All attempts to represent the Deity by any image or likeness, or the worship of these sacred objects was absolutely forbidden. The strongest possible warnings and promises guard the observance of the law.

In the third command the Hebrew idiom, "Thou shalt not take the name," means, "thou shalt not invoke the name of Jehovah thy God in vain." The meaning of the command turns on the expression "in vain." The Hebrew term thus translated means, (1) purposelessly and therefore flippantly and irreverently; (2) for destruction, as, for example, in cursing another; (3) for nothing, that is in swearing to what is false, and (4) in connection with any form of sorcery or witchcraft. It is possible that the command was intended to include all these different ways in which the sacred name and reputation of Jehovah might be desecrated by his people. The later Hebrew law of Leviticus 24[16] made death the penalty for blaspheming the name of Jehovah.

VII. **The Law of the Sabbath.** The fourth command, like that in Deuteronomy 5[12], emphasizes the obligation to observe the sabbath as a day holy to Jehovah. In this law the earliest significance of the institution is emphasized and its social and humane significance is only implied. The prophetic commentators, however, have brought out this later and nobler meaning very clearly. It is the day of rest for all who toil, whether master or slave or guest or wearied ox. A still later commentator has quoted, as an added reason for observing it, the late priestly account of Jehovah's resting after he had completed the work of creation (Gen. 2[2, 3]). In the parallel version in Deuteronomy, however, the reason urged rests upon the noblest ethical basis; it is the responsibility of the employer to the employed. The motive is the debt of gratitude which the Israelites owe to Jehovah who delivered them, a race of slaves, from the bondage of Egypt.

VIII. **The Obligation to Parents.** In their oldest form the first four commands define those personal obligations to Jehovah which are to be expressed in personal loyalty, in the worship, in speech, and in the institution of the sabbath. The fifth command enjoins respect and loyalty to parents. It recognizes the fact that obedience to human parents was necessary to the development of the proper reverence and obedience to the Divine Parent.

The primitive Hebrew laws (Ex. 21[15, 17]) punished by death the child who struck or cursed his father or his mother. The very old Sumerian law of Babylon made slavery the punishment for the son who repudiated his father. The fifth command provides no penalty, however, but appeals simply to the moral sense. The prophetic commentators add the promise of long life and prosperity to him who obeys.

IX. **Obligations to Others.** The second pentad deals with the relations of the individual to other members of society. All primitive peoples punished the crime of murder; but in dealing with lesser crimes most nations were more rigorous than the Hebrews, who ever had a high regard for the sanctity of human life (*cf.* St. O.T., IV. § 83). Adultery, with its baneful consequences, was also made a capital offence (*cf.* St. O.T., IV. §§ 70, 71). Not without reason, most primitive Semitic peoples punished this and kindred crimes against society even more severely than they did murder. The penalties for theft were double or fourfold restitution (*cf.* Dt. 22$^{1-4}$ St. O.T., IV. § 90).

The last command rises from the plane of action to the impelling motive. Even as did Jesus, it traces the crime back to the thought in the mind of man. To make the law definite later prophets have added a list of those things which the ordinary man was most in danger of coveting. In its simpler and original form the command is even more comprehensive and impressive.

§ XXVI. MOSES'S WORK AS JUDGE AND PROPHET

1. The visit of Jethro

Now when Jethro the priest of Midian, Moses's father-in-law, heard of all that God had done for Moses and for Israel his people, how that Jehovah had brought Israel out of Egypt, Jethro, Moses's father-in-law, took Zipporah, Moses's wife, and her two sons, of whom the name of one was Gershom [An alien resident there]; for he said, I have been a resident alien in a foreign land; and the name of the other was Eliezer [My God is a help]; for he said, The God of my father was my help, and delivered me from the sword of Pharaoh; and Jethro, Moses's father-in-law, came with his sons and his wife to Moses in the wilderness where he was encamped, at the mountain of God. And he said to Moses, I, thy father-in-law Jethro, am coming to you with your wife, and her two sons with her. And Moses went out to meet his father-in-law, and bowed before him, and kissed him; and when they had asked regarding each other's welfare, they came into the tent. Then Moses told his father-in-law all that Jehovah had done to Pharaoh and the Egyptians for Israel's sake, all the hardship they had encountered on the march, and how Jehovah had delivered them.

198

Then Jethro rejoiced because of all the goodness which Jehovah had done to Israel, in that he had delivered them from the power of the Egyptians. And Jethro said,

> Blessed be Jehovah
> Who hath delivered them from the power of Pharaoh;
> Who hath delivered the people from under the power of
>   the Egyptians.
> Now I am persuaded that Jehovah is greater than all gods,
> For in that, wherein they acted so arrogantly toward them,
>   hath he thrown them into confusion.

2. His song of thanksgiving and sacrificial offering

Moreover Jethro, Moses's father-in-law, took a burnt-offering and sacrifices for God, and Aaron came with all the elders of Israel to eat bread with Moses's father-in-law before God.

Now on the next day Moses sat as judge to decide cases for the people, and the people stood about Moses from morning until evening. But when Moses's father-in-law saw all that he was doing for the people, he said, What is this thing that you are doing for the people? Why are you sitting all alone, while all the people stand about you from morning until evening? And Moses answered his father-in-law, Because the people keep coming to me to inquire of God. Whenever they have a matter of dispute, they come to me, that I may decide which of the two is right, and make known the statutes of God, and his decisions.

3. Moses's duties as judge

Then Moses's father-in-law said to him, This thing which you are doing is not good. Both you and these people who are about you will surely wear yourselves out, for the task is too heavy for you; you are not able to perform it by yourself alone. Now hearken to me, I will give you good counsel, so that God will be with you: You be the people's advocate with God, and bring the cases to God, and you make known to them the statutes and the decisions, and show them the way wherein they must walk, and the work that they must do. Moreover you must provide out of all the people able, God-fearing, reliable men, hating unjust gain; and place such over them to be rulers of thousands, rulers of hundreds, rulers of fifties, and rulers of tens; and let them

4. Appointment of minor judges

judge the people at all times. Only every great matter let them bring to you; but every small matter let them decide themselves; so it will be easier for you, and they will bear the burden with you. If you do this thing—and God command you so—then you will be able to endure, and all these people also will go back to their places satisfied. So Moses hearkened to the advice of his father-in-law, and did all that he had said. And Moses chose able men out of all Israel, and made them heads over the people, rulers of thousands, rulers of hundreds, rulers of fifties and rulers of tens. And they judged the people at all times; the difficult cases they brought to Moses, but every small matter they decided themselves. Then Moses let his father-in-law depart, and he went his way to his own land.

5. Making of the tent of meeting
And Jehovah said to Moses, Say to the Israelites, 'Ye are a wilful people; if I go up into the midst of thee for one moment, I shall consume thee; therefore put off thy ornaments from thee, that I may know what to do to thee.' So the Israelites despoiled themselves of their ornaments from Mount Horeb onward, and with these Moses made a tent. . . .

6. Jehovah's revelation through Moses
Now Moses used to take the tent and pitch it outside the camp at some distance from the camp, and he called it the tent of meeting. And whenever any one wished to consult Jehovah, he would go out to the tent of meeting, which was outside the camp. And whenever Moses went out to the tent, all the people would rise and stand, every man at his tent door, and look after Moses until he had gone into the tent. And when Moses had entered into the tent, the pillar of cloud would descend, and stand at the door of the tent, while Jehovah spoke with Moses. And whenever the people saw the pillar of cloud standing at the door of the tent, all the people stood up and worshipped, every man at his tent door. Thus Jehovah used to speak with Moses face to face, as a man speaks to his friend. Then he would return to the camp; but his attendant Joshua, the son of Nun, a young man, did not leave the tent.

I. **Moses's Activity as Tribal Judge.** The present section is found for the most part in the Northern Israelite prophetic group of narratives.

It is, therefore, one of the older sources in the Pentateuch, and throws clear light upon the vexed question of Moses's relation to Hebrew legislation.

Its background is Mount Sinai, at the period immediately following the establishment of the covenant between Jehovah and the nation. As they are encamped at the foot of the sacred mountain, Moses's father-in-law, the priest of Midian and worshipper of Jehovah, the God of Sinai, visits Moses. It is significant that he, not Moses, takes the initiative in offering the sacrifices to the common God worshipped by the Hebrews and their Kenite kinsmen.

In the ancient East the duty of deciding questions of dispute between tribes and individual members of the tribes, always fell to the civil authorities. Even in ancient Babylon there does not appear to have been a distinct class of judges, but instead, every man in authority was called upon to discharge at certain times judicial, as well as administrative functions. The historical basis of this characteristically oriental usage is found in the customs of the desert. Then, as to-day, the head of the tribe was the one to whom all questions of dispute were referred. While he had no absolute authority to execute his decisions, he was accepted by both parties to the dispute as their arbiter, and his renderings were accepted as final. These decisions were in accordance with oral or customary law. Unusual and difficult cases, however, were necessarily decided according to the judgment of the arbiter. Thus, a great opportunity was given for each individual judge to establish new precedents and to contribute to the ever-growing body of customary law.

As the acknowledged leader of the different Hebrew tribes, it was inevitable that many legal cases would be referred to Moses. That this was so is definitely stated in the present narrative. Jethro, recognizing that Moses was overwhelmed by his judicial duties, wisely counselled that he should appoint certain reliable men as judges. These were to decide ordinary questions in accordance with the established precedents and customs. The difficult cases, presenting new problems, were still to be laid before Moses.

II. **Moses's Relation to Hebrew Legislation.** In this simple, definite way Moses made known to the Israelites the laws and principles which they were to observe. It illustrates very definitely Moses's relation to Hebrew legislation as a whole. The precedents, which he thus established, were based upon the divine principles which he, as Jehovah's prophet, was endeavoring to impress upon the conscience of his race. They were thus constantly held up before the eyes of the people, not in abstract but in concrete and permanent form. The precedents in time inevitably developed into fixed customs which regulated the life of the nation. As new needs arose, the principles underlying these customary laws were applied, and the resulting decisions supplemented still further the constantly growing body of customary law. Their present literary form indicates that in time the more important customary laws crystallized into decalogues, each containing ten short words, which were originally treasured in the memory of succeeding generations. When these decalogues and customary laws became so numerous that they could not easily be remembered, and when the Hebrews learned the art of writing, these laws were naturally put into written form. It is evident, however, that the development of written codes was one of the later stages in the history of Hebrew law.

It is unimportant whether or not Moses ever wrote down any of the laws found in the Old Testament. On this point the earliest writers have little to say beyond the statement that Moses inscribed the terms of the original covenant between Jehovah and the nation upon two tablets of stone. If Moses never wrote down a single statute, the claim that he was the father of Hebrew law is attested by the earliest Hebrew records and the evidence of later traditions. The prophet always precedes the lawgiver; the principle is enunciated before the detailed regulation appears, which formulates and applies the principle to the needs of the age. As Jehovah's prophet, Moses proclaimed those germinal principles which underlie the Old Testament laws. As judge, he formulated these principles in definite decisions, which in time grew into customary law, and then by slow stages were expanded into the ever-growing body of legislation. The process of growth was so gradual and the connection with Moses so close that each succeeding generation naturally and inevitably regarded Moses as the author of each and every code.

III. **The Tent of Meeting.** The early Judean narratives, in their present form, contain no references to the tent of meeting or dwelling. In the Northern Israelite history is found a very brief account of the making of this tent of meeting. Originally this account was evidently much fuller, but it has been curtailed to make way for the later priestly account of the dwelling or tabernacle. The earliest account states that the tent of meeting was made from the ornaments which the Israelites contributed. It was apparently a simple tent of goats' hair and was pitched at a little distance outside the camp. Thither the people went, as did the ancient Arabs to the *kāhin* or seer, to receive from Moses the divine teaching or decisions which he, as Jehovah's prophet, stood ready to give them. This simple story has been expanded by the later priestly writers into the elaborate plan and description of the tabernacle, to which the later part of the book of Exodus is largely devoted.

IV. Moses's True Prophetic Character. In this oldest form of the story of the tent of meeting is recorded the all-important fact that Moses was recognized by his own and later generations, as not only a judge and therefore a lawgiver, but above all as a prophet. Jehovah declares, in the ancient poem found in Numbers 12, that through the early prophet he made known his will by means of the vision or dream, but

> "Not so with my servant Moses;
> In all my house he is faithful.
> Mouth to mouth do I speak with him,
> Plainly and not in enigmas,
> And the form of Jehovah doth he behold."

Not through the various devices used by the ancient seers and augurs, but directly, as the spirit of Jehovah touched the spirit of Moses, came that message which made him the great prophetic leader and teacher of his race. The character of his message and nature of his work confirm the testimony of this ancient poem: in the method in which he saw the truth, in his sense of the immanent presence of God, and in his practical grasp of the existing conditions and forces, Moses stands side by side with the great prophets of the later age, such as Amos, Isaiah and Jeremiah. Although his conception of the character of God and of the truth was by no means as complete, as that of the later prophets, his unique relation to his race and their peculiar needs gave him an opportunity, shared by no other prophet in Hebrew history, to impress his personality and message upon his nation. His was the privilege not only of proclaiming but of executing. The experiences in Egypt and of the exodus and the grim life of the desert turned the eyes of his followers toward him as their God-given and divinely commissioned leader. In their need they looked to him for counsel and deliverance. Not only once, but throughout the years of the wilderness sojourn, he was able in public and in private, by word and by symbol, by command and by act, to impress upon his race the few fundamental truths that constitute the essence of his divine message.

§ XXVII. THE LIFE OF THE HEBREWS IN THE WILDERNESS

1. The plan of march

Then as they journeyed from the mountain of Jehovah, the ark of Jehovah went before them, to seek out a halting place for them. And whenever the ark started, Moses would say,

> Arise, O Jehovah,
> And let thine enemies be scattered;
> And let those who hate thee flee before thee.

And when it rested, he would say,

> Return, O Jehovah,
> To the ten thousand of thousands of Israel.

2. Complaints of the people

Now the rabble which was among them began to have a strong craving, and even the Israelites began to weep again, and to say, O that we had flesh to eat. We remember the fish which we used to eat in Egypt without cost: the cucumbers, and the melons, the leeks, the onions and the garlic; but now we pine away; there is not a thing to be seen except this manna.

3. Moses's discouragement and complaint

And the anger of Jehovah was greatly aroused. When therefore Moses heard the people weeping throughout their families, every man at the door of his tent, Moses was displeased. And Moses said to Jehovah, Why hast thou dealt ill with thy servant? and why have I not found favor in thy sight, that thou layest the burden of all this people upon me? Have I conceived all this people? Have I brought them forth, that thou shouldest say to me, Carry them in thy bosom, as a nursing-father carries the sucking child, to the land which thou swarest to their fathers? Whence should I have flesh to give to all this people? for they oppress me with their weeping, saying, 'Give us flesh that we may eat.' I am not able to bear all this people alone, because it is too heavy for me. And if thou deal thus with me, kill me, I pray thee, kill me, if I have found favor in thy sight; and let me not see my wretchedness.

Then Jehovah said to Moses, Say to the people, ' Sanctify yourselves for to-morrow and you shall eat flesh, for you have wept loudly in the hearing of Jehovah, saying, " O that we had flesh to eat! for it was well with us in Egypt." Therefore Jehovah will give you flesh that you may eat. Not one day nor two, nor five, nor ten, nor twenty days shall you eat, but a whole month, until it comes out at your nostrils, and is loathsome to you; because you have rejected Jehovah who is among you, and have wept before him, saying, " Why did we come out of Egypt?" ' Then Moses said, The people among whom I am, are six hundred thousand men on foot; yet thou hast said, ' I will give them flesh that they may eat a whole month.' Can flocks and herds be slain sufficient for them? or can all the fish of the sea be gathered sufficient for them? But Jehovah said to Moses, Is Jehovah's power limited? Now shalt thou see whether my promise to thee shall come to pass or not. **4. Jehovah's reply**

Then Moses went out, and told the people the words of Jehovah. And a wind went forth from Jehovah and brought quails from the sea and scattered them upon the camp, about a day's journey on this side, and a day's journey on the other side, round about the camp, even about two cubits above the surface of the earth. Therefore the people spent all that day and all the night, and all the next day, in gathering the quails. He who gathered least gathered about one hundred bushels; and they spread them all out for themselves about the camp. While they were still eating the flesh, before the supply was exhausted, the anger of Jehovah was aroused against the people, and Jehovah smote the people with a very great plague. Hence the name of that place was called Kibroth-hattaavah [Graves of the Craving], because there they buried the people who had the craving. From Kibroth-hattaavah the people journeyed to Hazeroth, and remained at Hazeroth. **5. The quails and the divine judgment**

Afterwards the people set forth from Hazeroth, and encamped in the wilderness of Paran. And the people were thirsty there for water, and murmured against Moses, and said, Why have you brought us up from Egypt to kill us with our children and cattle, with thirst? Moses answered, Why do you test Jehovah? So he called the name of the **6. Complaint of the people for lack of water** place Massah [Testing], because they tested Jehovah, saying, Is Jehovah among us or not?

7. The battle and victory

Then Amalek came and fought with Israel in Rephidim. And Moses said to Joshua, Choose men and go, fight with Amalek. To-morrow I will stand on the top of the hill, with the rod of God in my hand. So Joshua did as Moses had said to him, and fought with Amalek; and Moses, Aaron and Hur went up to the top of the hill. And whenever Moses held up his hand, Israel prevailed; and whenever he let down his hand, Amalek prevailed. But when Moses's hands became weary, they took a stone and put it under him, and he sat on it, while Aaron and Hur held up his hands, the one on the one side and the other on the other. So his hands were supported until the going down of the sun. And Joshua laid Amalek and his people low with the edge of the sword.

8. Cause of the hereditary hostility against the Amalekites

Then Jehovah said to Moses, Write this for a memorial in a book and rehearse it in the ears of Joshua: that I will utterly blot out the remembrance of Amalek from under heaven. Then Moses built an altar, and called the name of it Jehovah-nissi [Jehovah my Banner]; and he said, Jehovah hath sworn; Jehovah will have war with Amalek from generation to generation.

I. The Records of the Life in the Wilderness. It is not surprising that the records of the experiences of the Hebrews during this wilderness period are incomplete and often confusing. The later priestly writers, with their elaborate plans of the tabernacle and of the arrangement of the different tribes, represent the period as one of solemn procession through the desert wastes. There is little connection between their idealized picture and the actual wilderness background and the condition of the Hebrew tribes at this stage in their development.

Rather these later stories represent the projecting backward, upon this ancient background, of the ideas and institutions peculiar to the post-exilic Jews. The early prophetic narratives, embedded in the late priestly laws and traditions in the book of Numbers, give, however, certain glimpses of the real life and meaning of the period.

II. Geographical Background. The background is the wilderness which lies to the south of Canaan. It contains many miles of burning sands and rocky desert, but much of this territory in the past, as to-day, supports a large nomadic population. The term, *wilderness*, which in the Hebrew means *a lonely place*, unoccupied by cities or towns, truly describes it. In the north and east there are rolling, rocky plateaus and jagged mountain peaks. These are, for the most part, parched and treeless, but in the valleys are found at rare intervals gushing springs, which supply the simple needs of nomads. The South Country marked the gradual transition from the more barren wilderness on the south and west to Judah on the north. To the Hebrews it must have seemed, in contrast to the desert, a land of plenty. In later times it contained many strong and populous cities, but it ever remained a land where Nature was very niggardly with her gifts of food and water.

III. **The Life of the Wilderness.** The life of the Arab tribes, which to-day inhabit this same region, reveals in minutest detail the life of the ancient Israelites. Probably in ancient times the costume worn by the men was the same long tunic with the goats' hair mantle which protected them by day from the sun and rain. By night it was their bed. Beside the sacred springs the Hebrews pitched their black or striped goats' hair tents and lived for the most part out in the open air, exposed to the inclemency of the changing seasons, ever journeying from place to place in quest of food and water. As to-day, their chief article of diet was probably the laban or curds, which they made from the milk from the herds and flocks which they had brought with them when they came forth from the Land of Goshen. At the feast days and marriages and special celebrations, animals from the herd were slain. At the proper season they also doubtless hunted the quails and other game which is found in this wilderness region. Sometimes, when all their resources failed they gathered, like the modern Arab, the gum that exudes from the tamarisk tree or the lichens from the rocks, and from these, which probably represent the manna of the wilderness, they made a coarse flour and bread. This unpalatable food kept them alive until the winter rain again brought comparative plenty. It was a life of freedom, of constant activity, of privation and often of suffering. The lack of food and water was an ever-present spur, and constantly led them to turn with anxious longing toward the green hills and pasture lands of Palestine. It was a life full of danger and fear, not only lest grim Nature should fail to meet their natural wants, but lest their foes should overpower them. Barren though it was, the South Country was a territory for the possession of which many hostile tribes were contending with an intensity and cruelty proportionate to the scarcity of food and water. Any day, any hour, a hostile tribe might suddenly attack them, rob them of their possessions, slay the men and bear away the wives and children to lives of slavery and ignominy. Their life developed, therefore, the habit of constant watchfulness and the sense of dependence. It bound together all members of the tribe by the closest possible bonds. It also, in turn, bound the tribe to its tribal God by the powerful bonds of fear and dependence and gratitude.

IV. **Duration of the Sojourn.** As usual, only the latest narratives give any definite data regarding the duration of the sojourn in the wilderness. In the Old Testament the number forty is constantly used as the concrete equivalent of *many*. The absence of any definite data in the early prophetic narratives leaves the question of time entirely open. If, as seems probable, the date of the exodus was about 1200 B.C., the Israelite conquest of southern Palestine would not have been possible before about the middle of the twelfth century. Ramses III of the twentieth Egyptian dynasty, reigned between 1198 and 1167 B.C. He succeeded in re-establishing and maintaining Egyptian authority in southern Canaan. While it would have been possible for small desert tribes to gradually press in to the outlying districts of southern and eastern Palestine, no general settlement of aliens would have been allowed by the Egyptian authorities. It is not clear, however, that the Egyptian rule was established east of the Jordan, so that it is possible that a partial conquest of that region by the Hebrews may have followed very soon after the exodus. The story of the spies, also indicates that an attempt was made to invade Canaan from the south, but that this was only partially successful. The majority of the Hebrew tribes appear, as the later tradition states, to have remained in the wilderness and the South Country for at least a generation.

V. **Tribal Organization.** The oldest narratives suggest that the Hebrews quickly adapted themselves to the peculiar conditions of the wilderness. Probably dividing into different tribes, as the limited food and water supply of the desert made necessary, they subsisted by migrating from one pasture land to another, each tribe under its tribal leader.

The centre of their life was Kadesh, which has been identified in recent times with the modern *Ain Kadish*, a famous spring fifty miles south of Beersheeba. As in the earliest times, it is still regarded by the natives as sacred, as its name (Holy Spring) suggests. The spring itself gushes forth from the side of a sheer rock, and its waters go coursing down through a rather broad valley which it irrigates. This little oasis stands in striking contrast to the dry, barren, rocky territory about. While the water supply was not sufficient to meet the needs of a numerous people, its perennial spring and the tillable soil about, doubtless furnished enough to meet the needs of Moses and of the leaders who joined with him in ruling the allied tribes. There the people doubtless came to him with their cases of dispute or to learn through him Jehovah's will. Thither came the different tribes in the spring time and in the autumn, not empty handed, to present their gifts to Jehovah and to celebrate the sacred festivals. It appears to have been the common centre about which the different tribes revolved, and from which Moses exercised his leadership and direction.

VI. The Tradition of the Manna. The later traditions represent the Hebrews as subsisting upon food supernaturally supplied. The early Judean historians, on the contrary, clearly state that the Israelites lived on the natural products of the wilderness. The tradition that the Hebrews at this time numbered many thousands has clearly influenced the form of this narrative. It explains the fact that, while the source of the supply was natural, the quantity far exceeded that which the wilderness ordinarily supplies. Back of these stories of the manna and of the marvellous supply of water, is the historic truth that, in this barren environment and trying period of their history, Jehovah amply provided all that was needed for the welfare of his people. By means of these stories the prophetic historians bring out in clear relief that care and love which ever attends those who put their trust in the Divine Father.

VII. The Battle with the Amalekites. Another phase of the desert life of the Hebrews is reflected in the story of the battle with the Amalekites. Possibly this was for the possession of the sacred spring at Kadesh. These desert tribesmen figure in the later history, especially of Saul and David, as the inveterate foes of the Hebrews. They were found, not in the Sinaitic peninsula, but in the South Country on the border of Judah. This fact suggests that the occasion was an initial advance of the Hebrews toward Palestine. The episode is important because it reveals the warlike life of the wilderness period. The conflicts with these small desert tribes gave the Hebrews that experience and training which were essential if they were to win on the larger battle-fields of Palestine. Here, as elsewhere in their narratives, the prophetic historians focus attention on the supreme fact that it was Jehovah's strong arm which gave them the victory.

VIII. The Significance of the Ark. The early Judean narrative mentions the ark in connection with the journey through the wilderness;

209

but gives no description of its origin and form. The latest compiler of Exodus has evidently substituted for the older prophetic, the late priestly account of its construction. It was apparently a simple wooden chest, made from such wood as could be found in the desert. From its prominence and use by the Hebrews in their early conflicts with the Philistines (as recorded in the opening chapters of Samuel), it is clear that in that later day it enjoyed a reputation which could have been gained only through many generations. This evidence strengthens the testimony of the early Judean historian that the Hebrews, as they left Mount Sinai, bore with them some such rude chest or ark.

The presence of corresponding arks or ships among the ancient Babylonians, Egyptians and Phœnicians indicates that the institution was very old, and throws further light upon the original meaning of the symbol. Among the Egyptians each god had its sacred ship, on which the image of the god was borne in solemn procession up and down the Nile. In Babylonia corresponding arks or chests were similarly used to bear the images of the gods in the processions, which marched along the sacred streets on certain great feast days.

If the primitive decalogue of Exodus 34 comes from Moses, it would seem clear that from the first Jehovah was not represented by an image. The analogies and the references in the early sources indicate that the ark was apparently regarded either as the symbol of the presence of Jehovah or as the throne of the God of Sinai. In the minds of the early Hebrews, it may well have represented the transfer of Jehovah's place of abode from the sacred mountain to the temple at Jerusalem, in which the ark occupied a central place. Some such belief as this explains the ancient song in[1]. Before this symbol of Jehovah's presence Israel's foes were vanquished. Under Moses's direction it was the signal for the Hebrews to advance or to halt in their march. Above all, it symbolized to them in all their wanderings and varied vicissitudes the all-important fact that Jehovah, their God, was in their midst, guiding and directing them.

§ XXVIII. THE ATTEMPT TO ENTER CANAAN FROM THE SOUTH

1. The sending forth of the spies

Then Moses sent certain men to spy out the land of Canaan, and said to them, Go up now into the South Country and on up into the hill-country, and see what the land is and the people who dwell therein, whether they are strong or weak,

whether few or many, and what the land is in which they
dwell, whether it is good or bad; and what the cities are in
which they dwell, whether in camps or in strongholds; and
see what the land is, whether it is fertile or barren, whether
there is wood in it or not. Be brave and bring some of
the fruit of the land. Now it was the time of the first
ripe grapes.

So they went up by the South Country, and came to He- 2. Their journey
bron; and Ahiman, Sheshai and Talmai, the children of
Anak, were there. (Now Hebron was built seven years
before Zoan in Egypt.) And when they came to the valley
of Eshcol, they cut down from there a branch with one
cluster of grapes, and carried it upon a staff between two
men, and also some of the pomegranates, and some of the
figs. That place was called the valley of Eshcol [Grape-
cluster], because of the cluster which the Israelites cut
down from there.

And they returned to Kadesh, and brought back a report 3. Their report
to them, and showed them the fruit of the land. And they
told Moses, saying, We came to the land to which you sent
us; and surely it flows with milk and honey; and this is
the fruit of it. But the people who dwell in the land are
strong, and the cities are fortified, and very large; and, moreover, we saw the children of Anak there.

(The Amalekites were dwelling in the South Country;
and the Hittites and the Jebusites and the Amorites in the
hill-country; and the Canaanites were dwelling by the sea,
and beside the Jordan.)

Then Caleb stilled the people before Moses, and said, We
surely ought to go up and take possession of it; for we are
well able to overcome it. But the men who went up with
him said, We are not able to go up against the people; for
they are stronger than we. And there we saw Nephilim
[giants]; we were in our own sight as grasshoppers, and so
were we in their sight.

Then the people wept that night, saying, Why did Jehovah 4. Mur-
muring
of the
people
bring us to this land, to fall by the sword? Our wives and
our little ones will be a prey! Were it not better for us to
return to Egypt? And they said to one another, Let us make
a captain and return to Egypt.

5. Moses's counsel

But Moses said to them, If Jehovah delighteth in us, then he will bring us into this land, and give it to us; a land which flows with milk and honey. Fear not the people of the land, for they are our bread. Their defence is removed from over them, for Jehovah is with us; fear them not. But the people would not trust Jehovah.

6. Jehovah's condemnation of the Israelites

Therefore Jehovah said to Moses, How long will this people despise me? and how long will they refuse to trust me, in spite of all the signs which I have worked among them? I will smite them with a pestilence, and disinherit them, and will make thee a nation greater and mightier than they.

7. Moses's intercession for the people

But Moses said to Jehovah, Then the Egyptians will hear it (for thou broughtest this people in thy might from among them), and they will tell it to the inhabitants of this land. They have heard that thou, Jehovah, art in the midst of this people; for thou, Jehovah, art seen eye to eye, and thy cloud standeth over them, and thou goest before them in a pillar of cloud by day, and in a pillar of fire by night. Now if thou shalt kill this people as one man, then the nations which have heard the fame of thee will say, 'Because Jehovah was not able to bring this people into the land which he promised to them with an oath, therefore he hath slain them in the wilderness.' But now, I pray thee, let the power of the Lord be great, according as thou hast spoken, saying, 'Jehovah is slow to anger, and abundant in mercy, forgiving iniquity and transgression; although he does not leave it unpunished, visiting the iniquity of the fathers upon the children upon the third and fourth generation.' Pardon, I pray thee, the iniquity of this people, according to thy great mercy, and according as thou hast forgiven this people, from Egypt even until now.

8. The judgment upon the people

Jehovah said, I have pardoned according to thy word; but as surely as I live, and as surely as the whole earth shall be filled with the glory of Jehovah, of all the men who have seen my glory and my signs which I performed in Egypt and in the wilderness, and yet have tempted me these ten times, and have not hearkened to my voice, not one shall see the land which I promised to their fathers with an oath, neither shall any of those who despised me see it; but my servant Caleb, because he had another spirit in him, and hath followed me unreservedly, him will I bring into the land to which he went, and his descendants shall possess it. But your little ones, that ye said should be a prey, them will I bring in, and they shall know the land which ye have rejected. But as for you, your dead bodies shall fall in this wilderness. And your children shall be wanderers in the wilderness forty years.

Now when the Canaanite king of Arad, who dwelt in the South Country, heard that Israel had come by the way of Atharim, he fought against Israel, and took some of them captive.

Then Dathan and Abiram the sons of Eliab the son of Pallu, son of Reuben, took men, and rose up before Moses. And Moses sent to summon Dathan and Abiram the sons of Eliab; but they said, We will not come up; is it a small thing that you have brought us up out of a land flowing with milk and honey, to kill us in the wilderness, but you must even make yourself a prince over us? Moreover you have not brought us into a land flowing with milk and honey; will you throw dust in our eyes? we will not come up.

Then Moses was very angry and said to Jehovah, Do not respect their offering; I have not taken a single ass from them, neither have I hurt one of them. And Moses rose up and went to Dathan and Abiram, and the elders of Israel followed him. And he said to them, Depart, I pray you, from the tents of these wicked men, and touch nothing of theirs, lest you be swept away in all their sins. And Dathan and Abiram came out, and stood at the door of their tents, with their wives and sons and little ones.

Then Moses said, By this you shall know that Jehovah hath sent me to do all these works; that it was not of mine own choice. If these men die the common death of men, or if they share the usual fate of men, then Jehovah hath not sent me. But if Jehovah does something unprecedented, and the ground opens its mouth, and swallows them up, with all that belongs to them, and they go down alive to Sheol, then you shall understand that these men have despised Jehovah.

And it came to pass as he finished speaking all these words, that the ground which was under them was cleft. So they and all that belonged to them, went down alive into Sheol.

9. Defeat of the Israelites

10. Mutiny of Dathan and Abiram

11. Moses's protest and warning

12. His appeal to Jehovah for a divine decision

13. Fate of the rebels

ATTEMPT TO ENTER CANAAN FROM THE SOUTH

I. The Natural Approach to Canaan. As has already been noted, two ways opened before the Hebrews as they departed from Egypt. They chose the southern, the Way of the Red Sea, because it led to freedom and association with their kinsmen. They avoided the northern route, the Way of the Philistines, which was the more direct road to Canaan, because it was guarded by Egyptian garrisons and by strongly intrenched agricultural peoples, whom the nomad Hebrew clans could not hope to conquer.

From the first, Canaan, with its springs and fertile fields, was the loadstone which attracted the Hebrews. With Kadesh as a centre, they found their temporary home on the southern borders of this land of their hopes. The most natural and direct line of approach from Kadesh was directly northward. A journey of seventy-five or one hundred miles would bring them into the heart of southern Canaan. No strong, natural barriers barred their progress. Instead, the rolling, rocky South Country gradually merges into the rounded limestone hills of Judah.

II. The Report of the Spies. The story of the spies is the traditional record of the attempt of the Hebrews to enter Canaan from the south. Three distinct and variant versions of the tradition are found in Numbers, but they all agree regarding the essential facts. From Kadesh, Moses sent out certain men with Caleb at their head, to investigate conditions in the South Country and Canaan. Hebron they found in the possession of certain powerful clans. From the valleys of Judah they brought back convincing evidence of the vine culture which flourished there. In contrast to the barren life of the wilderness, even rocky Judah was a veritable paradise; but the cities were strong and fortified, and to the majority of the spies the conquest of Canaan seemed an impossibility. Caleb advocated an immediate advance; but the people were daunted by the report of the majority, and abandoned the hope of immediate conquest. A later prophetic editor, standing in the full light of later events, and inspired by a nobler faith, has introduced (6-8) a powerful arraignment of the people because of their cowardice and lack of faith at this critical moment in their history. The courage of Caleb was rewarded by the promise that his descendants should be established in southern Judah.

III. Reasons for the Failure. Egyptian inscriptions supplement the testimony of the oldest biblical records by revealing the real reasons why the Hebrews did not go up at once from the south to the conquest of Canaan. Chief among these was the fact that Egypt still maintained its rule in southern Palestine and thus bound together the different local clans and enabled them to offer a successful resistance to invasion from the desert. On the other hand, the Hebrews were not prepared to conquer the highly civilized peoples of Canaan. Excavation has revealed the strength and height of many of the walls which encircled their towns. Desert tribes have no means of attacking and capturing walled villages. The needs of their flocks and herds and the lack of military training make it impossible for them to maintain a protracted siege. The experiences of the Hebrews in Egypt had given them no training in warfare, but had tended to weaken rather than develop their courage. A generation of hardship in the desert under the inspiring direction of their prophet leader was necessary before they could become an efficient fighting force. It was also important that they should first intrench themselves in some semi-agricultural district and develop their resources and base of supply, before they could maintain a systematic and continuous attack.

IV. **The Tribes that Entered Palestine from the South.** The older narratives record an attempt on the part of the Israelites to capture Arad, one of the outlying Canaanite towns, and of their defeat at the hands of their foes. The testimony of these earliest narratives is that a majority of the Hebrew tribes remained for a generation or more in the wilderness, and ultimately entered Palestine from the east, rather than from the south. The prominence of Caleb, however, in the story of the spies and in the later account of the conquest of southern Canaan undoubtedly reflects the fact that the tribe of Caleb entered from the south, before the majority of the Hebrew tribes had settled in central Canaan. These Calebites were intrenched south of Hebron. Near them were found certain other Arab tribes, such as the Jerahmeelites, the Kenites and the Kenizzites. Possibly these were the vanguard of the Hebrew advance, or they may have already entered the South Country before the Hebrew tribes fled from Egypt. The subsequent records indicate that they affiliated with the Judahites and constituted a large and important part of that southern Israelite tribe.

V. **Rebellions Against Moses's Authority.** The rivalry of different tribes and the hardship of their life in the desert naturally begat strife and rebellion. Hostility between rival tribes is the rule rather than the exception in Arabia. The authority of the tribal sheik or leader is ill-defined, and depends chiefly upon the needs of the moment and the personal ability of the leader. In the face of discouragements it was almost inevitable that discontent should find open expression and that many of the tribal sheiks should oppose the authority of their prophetic

215

leader. This state of affairs is revealed in the many traditions of rebellions against Moses. Quick, decisive measures were doubtless adopted to put down these uprisings. It was by patience, tact and courage that the great leader finally overcame opposition and gradually welded the different tribes into a strong political unit.

VI. Significance of the Wilderness Sojourn. In the light of its historical background and the testimony of the earliest traditions, it is possible to estimate the significance to the Hebrews of their wilderness experiences. The necessities and hardships of their life gradually and inevitably gave them habits of courage, persistence and self-denial.

Their strenuous life developed physical strength and endurance, courage and skill in warfare. It impressed upon them the necessity and advantages of combined action, and facilitated the work of Moses in moulding the incipient nation. Their constant feeling of hunger and fear of attack deepened their sense of dependence upon divine power. Their simple religious life, which apparently centred in Kadesh, enabled Moses to impress upon them his own sense of Jehovah's constant presence and care for his people. On the other hand, as their judge and prophet, he was able definitely to illustrate those simple ethical principles, which appear from the first to have been the cornerstones of Israel's faith and civilization. Thus, in divine Providence, quietly out in the solitude and privation of the wilderness, under the leadership of one of the world's great prophets, a nation, ambitious, strong of limb and loyal to its tribal God and leader, was being prepared for the destiny which awaited it.

§ XXIX. THE JOURNEY FROM THE WILDERNESS AND BALAAM'S PROPHECY

1.
Moses's
request

Then Moses sent messengers from Kadesh to the king of Edom, Thus says your kinsman Israel, 'You know all the hardship that has befallen us: how our fathers went down into Egypt, and we lived in Egypt a long time; and the Egyptians ill-treated us and our fathers; but when we cried to Jehovah, he heard our voice and sent a Messenger and brought us out of Egypt; now we are in Kadesh, a city on the frontier of your territory. Pray, let us pass through your land. We will not pass through field or vineyard, and we will not drink of the water of the wells; we will go along the king's highway; we will not turn aside to the right hand or to the left, until we have passed your border.

But Edom said to him, You shall not pass through my territory, lest I come out with the sword against you. Then the Israelites said to him, we will go up by the main highway; and if I drink of your water, I and my cattle, then will I pay for it. Only—since it is nothing—I would like peacefully to pass through. But he said, You shall not pass through. Therefore Edom came out against him with a mighty host and a strong force. Thus Edom refused to give Israel passage through his territory; so Israel turned away from him. 2. Edom's refusal

Then they journeyed from Kadesh by the way leading to the Red Sea, to go around the land of Edom; but the people became discouraged, because of the journey. And the people spoke against Jehovah and Moses, Why have you brought us out of Egypt to die in the wilderness? for there is no bread and no water, and we loathe this worthless food. Then Jehovah sent fiery serpents among the people, and they bit the people, so that many Israelites died. And the people came to Moses and said, We have sinned, for we have spoken against Jehovah and against you; intercede with Jehovah that he take away the serpents from us. So Moses interceded for the people. And Jehovah said to Moses, Make a fiery serpent, and set it on a standard; and it shall come to pass, that any one who is bitten, when he seeth it, shall live. And Moses made a bronze serpent, and set it upon the standard; and it came to pass that, if a serpent had bitten any man, when he looked at the bronze serpent, he lived. 3. The fiery serpents

Then they encamped in the wilderness, which is opposite Moab on the east. From there they journeyed and encamped in the valley of the brook Zered. From there they journeyed and encamped on the other side of the Arnon, which is in the wilderness that stretches out from the territory of the Amorites; for the Arnon is the Moabite boundary, between Moab and the Amorites. Therefore it is said in the Book of Wars of Jehovah, 4. Experiences in the journey about Moab

> We passed through Waheb in Suphah,
> And the valleys of Arnon,

> And the slope of the valleys,
> Which extends to the site of Ar,
> And borders on the frontier of Moab.

And from thence the Israelites journeyed to Beer [Well]. Then Israel sang this song:

> Spring up, O well;
> Sing ye to it;
> To the well which the chieftains dug,
> Which the nobles of the people delved,
> With the leader's wand, with their staves.

And from Beer they journeyed to Mattanah; and from Mattanah to Nahaliel; and from Nahaliel to Bamoth; and from Bamoth to the valley which is in the region of Moab, to the top of Pisgah, which looks out upon the desert.

5. Moab's fear of Israel

Now Moab was seized with fear because of the Israelites. Therefore Moab said to the elders of Midian, Now will this multitude lick up all that is round about us, as the ox licks up the grass of the field. And Balak the son of Zippor was king of Moab at that time. And he sent messengers to Balaam the son of Beor, to the land of the Ammonites, saying, A people has come out from Egypt; behold, they have completely covered the face of the land, and are abiding over against me. Come, therefore, I pray, curse this people for me; (for they are stronger than I); perhaps I may be able to defeat and drive them out of the land. Then the elders of Moab and the elders of Midian departed with the fee for divination in their hands, and they came to Balaam, and repeated to him the words of Balak, Behold, the people that has come from Egypt is covering the face of the land; come now, curse them for me; perhaps I may be able to fight against them and drive them out. For I will reward you with very great honor, and whatever you say to me I will do. Come therefore, I pray, curse this people for me. And Balaam answered and said to the servants of Balak, If Balak should give me his house full of silver and gold, I could not go beyond the word of Jehovah my God, to do less or more.

Then he saddled his ass and went with them. But God's anger was aroused because he went, and the Messenger of Jehovah placed himself in the way as an adversary against him. Now he was riding upon his ass, and his two servants were with him. And when the ass saw the Messenger of Jehovah standing in the way, with his drawn sword in his hand, the ass turned aside out of the way, and went into the field. Then Balaam struck the ass to turn her into the way. But the Messenger stood in a narrow path between the vineyards, a wall being on this side, and a wall on that side. And when the ass saw the Messenger of Jehovah, she pressed herself against the wall and crushed Balaam's foot against the wall; so he struck her again. Then the Messenger of Jehovah went further, and stood in a narrow place, where there was no way to turn either to the right hand or the left. And when the ass saw the Messenger of Jehovah, she lay down under Balaam; and Balaam's anger was aroused, and he struck the ass with his staff. Then Jehovah opened the mouth of the ass, and she said to Balaam, What have I done to you, that you should have struck me these three times? And Balaam said to the ass, Because you have made sport of me; I would that there were a sword in my hand, for now I would kill you. And the ass said to Balaam, Am not I your ass, upon which you have ridden all your life long until to-day? Has it been my habit to deal thus with you? And he said, Nay. Then Jehovah opened the eyes of Balaam, and he saw the Messenger of Jehovah standing in the way, with his drawn sword in his hand; and he bowed his head and fell on his face. And the Messenger of Jehovah said to him, Why hast thou struck thine ass these three times? behold, I have come forth as an adversary, because thy conduct is perverse before me; and the ass saw me, and turned aside before me these three times. Unless she had turned aside from me, surely now I had even slain thee, and saved her alive. Therefore Balaam said to the Messenger of Jehovah, I have sinned; for I did not know that thou stoodest in the way against me; now therefore if it displeases thee, I will go back again. But the Messenger of Jehovah said to Balaam, Go with the men; but only the word I shall speak to thee, that thou shalt speak. And when Balak heard that Balaam was coming, he went out to meet him at Ir of Moab, which is on the boundary formed by the Arnon, which is at the extremity of the boundary, and said to him, Am I not able to honor you? Then Balaam went with Balak, and they came to Kiriath-huzzoth.

So Balak took Balaam to the top of Peor, which looks out over the eastern desert. Now when Balaam saw that it pleased Jehovah to bless Israel, he did not go to consult omens as he had done time and again, but he turned toward the wilderness. And when Balaam lifted up his eyes, he saw Israel dwelling according to their tribes; and the spirit of God came upon him, and he uttered his oracle saying,

> The oracle of Balaam the son of Beor,
> Even the oracle of the man who seeth truly,
> The oracle of him who heareth the words of God,
> Who seeth the vision of the Almighty,
> Falling down and having his eyes open:
> How beautiful are thy tents, O Jacob,
> Thy dwellings, O Israel!
> Like valleys are they spread out,
> Like gardens by the river-side,
> Like lign-aloes which Jehovah hath planted,
> Like cedars beside the waters.
> Water shall flow from his buckets,
> And his seed shall be sown in abundant waters,
> And his king shall be higher than Agag,
> And his kingdom shall be exalted.
> God who brought him forth out of Egypt
> Is for him like the strength of the wild-ox.
> He shall devour the nations, his adversaries,
> And shall break their bones in pieces,
> And shatter his oppressors.
> He croucheth, he lieth down like a lion,
> And like a lioness, who shall stir him up?
> Blessed is every one who blesseth thee,
> And cursed is every one who curseth thee.

Then Balak's anger was aroused against Balaam, and he smote his hands together; and Balak said to Balaam,

I called you to curse my enemies, and, behold, you have done nothing but bless them. Now therefore flee to your home. I intended to honor you greatly; but, as it is, Jehovah hath kept thee back from honor. But Balaam said to Balak, Did I not say to your messengers whom you sent to me, ' If Balak should give me his house full of silver and gold, I could not go beyond the word of Jehovah, to do either good or bad of my own will; what Jehovah speaketh that must I speak?' And now, behold, I am going to my people: come let me tell you beforehand what this people will do to your people in the days to come. And he uttered his oracle, saying,

> The oracle of Balaam the son of Beor,
> Even the oracle of the man who seeth truly,
> The oracle of him who heareth the words of God,
> And knoweth the knowledge of the Most High,
> Who seeth the vision of the Almighty,
> Falling down and having his eyes open:
> I see him, but not now;
> I behold him, but not near;
> A star cometh forth out of Jacob,
> And a sceptre ariseth out of Israel,
> And shattereth the temples of Moab,
> And the skull of all the sons of Seth.
> And Edom shall become a possession,
> Seir, his enemies, shall also become a possession,
> While Israel doeth valiantly.
> And out of Jacob shall one have dominion,
> And shall destroy the remnant from the city.

I. **Reasons for the Journey.** The opportunity to secure a base from which to invade Palestine, first offered itself to the Hebrews in the east-Jordan territory. The Amorites, possibly to escape Egyptian rule, seized the rolling uplands east of the Jordan. By the Moabites and Ammonites these invaders were naturally regarded as aliens. Hence in case of attack from their neighbors the Amorites could expect no aid. According to the earliest records, it was from these aliens that the Hebrews wrested the fertile lands on which they made the transition from the life of the wilderness to the settled agricultural civilization of Palestine.

THE JOURNEY FROM THE WILDERNESS

To reach the east-Jordan territory, the nearest way led across the northern territory of Edom and south of the Dead Sea. The Edomites, suspicious of the Israelites, refused them a passage. The journey around the southern end of Edom was long and toilsome, but the Hebrews chose it rather than battle with the Edomites.

II. **The Journey Around Edom.** The prophetic historians have preserved a few stories and fragments from the folk songs connected with the events of this journey. Again the people were discouraged and rebelled against Jehovah and Moses. The calamity which overtook them is interpreted as a divine judgment. The tradition states that fiery serpents came among them and bit them. Divine forgiveness and deliverance came only in response to the earnest prayers of Moses. In II Kings 18⁴ it is stated that Hezekiah, under the inspiration of the preaching of Isaiah, "broke in pieces the brazen serpent that Moses had made, for up to that time the Israelites had offered sacrifices to it, and they called it Nehushtan (*the brazen one*)." From this reference it appears that the present story is the traditional interpretation of the origin and meaning of this ancient symbol. The fact that it was destroyed in connection with Hezekiah's reform work indicates that the later age, under the preaching of the prophets, realized its true character. The early prophetic historians preserved the story because it illustrated vividly and concretely the duty of following God's leadership, without complaint even amidst the most adverse conditions. It also revealed that divine love which ever responds to the cry of contrition. Thus to the old heathen symbol these early prophets gave an interpretation which anticipates the later Gospel message.

The Song of the Well was probably sung by the women, as they went out to draw water from the famous well at Beer. It commemorates either the time when the well was originally dug, or the combined action of the leaders and people at some period of protracted drought. A list is also given of the stations in the caravan route which led from the desert northward.

III. **The Two Versions of the Balaam Stories.** In its present setting, the remarkable Balaam story is one of the episodes of the journey from Kadesh to the Jordan. Two complete and variant versions of this story are found in the book of Numbers. The Northern Israelite version makes Balaam a famous prophet from Pethor beside the Euphrates. He therefore lived on the borders of the land of Aram, from whence came the ancestors of the Hebrews. At the divine command he responded to the invitation of the king of Moab; but instead

222

of cursing, he pronounced a blessing which foretold the future prosperity and military glory of the Israelites. In the older, the early Judean narrative, Balaam was a famous Ammonite seer called to curse the Israelites. Brought to his senses by the voice of his patient ass, which is thought of as gifted with speech, even as the serpent in the early Judean story of man's fall, Balaam uttered a true and noble prediction concerning Israel's future victories under the leadership of Saul and David.

IV. The Balaam Oracles. Underlying the ancient story is the common belief that a curse, especially if it proceeds from the lips of one who has great influence with the Deity, possesses a malign power. The Balaam story also indicates that the early Hebrew historians held that divine revelation was not limited to seers and prophets of their own race. The setting and poetic form of Balaam's predictions are characteristic of ancient oracles. Although the exact meaning of the Hebrew is obscure, the opening words seem to indicate that the seer was in a state of trance, repeating that which he saw in his vision. The oracles, interpreted into prose, predict the fertility of the land of Palestine and the great numbers of the Hebrews. They fix the attention on the Hebrew king who was to bind together the different tribes of Israel and conquer their hostile neighbors, the Moabites and the Edomites. The picture is not of spiritual but of material splendor and conquest. The portrait of the victorious ruler is true of but one man in Israel's history, and that is the great conqueror David. His cruel treatment of Israel's fallen foes is made the theme of exultation rather than of condemnation. Its spirit is that of victorious Israel in the days when the united kingdom stood at the zenith of its power. The words well fit the lips of a court poet greeting the victorious army of Israel, as it came back under the leadership of Joab, sated with victory and bearing the spoils of conquest. Like Shakespeare's prediction of the glories of the reign of Queen Elizabeth (Henry VIII), they are placed with great dramatic effect in the mouth of an ancient seer.

V. The People of Destiny. As in Noah's blessing, it is clear that Israel's later experiences as a nation lie back of these ancient songs. They reflect the hopes of the Hebrews at the height of their military glory. There is no trace of the disasters that followed the death of Solomon. The influences of the higher ethical standards and of the law of love, which characterize the writings of later prophets, priests and sages, are nowhere apparent. Yet in these ancient oracles, Israel's consciousness of a unique calling and destiny is clearly expressed. Apart from and hostile to the rest of the world, the Hebrew nation stands like a crouching lion, yet assured of Jehovah's unique blessing and protection. The roots of that hope are found in the remarkable experiences of the past, and especially in the great deliverance from Egypt. The popular belief has deepened into a conviction that, not by chance but as the realization of divine destiny, the handful of fugitive slaves, in the face of overwhelming obstacles, have grown into a great and powerful nation. This sense of destiny and the conviction that they are Jehovah's peculiar people have already become so strong, that even the earliest prophets, projecting it backward, voice it, not only on the lips of an Abraham, Jacob and Moses, but even on the lips of a heathen seer. Israel's history as a whole is a sublime illustration of the truth that to believe is to achieve, even though the ultimate realization may be very different from the original hope.

§ XXX. EAST-JORDAN CONQUESTS AND MOSES'S FAREWELL

1. Victory over Sihon

Then Israel sent messengers to Sihon king of the Amorites, saying, Let me now pass through your land. We will not turn aside into field or vineyard; we will not drink from the water of the wells; we will go by the king's highway, until we have passed through your territory. But Sihon would not allow Israel to pass through his territory. Therefore Sihon gathered all his people together, and went out against Israel in the wilderness, and came to Jahaz, where he fought against Israel. And Israel smote him with the edge of the sword, and seized his land from the Arnon to the Jabbok, even to the Ammonites.

2. The occupation of Sihon's land

Then Israel took and dwelt in all the cities of the Amorites, in Heshbon, and in all its dependent villages. For Heshbon was the city of Sihon the king of the Amorites, who had fought against the former king of Moab, and taken all his land out of his hand, even to the Arnon. Therefore the bards sing:

> Come to Heshbon!
> Let it be rebuilt!
> Let the city of Sihon be re-established!
> For fire went out from Heshbon,
> Flame from the city of Sihon;
> It devoured Moab,

The lords of the high places of Arnon.
Woe to thee Moab!
Undone art thou, O people of Chemosh,
Who has made his sons fugitives
And his daughters captives,
So their offspring have perished from Heshbon to
    Dibon
And their wives . . . to Medeba.

Thus Israel came to live in the land of the Amorites.

And the children of Machir the son of Manasseh went to Gilead and took it, and dispossessed the Amorites who were therein. And Jair the son of Manasseh went and took their tent-villages and called them Havvoth-jair [Tent-villages of Jair]. And Nobah went and took Kenath, and its dependent towns, and called it Nobah after his own name. *3. Conquest of Gilead and Bashan*

Then Jehovah said to Moses, Behold, thy time approacheth that thou must die; call Joshua, and present yourselves in the tent of meeting, that I may give him a charge. And Moses and Joshua went and presented themselves in the tent of meeting. And Jehovah appeared in the tent in a pillar of cloud; and the pillar of cloud stood over the door of the tent. And he gave Joshua the son of Nun a charge saying, Be courageous and strong; for thou shalt bring the Israelites into the land which I promised them with an oath; and I will be with thee. *4. Jehovah's command to Moses*

Then Moses went up to the top of Pisgah. And Jehovah showed him all the land. And Jehovah said to him, This is the land which I promised with an oath to Abraham, Isaac, and Jacob, saying, ' I will give it to thy descendants'; I have caused thee to see it with thine eyes, but thou shalt not go over thither. So Moses the servant of Jehovah died there in the land of Moab. And Jehovah buried him in the ravine in the land of Moab over against Beth-Peor; but to this day no man knows of his burial-place. And there has not arisen a prophet since in Israel like Moses, whom Jehovah knew face to face. *5. The closing scenes of Moses's life*

I. **Victories over the Amorites.** Later conquests may perhaps be reflected in the tradition of the victory over the Amorites, but there

225

is doubtless an underlying basis of historic fact. The ancient song in*
is probably an extract from an older and fuller poetic source to which
the prophetic writers had access. This extract apparently refers to the
victories which the Hebrews won over the Moabites. It implies that
the Israelites had already captured Heshbon, the Amorite capital, and
made it the base of attack against the Moabites in the south. As in the
book of Joshua, the historical perspective may be foreshortened, so that
the events of a century or more are represented as taking place in one
year. It seems probable that at least some of the Hebrew tribes succeeded in capturing certain territory to the east of the lower Jordan and
there intrenched themselves, preparatory to the westward movement
toward Canaan.

II. **Importance of the East-Jordan Conquest.** As has already
been noted, throughout all its history the east-Jordan land has been the
territory in which the nomads from the desert have made the gradual
transition from their wandering life to the settled occupations of an
agricultural people. The plateaus furnish abundant grass for the herds
and flocks. At many points there are fruitful fields which yield abundant
crops of grain. Here the nomad learns how to till the soil and tastes
the joys of settled agricultural life. From these eastern highlands the
Hebrew immigrants looked longingly across the deep valley of the
Jordan to the rolling hills of Judea and Samaria. The pressure behind,
of other tribes moving in from the desert, and the rapid increase in their
own numbers, which would result from a more settled and favorable
method of life, were powerful forces impelling the Hebrews to cross the
Jordan and seek homes among the hills to the west.

III. **Moses's Farewell.** Tradition records that on these heights
east of the Jordan, Moses was given his first and last view of the promised
land of Canaan. In the older traditions, the account of his farewell
and death is very brief. Joshua the son of Nun, who had attended Moses
in the tent of meeting, is given command to lead the Israelites across the
Jordan into the land of their hopes. With the assurance that the ultimate goal of their wanderings would soon be attained, the servant of
Jehovah laid down the heavy burden, which he had borne so nobly.
Tradition fails to recall the spot where Israel's great leader was buried.
Mystery surrounds the death scene of the great prophet. Like Elijah
of the later story, the background of his activity was the lonely, mysterious wilderness, with its caves and dry, jagged mountains. On the
borders of civilized life, he suddenly disappears and his work is
done.

IV. Literary Setting of the Book of Deuteronomy. Later generations, recognizing that Israel's early judge and prophet had laid the foundations for all later Hebrew legislation, naturally regarded him as the author of that remarkable collection of exhortations and laws found in the book of Deuteronomy. Its literary setting is dramatic and appropriate. The laws and exhortations anticipate the various needs that arose in the later experiences of the Israelites in Canaan. As the Hebrews were about to pass from the wilderness to the conquest of Canaan, Moses is represented as giving these detailed laws in the form of a long prophetic address. In a very real sense the implications of this literary setting are historically true. Later prophets like Amos, Hosea and Isaiah still further interpreted the fundamental principles of Israel's faith. Their disciples formulated these principles in the definite laws found in the book of Deuteronomy. It was, however, the initial work of Moses that made this later national and social development possible. It was his spirit and faith that inspired his race to conquer and to achieve. It was his simple prophetic message that lay at the foundations of the growing body of Israel's legislation. Though in divine Providence other voices and other pens determined the final form of the laws, they nevertheless represent Moses's message to his race in the midst of its new life and environment.

V. The Real Work of Moses. Every student of the Old Testament is familiar with the profound impression which Moses made upon succeeding generations. It is more difficult to determine the real nature of the work which he did for his own age and race. About his person have gathered so many traditions, that it is also difficult to gain a clear conception of his personality. In the preceding sections an attempt has been made to trace his character and work in the light of the oldest narratives. Contemporary historical conditions and analogies in the experiences of later prophets also aid in this task. Moses was doubtless a man of his times, subject to the limitations of the primitive age in which he lived. Yet, like every true prophet, he rose as a towering mountain peak above his contemporaries, and with inspired vision caught glimpses of truth which made him a man of conviction with a message to his race.

Prophet that he was, he saw conditions as they were, and having seen, he did not hesitate to speak and act. Like every inspired leader of men, he was doubtless gifted with a constructive imagination, which enabled him to picture, to a certain extent, the noble destiny in store for his people. Above all, he was conscious of a Divine Power ruling over Nature and the destinies of his race, of a God not only powerful but per-

227

sonally interested in delivering the oppressed and in righting the wrongs of those who put their trust in him. In the mind of Moses the keen sense of his people's need, on the one hand, and of Jehovah's presence and character on the other, crystallized into a conviction that the God of Sinai was able and would deliver his people. Moses also recognized that he himself was called to be the herald of this great truth. His conviction and message were similar to those of the true prophets of a later age. His method was adapted to the peculiar conditions of his day. He was called, not merely to proclaim, but to lead. The dramatic experiences of his followers in the exodus and wilderness life confirmed his authority and gave him a supreme opportunity to impress his message upon them.

The very simplicity of his message added to its strength. Briefly expressed, it appears to have been: (1) Jehovah is able and eager to deliver his people from their bondage and to lead them to a land of freedom and opportunity. (2) The people must be loyal to Jehovah, rendering to him their full worship, expressed in gifts and ritual.

In addition, it is probable that Moses emphasized the necessity of their showing loyalty to Jehovah by the just treatment of their fellowmen. Thus it would appear that Israel's faith was from the first unique, because of this close blending of ethics and religion. As prophet, judge and leader, Moses touched every side of the life of his nation and left an impress which was simply deepened by later experiences.

VI. **The Desert Training.** The Hebrews acquired in the desert characteristics which may be traced in all the later stages of their history. There is a certain sternness and austerity in their character which they have never lost. Their tendency to stand aloof and to regard all other peoples as hostile is but the survival of a habit first engendered by the life of the desert, where every alien tribe is regarded as a foe. Their intense racial loyalty is another mark of the primitive tribal instinct. Throughout their history they showed themselves restive under any strongly organized central authority. Only under the pressure of direst necessity did the different tribes consent to lay down their individual independence and acknowledge a common authority.

From the desert they also brought that spirit of freedom and democracy which is so marked under the tribal organization. Each man is the equal of his fellow, and the tribal leader rules only by common consent and as a servant of the whole. To preserve this sacred heritage of democracy, the Israelites repeatedly passed through bloody and disastrous revolutions.

THE DESERT TRAINING

Even though they came under the sway of the polytheistic Canaanite civilization, their desert instinct, which led them to revere but one God, as the God of the tribe and nation, repeatedly asserted itself in response to the appeals of their prophets. Loyalty to Jehovah was therefore their supreme heritage from their desert days and from their great prophet Moses. It was also the foundation stone upon which was reared Israel's later political, social and ceremonial institutions. Standing on this same foundation, the inspired Hebrew prophets, priests and sages in later days developed that noble, ethical religion which is Israel's supreme contribution to the faith and progress of humanity.

APPENDIX

I

THE LATE PRIESTLY STORY OF CREATION

THESE ARE THE GENERATIONS OF THE HEAVENS AND OF THE EARTH WHEN THEY WERE CREATED

In the beginning God created the heavens and the earth. And the earth was waste and void, and darkness was upon the face of the deep; and the Spirit of God was brooding over the face of the waters. *1. Introduction: original chaos*

Then God said, Let there be light, and there was light. And God saw that the light was good. God caused the light to separate from the darkness. And God called the light Day, and the darkness he called Night. And there was evening and there was morning, a first day. *2. Work of the first day: separation of light from darkness*

Then God said, Let there be a firmament in the midst of the waters, and let it divide the waters from the waters. Thus God made a firmament, and caused the waters which were under the firmament to separate from the waters which were above the firmament, and it was so. And God called the firmament Heaven. And there was evening and there was morning, a second day. *3. Second day: creation of a firmament*

Then God said, Let the waters under the heavens be gathered together into one place, that the dry land may appear. And it was so. And God also called the dry land Earth, and the gathering together of the waters he called Sea. And God saw that it was good. Moreover God said, Let the earth put forth vegetation: herbs which yield seed, and fruit-trees which bear fruit on the earth after their kind, wherein is their seed. And it was so. Thus the earth brought forth vegetation, herbs which yield seed after their *4. Third day: separation of land and water and growth of vegetation*

231

kind and trees which bear fruit after their kind, wherein is their seed. And God saw that it was good. And there was evening and there was morning, a third day.

5. Fourth day: creation of the heavenly bodies

Then God said, Let there be lights in the firmament of heaven to distinguish between day and night. Let them also be for signs, and for seasons, and for days and years; and let them be lights in the firmament of heaven to shed light upon the earth. And it was so. Thus God made the two great lights: the greater to rule the day, and the lesser light to rule the night; also the stars. And God set them in the firmament of heaven to shed light upon the earth, and to rule over the day and over the night, and to distinguish between light and darkness. And God saw that it was good. And there was evening and there was morning, a fourth day.

6. Fifth day: creation of the creatures of the air and water

Then God said, Let the waters swarm with swarms of living creatures, and let birds fly over the earth in the open firmament of heaven. Thus God created the great sea-monsters, and all living, moving creatures with which the waters swarm, after their kind, and every winged bird after its kind. And God saw that it was good. And God blessed them, saying, Be fruitful, and become numerous, and fill the water in the sea, and let the birds become numerous on the earth. And there was evening and there was morning, a fifth day.

7. Sixth day: creation of land animals, reptiles and insects
8. Creation of man with divine intelligence and will, and with authority

Then God said, Let the earth bring forth living creatures after their kind: cattle and creeping things and beasts of the earth after their kind. And it was so. Thus God made the beasts of the earth after their kind, and the animals after their kind, and everything that creeps upon the ground after its kind. And God saw that it was good.

Moreover God said, Let us make man in our image, after our likeness, that they may have dominion over the fish of the sea, and over the birds of the heavens, and over the cattle, and over all the beasts of the earth, and over all the creeping things that creep upon the earth. Thus God created man in his own image, in the image of God created he him; male and female created he them. God also blessed them, and said to them, Be fruitful, and become numerous, and fill the earth, and subdue it; and have

232

dominion over the fishes of the sea, and over the birds of the heavens, and over every living thing that creeps upon the earth.

God also said, Behold, I give to you every herb yielding seed, which is upon the face of all the earth, and every tree, in which is fruit yielding seed; it shall be food for you. And to every beast of the earth, and to every bird of the heavens, and to everything that creeps on the earth, wherein there is life, I give every green herb for food. And it was so. And when God saw everything that he had made, behold, it was very good. And there was evening and there was morning, a sixth day. *9. Man and animals to be herbivorous* *10. Universe originally perfect*

Thus the heavens and the earth were finished, and all their host. When on the seventh day God had finished his work which he had done, he rested on the seventh day from all his work which he had done. God also blessed the seventh day, and hallowed it; because in it he rested from all his work which he, God, had done in the process of creation. *11. Seventh day: rest*

II

A PRACTICAL BIBLICAL REFERENCE LIBRARY

Purpose of a Reference Library. The number of books on biblical and related subjects is appallingly great. Many of them are intended simply for technical students; some are out of date, and others are more misleading than helpful. The most difficult problem that confronts the ordinary reader is to determine what books are the most reliable and helpful for the elucidation of the Bible. Not many, but a few clear, interestingly written books are required, which will put the student into possession of the important information which comes from the related fields of biblical geography, contemporary history, archæology and modern biblical research. Together the books of a practical reference library should give a comprehensive survey of the entire biblical field, and above all they should focus attention upon the Bible itself and aid in interpreting that spiritual truth which constitutes its chief and abiding value.

Books for Constant Reference. In the corresponding first volume of the *Student's Old Testament*, entitled *The Beginnings of Hebrew History*, teachers and readers will find the more detailed introductions to the first three books of the Old Testament and the reasons which have led to the separation of the older from the later narratives and additions. Variant versions of the same incidents are printed in parallel columns and the important interpretative and textual notes are placed at the foot of each page. In the Appendix is also given a selected bibliography with detailed references to both English and foreign works, and citations from the more important extra-biblical documents. For the contemporary Babylonian and Egyptian history, the Bible student should also have on his table Goodspeed's *History of the Babylonians and Assyrians* and Breasted's *History of the Ancient Egyptians*. A good, modern Bible dictionary is likewise indispensable. Hastings' shorter edition (to be issued soon), or preferably the larger edition of five volumes is undoubtedly the most satisfactory.

Additional Books of Reference: Introductions. In addition to the books for constant reference, the teacher and student and general reader should be able to refer readily to a score or more of the most important books in English, which throw light upon different subjects connected with the period represented by this volume. These volumes should be found at least in every working college, Sunday-school, or public library. As a general introduction to the problems which are commanding the attention of thoughtful men and women to-day, either Dods, *The Bible, Its Origin and Nature*, or Kent, *The Origin and Permanent Value of the Old Testament*, will be found useful. In many ways the most illuminating, brief, popular introduction to the individual books of the Old Testament is that by Professor McFadyen. Equally clear and attractive, and somewhat more detailed and compact is the *Introduction to the Old Testament* by Professor Cornill. For Bible classes Hazard and Fowler, *The Books of the Bible*, is an exceedingly useful hand-book. A more technical treatment of the subject is found in Driver, *Introduction to the Literature of the Old Testament*. The articles in Hastings, *Dictionary of the Bible*, on the individual books also furnish a valuable and yet popular introduction. For the purely literary study, the more recent work by Professor Gardiner on *The Bible as English Literature* is exceedingly suggestive, and supplements, from the modern point of view, the older epoch-making work of Professor Moulton on the *Literary Study of the Bible*.

Contemporary Literature and History. For the contemporary Babylonian literature Johns, *Babylonian and Assyrian Laws, Contracts and Letters;* King, *The Letters and Inscriptions of Hammurabi;* and

APPENDIX

The Seven Tablets of Creation; King and Hall, *Egypt and Western Asia in the Light of Recent Discoveries;* Ball, *Light from the East,* and Clay, *Light on the Old Testament from Babel,* are the chief authorities. Winckler, *The Tel-El-Amarna Letters,* contains an excellent translation of these important documents. The contemporary Egyptian documents will be found either in Breasted's *History of the Ancient Egyptians* or in his more voluminous *History of Egypt* or in his *Ancient Records.* In addition to the histories of Breasted and Goodspeed, already mentioned, the reader will find Paton's compact and reliable little *Early History of Syria and Palestine* exceedingly suggestive. Maspero's large and beautifully illustrated volumes on the *Dawn of Civilization* and *The Struggle of the Nations* are still delightful mines of information. Winckler's recently translated *History of Babylonia and Assyria* also supplements, although it does not supplant Goodspeed's earlier work. Sayce, *Babylonians and Assyrians,* presents in concise form the life and customs of these ancient peoples, and Jastrow, *Religion of Babylonia and Assyria,* gives a clear picture of their beliefs and religious institutions.

Hebrew History. For a brief, popular treatment of early Hebrew history, Wade, *Old Testament History,* and Cornill, *History of the People of Israel,* are suggestive and useful. Smith, *Old Testament History,* is more critical and thorough in its method.

The Early Hebrew Traditions. The literature in this field is especially rich. Davis, *Genesis and Semitic Traditions,* and Ryle, *The Early Narratives of Genesis,* are popular yet exceedingly suggestive interpretations of the opening stories in the Old Testament. Gunkel, *The Legends of Genesis,* and Peters, *Early Hebrew Stories,* throw much new light upon the origin and interpretation of these early narratives. In his *Early Traditions of Genesis,* Professor Gordon has made a fresh and illuminating study, especially from the philosophical and theological side, of these early chapters. Worcester, *Genesis in the Light of Modern Knowledge,* contains a full collection of parallel traditions, gathered both from the ancient Orient and Occident.

By far the best English commentary on the book of Genesis is that by Professor Driver, although the older work by Professor Dillmann and the brief hand-book by Professor Dods are still of great value. The volume in the *International Critical Commentary* by Professor Gray on Numbers contains a thorough treatment of the difficult problems presented by that book.

APPENDIX

III

GENERAL QUESTIONS AND SUBJECTS FOR SPECIAL RESEARCH

For readers and students questions are of value either in focussing the attention, while reading, on those subjects which are of vital importance, and in formulating definitely the results of the reading; or else in guiding and inspiring the student to enter new but related fields of research.

The following questions have been prepared and classified with these two distinct ends in view. They follow the chapter or general section divisions of the *Historical Bible*. The biblical text or the accompanying notes furnish the data for answering the *General Questions*. This first group of questions also aims to suggest in outline a practical order in which the important subjects presented by each chapter may be considered in the class-room or in general discussion. The themes for practical discussion and suggestions regarding the personal application of the teachings contained in each section will be reserved for the teacher's manual, which will be issued later.

The *Subjects for Special Research* point to the larger horizon with which the teacher should be familiar, and give the detailed references which are most helpful in gaining this wider vision. They also suggest certain related lines of study which are of interest and value to the general reader and student. In class-room work many of these topics may be profitably assigned for personal research and report. The references are to pages, unless otherwise indicated. Ordinarily several parallel references are given, that the student may be able to utilize the book at hand. More detailed classified bibliographies will be found in Sanders and Fowler's *Outlines of Biblical History and Literature* and in Appendix I of *Student's Old Testament*, Vol. I.

INTRODUCTION

I. The Old Testament World. GENERAL QUESTIONS: 1. In what ways did the character of the land in which they lived influence primitive peoples? Cite illustrations. 2. Describe the boundaries and general character of the Old Testament world? 3. The Lower Tigris-Euphrates valley, Mesopotamia and Egypt, and the type of civilization which they each produced. 4. The general characteristics of Syria and Pal-

APPENDIX

estine. 5. The migrations of the different Semitic peoples from their original home, and their final settlement.

SUBJECTS FOR SPECIAL RESEARCH: 1. A detailed comparison of the physical characteristics of the Tigris-Euphrates and the Nile valleys. Goodspeed, *Hist. Babs. and Assyrs.*, 3–13; Erman, *Life in Anc. Egypt*, 5–28; Breasted, *Hist. of the Anc. Egyptians*, 3–13; *Hist. of Egypt*, 3–12; Hastings, *D.B.*, I, 214, 653–5; Maspero, *Dawn of Civilization*, 1–46, 702–84; Articles in standard encyclopædias. 2. The great zones of Palestine and their physical peculiarities. Kent, *Hist. Heb. Peop.*, *United Kgd.*, 18–26; Smith, *Hist. Geog. of the Holy Land*, 6–13, 46–59; Hastings, *D.B.*, III, 640–8; *Encyc. Bib.*, III, 3534–44; Stewart, *Land of Israel* 3. Relation of the Semitic peoples to the other branches of the human race, and the physical and mental characteristics of the Semites. Hastings, *D.B.*, Extra Vol., 72–91; Barton, *Sketch of Semitic Origins*, Ch. I; Keane, *Ethnology*, 391–5; Brinton, *Cradle of the Semites*.

II. The Babylonian Background of Early Hebrew History.

GENERAL QUESTIONS: 1. Describe the ancient Babylonian system of writing, and explain why it developed at so early a period in the lower Tigris-Euphrates valley. 2. The more striking characteristics of the ancient Babylonian civilization. 3. The Babylonian conception of the universe. 4. The different classes in early Babylonia. 5. The three or four distinct stages of political development which may be traced in Babylonia. 6. The empire and reign of Sargon I. 7. The character, conquests, policy, building enterprises and code of Hammurabi. 8. The important dates in Babylonian and Assyrian history. 9. Babylonia's contributions to human civilization.

SUBJECTS FOR SPECIAL RESEARCH: 1. The records of the earliest Semitic civilization and their discovery. Goodspeed, *Hist. of Babs. and Assyrs.*, 14–36; Hastings, *D.B.*, I, 220–4; *Encyc. Bib.*, I, 425–9; Jastrow, *Relig. of Bab. and Assyr.*, 6–19. 2. The Sumerians. King and Hall, *Egypt and Western Asia*, 143–50; Hastings, *D.B.*, I, 214–5; Winckler, *Hist. of Bab. and Assyr.*, 12–17. 3. Early Babylonian Chronology. King and Hall, *Egypt and Western Asia*, 184–90, 246–8; King, *Studies in Eastern Hist.*, II, 76–137. 4. The Early Babylonian Cities. Goodspeed, *Hist. of Babs. and Assyrs.*, 49–54. 5. Code of Hammurabi. Kent, *St. O. T.*, IV, *Israel's Laws and Legal Precedents*, 3–7, 291–7; Johns, *Bab. and Assyr. Laws, Contracts and Letters;* King and Hall, *Egypt and Western Asia*, 274–316; Cook, *The Laws of Moses and the Code of Hammurabi.* 6. The Kassites. Goodspeed, *Hist. of Babs. and Assyrs.* 121–7; Winckler, *Hist. of Bab. and Assyr.*, 71–92.

APPENDIX

III. The Egyptian Background. GENERAL QUESTIONS: 1. Describe the beginnings of Egyptian history. 2. Building enterprises of the fourth Egyptian dynasty. 3. Rule of the twelfth dynasty. 4. Origin and rule of the Hyksos. 5. The development of the Egyptian empire and the rule of Ramses II. 6. The great political changes in Old Testament world about 1200 B.C.

SUBJECTS FOR SPECIAL RESEARCH: 1. The character of the earliest Egyptian civilization. Breasted, *Hist. of the Anc. Egyptians*, 29–51; *Hist. of Egypt*, 25–50. 2. The building of the great pyramids. *Encyc. Brit.*, article "Pyramids"; Breasted, *Hist. of Anc. Egyptians*, 103–16; *Hist. of Egypt*, 111–23. 3. The Egyptian mines in the Sinaitic peninsula. Breasted, *Hist. of the Anc. Egyptians*, 160; Erman, *Life in Anc. Egypt*, 468–9; Petrie, *Researches in Sinai*. 4. Egyptian armies and methods of conquest under the eighteenth dynasty; Erman, *Life in Anc. Egypt*, 520–34; Breasted, *Hist. of Anc. Egyptians*, 223–43; *Hist. of Egypt*, 233–5, 243. 5. Probable origin of the Hittites. Article "Hittites," in *Encyc. Brit.*; Hastings, *D.B.*, II, 390–2; *Encyc. Bib.*, II, 2094–2100.

IV. The Early Palestinian Background. GENERAL QUESTIONS: 1. Describe the different sources of information regarding the pre-Hebrew history of Palestine. 2. The dates and ways in which the culture of Babylonia touched Syria and Palestine in the pre-Hebrew period. 3. The Amorite and Canaanite invasions of Palestine. 4. Life in Palestine about 2000 B.C. 5. The nature and effects of Egyptian rule in Palestine. 6. The light thrown upon conditions in Palestine by the el-Amarna letters. 7. The relative date of Israel's appearance, and the characteristics of the civilization which the Hebrews found in Palestine.

SUBJECTS FOR SPECIAL RESEARCH: 1. Excavations at Lachish. Hastings, *D.B.*, III, 15, 16; Petrie, *Tell-el-Hesy*; Bliss, *A Mound of Many Cities*. 2. At Gezer. Quarterly Statements of the Palestinian Exploration Fund during the years 1905–8; Macalister, *Bible Side-lights from the Mound of Gezer*. 3. The light shed by the Babylonian and Egyptian inscriptions upon early Palestine. Paton, *Early Hist. of Syria and Pal.*, 49–62; Maspero, *Struggle of the Nats.*, 14–19. 4. The Amorite-Canaanite Period. Paton, *Early Hist. of Syria and Pal.*, 24–46, 63–72; McCurdy, *Hist. Prophecy and the Monuments*, I, 152–223. 5. The Egyptian Rule in Palestine. Hastings, *D.B.*, I, 660–2; *Encyc. Bib.*, II, 1238–42; Paton, *Early Hist. of Syria and Pal.*, 74–102; Breasted, *Hist. of the Anc. Egyptians*, 251–2; *Hist. of Egypt*, 233–50. 6. History and contents of the el-Amarna letters. Breasted, *Hist. of Egypt*, 332–7.

APPENDIX

382–9; Winckler, *The Tell-El-Amarna Letters;* Petrie, *Syria and Egypt from the Tell-el-Amarna Letters;* Clay, *Light on the O. T. from Babel,* 251–82. 7. Compare the contemporary Mycenæan civilization with that of the Eastern empires. Goodspeed, *Hist. of the Anc. World,* 77–80; Bury, *Hist. of Greece,* 11–53; Morey, *Outlines of Greek History,* 86–94.

V. **Israel's Religious Heritage.** GENERAL QUESTIONS: 1. Describe the different ways in which religion influenced the life and civilization of the ancient Babylonians. 2. The religion of the Sumerians. 3. The gods and cultus of the early city states. 4. Political forces that developed the Babylonian pantheon. 5. The religion of the Canaanites. 6. Contributions of these earlier Semitic religions to Israel's faith.

SUBJECTS FOR SPECIAL RESEARCH: 1. A definition of religion, *cf.* dictionaries and encyclopædias; Clarke, *Outlines of Christian Theol.;* Brown, *Christian Theol. in Outline;* Menzies, *Hist. of Relig.* 2. A comparison between the growth of the Babylonian and Egyptian religions. Hastings, *D.B.,* 1, 215–6, 665–7; *Encyc. Bib.,* I, 431–7, II, 1214–9; Sayce, *Babs. and Assyrs.,* 231–64; Jastrow, *Relig. of the Babs. and Assyrs.; Encyc. Brit.,* VII, 714–8; Budge, *The Gods of Egypt;* Erman, *Life in Anc. Egypt.* 3. The history of the temple at Nippur. Peters, *Nippur,* I, II; Hilprecht, *Explorats. in Bible Lands,* 289–568. 4. Describe an ancient Canaanite sanctuary and its cultus. Marti, *Relig. of the O. T.,* 80–96; *Encyc. Bib.,* II, 2064–9; Curtiss, *Primitive Sem. Relig. To-day,* 133–43.

VI. **The Oldest History of Israel.** GENERAL QUESTIONS: 1. Describe the way in which ancient Semitic histories grew. 2. The four distinct lines of evidence which aid in distinguishing the quotations from the older and later sources. Illustrate. 3. Scope and literary characteristics of the oldest history of the Hebrews. 4. Its primary aim and value. 5. The different sources from which its narratives were drawn. 6. Its date and place of composition.

SUBJECTS FOR SPECIAL RESEARCH: 1. History of the discovery of the different sources. Carpenter and Harford-Battersby, *Hexateuch,* I, 1–17, 33–48. 2. Israel's heritage of oral traditions. Kent, *St. O. T.,* 3–12; Gordon, *Early Trads. of Gen.,* 36–61, 75. 3. The transmission and crystallization of Israel's traditions into literature. *St. O. T.,* I, 13, 16–20; Gordon, *Early Trads. of Gen.,* 62–74. 4. Their literary characteristics. *St. O. T.,* I, 13–15; Gardiner, *The Bible as Eng. Lit.,* 34–76; Gordon, *Early Trads. of Gen.,* 76–87. 5. The Early Judean Prophetic Narratives. *St. O. T.,* I, 31–7; Carpenter and Harford-Battersby, *Hexateuch,* 97–110; Driver, *Genesis,* xii–xxii.

APPENDIX

VII. The Later Parallel Histories. GENERAL QUESTIONS: 1. Describe the characteristics of the northern prophetic history. 2. Its aims and contents. 3. Method in which the two prophetic histories were combined. 4. Characteristics and aims of the late priestly history. 5. Result of the final blending of the older and later histories. 6. Practical value of distinguishing and separating the older from the later histories.

SUBJECTS FOR SPECIAL RESEARCH: 1. The detailed characteristics and origins of the Northern Israelite prophetic history.* *St. O. T.*, 37–41; Carpenter and Harford-Battersby, *Hexateuch*, I, 110–20. 2. Of the late priestly history, *St. O. T.*, I, 43–8; Carpenter and Harford-Battersby, *Hexateuch*, I, 121–57. 3. The blending of the Gospel narratives in Tatian's Diatessaron. *Journal of Bib. Lit.*, 1890, pp. 201–15; Carpenter and Harford-Battersby, *Hexateuch*, 8–11; Hill, *The Earliest Life of Christ*. 4. Prepare a chronological table or diagram showing the approximate dates of the original documents and the work of the compilers who have given the first four books of the Old Testament their present form. *St. O. T.*, I, Frontispiece.

THE BEGINNINGS OF HEBREW HISTORY

§ I. The Story of Man's Creation. GENERAL QUESTIONS: 1. What evidence is found in the story that it is very old and that its author was a prophet? 2. What appears to have been the oldest Hebrew tradition regarding the creation of the earth and heavens? 3. Make a table giving in parallel columns the testimony of the Early Judean (§ I), the late priestly (Appendix I), the early Babylonian (I[vi]) and the later Babylonian (I[vii]) accounts of creation, regarding (1) name of the creator; (2) method of creation; (3) order, and (4) aim. 4. What did the tree of life and the tree of the knowledge of good and evil represent? 5. What are the teachings of the story regarding (1) God, (2) man, and (3) the basis of the marriage relation.

SUBJECTS FOR SPECIAL RESEARCH: 1. The Babylonian Creation Stories. *St. O. T.*, I, 360–70; Hastings, *D. B.*, I, 501–7; *Encyc. Bib.*, I, 938–41; Worcester, *Genesis*, 110–47; Clay, *Light on the O. T. from*

---

* In the more technical articles on the sources, the early Judean prophetic narratives are designated by J, and the later additions to it by J[s] or J[2]; the Northern Israelite or early Ephraimite prophetic narratives by E, and its supplements by E[s] or E[2]; the compiler, who combined J and E by R[JE]; the late priestly narratives by P, and its supplements by P[s] or P[2].

APPENDIX

Babel, 59–76. 2. Parallel stories among other nations. Hastings. *D. B.*, extra vol., 177–81; *Encyc. Bib.*, I, 942–4; Worcester, *Genesis*, 95–110; Lenormant, *The Beginnings of Hist.* 3. The modern scientific theory of the origin of man. Peschel, *Races of Man*, 1–34; Morris' *Man and His Ancestor;* Clay, *Man, Past and Present.*

§ II. **Man's Sin and Its Consequences.** GENERAL QUESTIONS: 1. Describe the literary characteristics of this story. 2. Its real theme and object. 3. The rôle of the serpent. 4. Define (1) temptation, (2) sin. 5. The nature and effects of sin as illustrated by the story.

SUBJECTS FOR SPECIAL RESEARCH: 1. The ancient parallels to the story. *St. O. T.*, I, 370–3; Driver, *Genesis*, 44, 51–7, 60–1; Worcester, *Genesis*, 184–256. 2. The Babylonian and Egyptian idea of sin. Hastings, *D. B.*, extra vol., 566–7; Jastrow, *Relig. of the Babs. and Assyrs.*, 312–27; Breasted, *Hist. of Egypt*, 173–5. 3. The later Jewish conception of the origin of sin. Porter, in "Biblical and Semitic Studies" (*Yale Bi-Centennial Publications*), 98–156; Hastings, *D. B.*, IV, 531–2; Tennent, *Sources of the Doctrines of the Fall and Original Sin.* 4. Milton's interpretation of the story in *Paradise Lost.*

§ III. **The Story of Cain and Abel.** GENERAL QUESTIONS: 1. Describe the state of society reflected in this story. 2. The evidence that Cain and Abel originally represented tribes or nations. 3. The development of Cain's character. 4. Cain's attitude toward society, and the cause of his fear. 5. The ancient and modern methods of punishing murder. 6. Jehovah's choice, as illustrated by the story.

SUBJECTS FOR SPECIAL RESEARCH: 1. The evidence that the story is of early Hebrew rather than of Babylonian origin. *St. O. T.*, I, 61; Driver, *Genesis*, 71–2; Worcester, *Genesis*, 269–77. 2. The Semitic law of blood-revenge. *St. O. T.*, IV, 91, 114–6; Gordon, *Early Trads. of Genesis*, 201–6; Smith, *Religion of the Semites*, 72, 420. 3. Tribal marks, *Encyc. Bib.*, I, 973–4; Gordon, *Early Trads. of Genesis*, 206–11.

§ IV. **The Traditional Origin of Early Semitic Institutions.** GENERAL QUESTIONS: 1. Describe the origin and object of the genealogical list. 2. Compare the Hebrew and Phœnician traditions regarding the origin of the arts. 3. Give the probable origin of the story of Enoch. 4. The meaning of the different traditions connected with Lamech. 5. The interpretation of the story of Noah, the first tiller of the soil. 6. Teachings of the story.

SUBJECTS FOR SPECIAL RESEARCH: 1. The Babylonian list of the ten antediluvian kings. *St. O. T.*, I, 58; Maspero, *Dawn of Civiliz.*, 591–4. 2. Compare the ancient theories of the origin of the arts with

APPENDIX

those of modern science of society. Peschel, *Races of Man;* Taylor, *Primitive Man;* Deniker, *Races of Man;* Keane, *Ethnology.* 3. Israel's popular folk-songs. *St. O. T.*, I, 16; Hastings, *D.B.*, IV, 11–12.

§ V. **The Story of the Great Flood.** GENERAL QUESTIONS: 1. Give the probable origin and prophetic interpretation of the story regarding the sons of God and the daughters of men. 2. Compare the two biblical versions of the flood story. 3. The early Babylonian and the early Hebrew versions. 4. What was the probable origin of the flood story. 5. By the aid of the Babylonian parallels trace its history. 6. What are the fundamental differences between the biblical and other flood stories. 7. What are the teachings of each of the two biblical accounts of the flood?

SUBJECTS FOR SPECIAL RESEARCH: 1. The history of the Babylonian flood story. *St. O. T.*, I, 373–8; Hastings, *D.B.*, II, 17–18; Worcester, *Genesis*, 374–411; Maspero, *Dawn of Civiliz.*, 566–72. 2. Flood stories among other peoples. Worcester, *Genesis*, 361–73; Hastings, *D.B.*, II, 18–22, extra vol., 181–2. 3. The scientific accuracy of the biblical narratives. Ryle, *Early Narratives of Gen.*, 112–3; Davis, *Gen. and Semitic Trads.*, 130–1; Driver, *Genesis*, 82–3, 99; Sollas, *Age of the Earth*, 316 *ff.;* Süss, *Race of the Earth*, I, 20–40, 63–5, 69, 71–2.

§ VI. **The Traditional Origin of the Nations.** GENERAL QUESTIONS: 1. What mound probably gave rise to the story of the tower of Babel? 2. What does the Hebrew story seek to explain? 3. Indicate the principles of classification followed in the table of the nations. 4. The identification and home of the different nations. 5. The ethnographic, geographic and religious value of the table.

SUBJECTS FOR SPECIAL RESEARCH: 1. Parallels to the story of the Tower of Babel. Worcester, *Genesis*, 497–521; Clay, *Light from Babel*, 89–124. 2. The modern theory regarding the origin of languages and races. Taylor, *Primitive Man;* Peschel, *Races of Men*, 102–14, 129–31; Deniker, *Races of Man;* Keane, *Ethnology.* 3. Corresponding tables among other nations. Gordon, *Early Trads. of Gen.*, 87–9. 4. Different identifications of Ophir. Hastings, *D.B.*, III, 626–8; *Encyc. Bib.*, III, 3513–5; Driver, *Genesis*, xix; Keane, *The Gold of Ophir;* Peters, *Eldorado of the Ancients.* 5. Classify the traditions in §§ I–VI according to their probable Babylonian, Aramean or Hebrew origin. 6. Their value (1) as literature; (2) as historical sources; (3) as illustrations of religious and ethical principles. *St. O. T.*, I, 3–12; Worcester, *Genesis*, 55–69; Gunkel, *Legends of Genesis.*

§ VII. **Abraham's Call and Settlement in Canaan.** GENERAL QUESTIONS: 1. Describe the probable origin and history of the Abraham stories. 2. The later traditions regarding Abraham. 3. The probable origin of the two names, Abraham and Abram. 4. The original home of the Hebrews. 5. Meaning of the divine promises to Abraham. 6. Compare the spirit and ambitions of Abraham and Lot.

SUBJECTS FOR SPECIAL RESEARCH: 1. The four great divisions of the book of Genesis. *St. O. T.*, I, 21–3; Worcester, *Genesis*, 55–69; *cf.* O. T. Introductions. 2. Abraham's genealogy. Bible dictionary articles, "Nahor," "Milcah," "Sarah." 3. Abraham in late Jewish tradition. Hastings, *D. B.*, I, 16, 17; James, *The Testament of Abraham.* 4. Sacred trees and the oaks of Mamre. Hastings, *D. B.*, III, 224–5; Smith, *Relig. of the Semites*, 185–95; *Encyc. Bib.*, III, 3352–4; Thomson, *Land and the Book*, II, 104, 171–2, 222, 474; Curtiss, *Primitive Semitic Relig. To-day*, 91, 93.

§ VIII. **The Promise of a Son to Sarah.** GENERAL QUESTIONS: 1. Describe the geographical background of the story of Hagar. 2. The purpose of the story. 3. Does Hagar represent an individual or a tribe? 4. The character and quality of Abraham's hospitality. 5. The Greek parallel to the story of the divine guests. 6. Ideas of God reflected in these stories.

SUBJECTS FOR SPECIAL RESEARCH: 1. History of the Ishmaelites. Hastings, *D. B.*, II, 502–5; *Encyc. Bib.*, II, 2211–2. 2. The Northern Israelite account of the expulsion of Hagar. *St. O. T.*, I, 93–4. 3. The historical character of Genesis 14. *St. O. T.*, I, 84–6; Driver, *Genesis*, 156–73; Paton, *Early Hist. of Syria and Palestine*, 31–46.

§ IX. **The Destruction of Sodom.** GENERAL QUESTIONS: 1. Describe the scene of the story. 2. Character of the ancient Canaanites. 3. Aim of the story. 4. Abraham's intercession. 5. Historical value of the story. 6. Its moral and religious teachings.

SUBJECTS FOR SPECIAL RESEARCH: 1. Geological history of the Jordan and Dead Sea valley. Smith, *Hist. Geography*, 467–71. 2. The Dead Sea. Hastings, *D. B.*, I, 575–7; *Encyc. Bib.*, I, 1042–6; Smith, *Hist. Geography*, 499–516. 3. Parallels to the biblical story. Cheyne, in *New World*, June, 1892. 4. The early history of the Moabites. Hastings, *D. B.*, III, 408–10; *Encyc. Bib.*, III, 3175–7. 5. The early history of the Ammonites, Hastings, *D. B.*, I, 82–3; *Encyc. Bib.*, I, 142–4.

§ X. **Birth and Sacrifice of Isaac.** GENERAL QUESTIONS: 1. What was the meaning of the Semitic rite of human sacrifice? 2. What ancient peoples practised it? 3. When did the Hebrew people begin to condemn it? 4. What are the aims of the present story? 5. Describe Abraham's character as portrayed in the early prophetic stories.

APPENDIX

SUBJECTS FOR SPECIAL RESEARCH: 1. The original meaning of sacrifice. *St. O. T.*, IV, 238; Hastings, *D. B.*, IV, 329–31; *Encyc. Bib.*, IV, 4216–26; Smith, *Religion of the Semites*, 213–43, 252–440; Gordon, *Early Trads. of Genesis*, 212–6. 2. The priestly account of the circumcision of Isaac. *St. O. T.*, I, 82–4, 89; Driver, *Genesis*, 184–91; Hastings, *D. B.*, I, 442–4. 3. Abraham's character as portrayed by the late priestly historian. Hastings, *D. B.*, I, 14; *Encyc. Bib.*, I, 25.

§ XI. **Securing a Wife for Isaac.** GENERAL QUESTIONS: 1. Describe the literary characteristics of the story and its seven distinct scenes. 2. The character of Abraham's servant. 3. The Semitic marriage customs reflected in the story. 4. Contrast the characters of Abraham and Isaac.

SUBJECTS FOR SPECIAL RESEARCH: 1. The land of Aram. Hastings, *D. B.*, I, 138–9; *Encyc. Bib.*, I, 276–8. 2. Oriental methods of courtship. Hastings, *D. B.*, III, 270–2; *Encyc. Bib.*, III, 2942–6; Smith, *Kinship and Marriage in Early Arabia*. 3. Characteristics of the South Country (*Negeb*). Hastings, *D. B.*, III, 505–6; *Encyc. Bib.*, III, 3374–9. 4. Stories regarding Isaac. *St. O. T.*, I, 76–81; Hastings, *D. B.*, II, 483–5; *Encyc. Bib.*, II, 2174–9.

§ XII. **Jacob and His Brother Esau.** GENERAL QUESTIONS: 1. What two nations traced their descent from Jacob and Esau? 2. In what sense was Esau the older, and what superior rights did the descendants of Jacob enjoy? 3. Describe the ancient Semitic idea of the birthright and of a father's dying blessing. 4. What special promise had been given to the race? 5. What different means did Jacob employ to secure the rights of the eldest? 6. The effect upon Esau and Jacob. 7. Compare the characters of the two brothers, as sketched in this narrative. 8. In what respects is Jacob a true representative of the Hebrew race?

SUBJECTS FOR SPECIAL RESEARCH: 1. Compare the two accounts of Jacob's theft of the birthright. *St. O. T.*, I, 103–7. 2. Trace the early history of the Edomites. Hastings, *D. B.*, I, 644–5; *Encyc. Bib.*, II, 1181–4. 3. Law of inheritance among the early Semites. *Encyc., Bib.*, III, 2728–9; Hastings, *D. B.*, II, 470–3; Johns, *Bab. and Assyr. Laws, Contracts and Letters*, 161–7.

§ XIII. **Jacob's Experiences as a Fugitive.** GENERAL QUESTIONS: 1. Describe the situation of Bethel. 2. The meaning and traditional origin of the name. 3. The meaning and fulfilment of the promise to Jacob. 4. Jacob's wooing of Rachel. 5. The meaning of the traditions regarding the ancestry of the different Hebrew tribes. 6. Indications

APPENDIX

that Jacob is (1) an individual, or (2) simply the traditional ancestor of the twelve tribes.

SUBJECTS FOR SPECIAL RESEARCH: 1. Origin and nature of the ancient Hebrew sanctuaries. Peters, *Early Heb. Story*, 81–116; Hastings, *D. B.*, IV, 395–7, extra vol., 615–8; Libbey and Hoskins, *Jordan Valley and Petra*, I, 171–207. 2. The meanings of the names of the twelve tribes. *Cf.* articles in Bible dictionaries. 3. Compare the different portraits of Jacob in the early prophetic and late priestly narratives. *St. O. T.*, I, 103–13; Hastings, *D. B.*, II, 526–35; *Encyc. Bib.*, II, 2306–11.

§ XIV. **Jacob's Return to Canaan.** GENERAL QUESTIONS: 1. Give the reasons for Jacob's flight from Laban. 2. What was the nature and meaning of the struggle beside the Jabbok? 3. Is there a marked contrast between Jacob's character before and after this experience? 4. Describe Jacob's faults and virtues. 5. In what respects was he inferior to Esau. 6. Why was Jacob best fitted to be the traditional ancestor of the Hebrew race?

SUBJECTS FOR SPECIAL RESEARCH: 1. The Arameans. Hastings, *D.B.*, I, 138–9; *Encyc. Bib.*, I, 276–280; Peters, *Early Heb. Story*, 45–7, 115–6, 133–4; Maspero, *Struggle of the Nats.*, 126. 2. The household gods or teraphim. Hastings, *D. B.*, IV, 718; *Encyc. Bib.*, IV, 4974–5; Moore, *Judges*, 379–81. 3. Sites of Mizpah, Mahanaim, Penuel and Succoth. Driver, *Genesis*, 300–2; articles in Bible dictionaries. 4. Contrast the characters of Abraham and Jacob.

§ XV. **Joseph Sold by His Brothers.** GENERAL QUESTIONS: 1. Describe the literary characteristics of the Joseph stories. 2. Joseph's early home life and character. 3. The character and attitude of his brothers. 4. Situation of Dothan. 5. The effect of the life in Egypt upon Joseph's character.

SUBJECTS FOR SPECIAL RESEARCH: 1. Eastern dress. Hastings, *D. B.*, I, 623–8; *Encyc. Bib.*, I, 1135–41; Maspero, *Dawn of Civiliz.*, 55–8, 265, 685. 2. The early caravan and trade routes in the ancient Semitic world. Hastings, *D. B.*, extra vol., 368–75. 3. Society and religion in Egypt under the eighteenth dynasty. Breasted, *Hist. of the Ancient Egyptians*, 193–206; *Hist. of Egypt*, 233–52; Erman, *Life of the Ancient Egyptians*, 102–29.

§ XVI. **Joseph Made Governor of Egypt.** GENERAL QUESTIONS: 1. Describe the dreams of Joseph's fellow-prisoners and the interpretations. 2. The oriental estimate of dreams. 3. Pharaoh's dreams. 4. Joseph's plans for the period of famine. 5. His policy in adapting

APPENDIX

himself to the peculiar customs of Egypt. 6. The Egyptian system of land tenure. 7. Joseph as an administrator.

SUBJECTS FOR SPECIAL RESEARCH: 1. The ancient and modern attitude toward dreams. Hastings, *D. B.*, I, 622–3; *Encyc. Bib.*, I, 1118; Driver, *Genesis*, XXI, 342; *cf.* modern psychologies. 2. Recorded famines in Egypt. Breasted, *Hist. of Egypt*, 160–1; Hastings, *D. B.*, II, 773–4; *Encyc. Bib.*, II, 2591; Driver, *Genesis*, 346–7. 3. The possessions and privileges of the priests in Egypt. Maspero, *Dawn of Civiliz.*, 124–6, 266, 305; Erman, *Life of the Ancient Egyptians*, 104–5, 292–3, 298–304; *Herodotus*, II, 168.

§ XVII. **Joseph and His Brothers.** GENERAL QUESTIONS: 1. Describe Joseph's early interviews with his brothers. 2. Aim and justification of his hiding the money in their sacks. 3. The portrait of the aged Jacob. 4. The character of Judah and his appeal for Benjamin. 5. The final scene between Joseph and his brothers. 6. Qualities in Joseph's character reflected in the story.

SUBJECTS FOR SPECIAL RESEARCH: 1. Divination. Driver, *Genesis*, 358; Hastings, *D. B.*, I, 611–13; *Encyc. Bib.*, I, 1117–21; Strabo, XVI, 39. 2. Effect of famine in the East. *Cf.* reports of recent famines in India; Kipling, "William the Conqueror," in *The Day's Work*. 3. Egyptian methods of eating. Erman, *Life of the Anc. Egyptians*, 193, 250–5. 4. Houses of wealthy Egyptians. Erman, *Life of the Anc. Egyptians*, 153, 177–88; Breasted, *Hist. of Egypt*, 88–90. 5. Oriental methods of showing emotion. *Encyc. Bib.*, III, 2694–6; 3220–2; Hastings, *D. B.*, III, 453–4.

§ XVIII. **Joseph's Loyalty to His Kinsmen.** GENERAL QUESTIONS: 1. Why was Joseph's treatment of his kinsmen especially noble? 2. Describe the land of Goshen and the life of the Hebrews while there. 3. Interrelations between Egypt and Asia at this period. 4. The meaning of Jacob's dying blessing. 5. The distinctly Egyptian elements in the Joseph stories. 6. Parallels to the story of Joseph in ancient contemporary literature. 7. The date of Joseph. 8. The literary, historical, archæological and religious value of the Joseph stories.

SUBJECTS FOR SPECIAL RESEARCH: 1. Semitic ideas and influences in Egypt during the reigns of Amenhotep III and IV. Breasted, *Hist. of Ancient Egyptians*, 248–79; *Hist. of Egypt*, 328–37, 352–79. 2. The Egyptian method of embalming and burial. Maspero, *Dawn of Civiliz.*, 112, 361; *Struggle of the Nations*, 509–26; *Encyc. Bib.*, II, 1284–5; *Herodotus*, II, 86–89; Budge, *The Mummy*, 160 *ff.* 3. Compare the character, fortunes and services of Joseph and Ulysses. Driver, *Genesis*, 320–1, 400–1; Hastings, *D. B.*, II, 770.

THE BONDAGE AND DELIVERANCE FROM EGYPT

§ XIX. **The Oppression of the Hebrews in Egypt.** GENERAL QUESTIONS: 1. Describe the general characteristics of the three biblical accounts of the bondage and exodus. 2. Effect of the policy of the rulers of the nineteenth dynasty upon the serf class in Egypt. 3. The store cities of Pithom and Ramses. 4. The evidence that Ramses II was the Pharaoh of the oppression. 5. The historical facts underlying the biblical stories of the sojourn in Egypt. 6. Influence of the Egyptian sojourn upon the life and faith of the Hebrews.

SUBJECTS FOR SPECIAL RESEARCH: 1. Excavations at Pithom. Hastings, *D. B.*, III, 886–7; Naville, *Store-City of Pithom and the Route of the Exodus;* Hogarth, *Authority and Archæology*, 54–5, 61, 68. 2. The reign and policy of Ramses II. Breasted, *Hist. of the Anc. Egyptians*, 303–26; *Hist. of Egypt*, 423–63; Maspero, *Struggle of the Nats.*, 385–430; Hastings, *D. B.*, I, 662; *Encyc. Bib.*, II, 1241–2. 3. A comparison of modern industrial conditions with those in Egypt under Ramses II. Brown, *Social Message of the Modern Pulpit.*

§ XX. **Moses's Childhood and Training.** GENERAL QUESTIONS: 1. Describe Moses's boyhood training. 2. The justification and significance of Moses's slaying the Egyptian taskmaster. 3. Moses's adoption into the Midianite clan. 4. Did Moses first learn of Jehovah from the Midianites? 5. Influence of his life in the wilderness upon the character and faith of Moses.

SUBJECTS FOR SPECIAL RESEARCH: 1. The story of the childhood of Sargon I. Marti, *Relig. of the O. T.*, 18–21; Peters, *Early Heb. Story*, 192–4; Maspero, *Dawn of Civiliz.*, 597–8. 2. The Egyptian system of education. Breasted, *Hist. of the Anc. Egyptians*, 92–4, 395; *Hist. of Egypt*, 98–100; Maspero, *Dawn of Civiliz.*, 288; Erman, *Life of the Anc. Egyptians*, 328–68. 3. The Midianites. Hastings, *D. B.*, III, 365–6; *Encyc. Bib.*, III, 3079–81. 4. Origin of the Jehovah religion. Budde, *Relig. of Israel*, 1–38; Gordon, *Early Traditions of Gen.*, 106–10; Hastings, *D. B.*, extra vol., 626–7.

§ XXI. **Moses's Call to Deliver the Hebrews.** GENERAL QUESTIONS: 1. Describe the three different accounts of the way in which the divine revelation came to Moses. 2. The vital points in which they all agree. 3. The causes of Moses's hesitation, and the different ways

APPENDIX

in which his objections are met. 4. In the light of the situation and in the language of to-day, describe Moses's training and call to be a prophet leader. 5. Pharaoh's defiant refusal to let the Hebrews go.

SUBJECTS FOR SPECIAL RESEARCH: 1. The magicians of Egypt. Erman, *Life in Anc. Egypt*, 352–6, 373–4; Hastings, *D. B.*, III, 207. 2. Meaning of the divine names. Driver, *Genesis*, 402–9; *Encyc. Bib.*, III, 3323–6; Hastings, *D. B.*, extra vol., 625–6. 3. Compare Moses's call with that of Isaiah (Is. 6) and Jeremiah (Jer. 1). 4. The serf class in Egypt. Breasted, *Hist. of the Anc. Egyptians*, 236, 254; *Hist. of Egypt*, 308–9, 339, 496–7; Maspero, *Dawn of Civiliz.*, 309, 326–7.

§ XXII. **The Egyptian Plagues.** GENERAL QUESTIONS: 1. Describe the form of the plague stories in each of the groups of Hebrew narratives. 2. The early Judean account of each of the seven plagues. 3. The peculiar sanitary conditions in the land of Egypt. 4. The natural and national calamities reflected in the plague stories. 5. The effect of these calamities upon (1) the Egyptians and (2) the Hebrews. 6. The origin and new significance of the passover.

SUBJECTS FOR SPECIAL RESEARCH: 1. Plagues in antiquity and the popular explanations of them. Hastings, *D. B.*, III, 887–92; *Encyc. Bib.*, III, 3784–9. 2. Conditions in Egypt at the end of the nineteenth dynasty. Breasted, *Hist. of the Anc. Egyptians*, 333–5; *Hist. of Egypt*, 464–79. 3. The Pharaoh's place in the religious hierarchy of Egypt. Breasted, *Hist. of the Anc. Egyptians*, 63–4; *Hist. of Egypt*, 62, 122–3, 456; Maspero, *Dawn of Civiliz.*, 266, 304. 4. History of the Semitic spring festival. *St. O. T.*, IV, 258; Hastings, *D. B.*, III, 688–90; *Encyc. Bib.*, III, 3589–3600; Barton, *Semitic Origins*, 110–1; Gray, *Numbers*, 404–7.

§ XXIII. **The Exodus.** GENERAL QUESTIONS: 1. Describe the escape from Egypt, as recorded in the earliest biblical narrative. 2. Modern parallels. 3. Probable number of the Hebrew fugitives. 4. The direction and manner of the march through the wilderness. 5. Meaning of the song of deliverance. 6. Effect of the great deliverance upon Hebrew character, literature and faith.

SUBJECTS FOR SPECIAL RESEARCH: 1. Compare the priestly with the early prophetic accounts of the exodus. *St. O. T.*, I, 172–6. 2. Caravan travel through the desert. Palmer, *The Desert of the Exodus;* Stanley, *Sinai and Palestine;* Doughty, *Wanderings in Arabia.* 3. The references to the exodus in later Hebrew literature. *Cf.* article, "Exodus," in Bible dictionaries.

APPENDIX

§ XXIV. **The Revelation and Covenant at Sinai.** GENERAL
QUESTIONS: 1. Describe and explain the growing importance of Sinai
in Hebrew thought. 2. The probable situation of the sacred mountain.
3. The different accounts of the way in which Jehovah revealed himself
to his people, and their meaning. 4. The establishment of the covenant between Jehovah and Israel. 5. The original decalogue defining
Israel's obligations to Jehovah. 6. History of this decalogue. 7. Probable origin and early significance of the sabbath.

SUBJECTS FOR SPECIAL RESEARCH: 1. The recent excavations in the
Sinaitic peninsula. Petrie, *Researches in Sinai*. 2. The late traditions of the march through the wilderness. *St. O. T.*, I, 176–8. 3. The
covenant in early Semitic life. Hastings, *D. B.*, I, 509–15; extra vol.,
630–2; *Encyc. Bib.*, I, 928–36; Trumbull, *The Blood Covenant*. 4. The
four biblical versions of the revelations and covenant at Sinai. *St. O. T.*,
I, 181–8. 5. History of the sabbath. *St. O. T.*, IV, 257–8; Hastings,
D. B., IV, 317–19; *Encyc. Bib.*, IV, 4177–9; Gordon, *Early Trads. of
Genesis*, 216–23.

§ XXV. **Man's Individual Duties to God and Man.** GENERAL
QUESTIONS: 1. Compare the two decalogues given, according to tradition, to Moses. 2. Explain why the prophetic decalogue is assigned
the first place in Exodus. 3. Describe its probable date and authorship. 4. Its original simple form, and the expanded versions in Exodus
20 and Deuteronomy 5. 5. Man's primary duties (1) to God, (2) to
parents and (3) to others. 6. The place of this decalogue in the Jewish and Christian religions.

SUBJECTS FOR SPECIAL RESEARCH: 1. Different possible divisions of
the decalogue. Hastings, *D. B.*, I, 580–2; *Encyc. Bib.*, I, 1049–52.
2. Jesus's version of the different commands of the prophetic decalogue.
Cf. Matt. 5^{17-48}, 6^{19-21}, $12^{1-12, 31, 32}$, 15^{3-5}, 22^{36-39}, 12–31. 3. Similar formu-
lations of primary duties in other literatures.

§ XXVI. **Moses's Work as Judge and Prophet.** GENERAL QUES-
TIONS: 1. Describe the visit of Moses's father-in-law. 2. Moses's
activity as judge. 3. The way in which laws come into existence among
primitive people. 4. In what sense is Moses the father of Hebrew law.
5. Describe the origin and use of the tent of meeting. 6. Moses's work
as a prophet.

SUBJECTS FOR SPECIAL RESEARCH: 1. The origin and growth of Hebrew law. *St. O. T.*, IV, 8–15; Hastings, *D. B.*, III, 64–7; *Encyc. Bib.*,
III, 2714–8. 2. The appointment and duties of Babylonian and Hebrew judges. *St. O. T.*, IV, 86–8; Johns, *Bab. and Assyr. Laws*,

APPENDIX

Contracts and Letters, 80–4; Sayce, *Babylonians and Assyrians*, 195–9.
3. The late priestly tradition of the tent of meeting or dwelling. *St. O. T.*, IV, 149–57; Hastings, *D. B.*, IV, 654–68; Brown, *The Tabernacle*. 4. Definition of prophet. *Cf.* § XXI³; Hastings, *D. B.*, IV, 108–9; *Encyc. Bib.*, III, 3853–9.

§ XXVII. **The Life of the Hebrews in the Wilderness.** GEN-ERAL QUESTIONS: 1. Describe the scene of the wilderness wanderings. 2. Life in this region. 3. The spring of Kadesh. 4. Traditions regarding the food supply. 5. Contests with native tribes. 6. Form and significance of the ark. 7. Duration of the wilderness sojourn.

SUBJECTS FOR SPECIAL RESEARCH: 1. Contents of the book of Numbers. *St. O. T.*, I, 24; Hastings, *D. B.*, III, 567–73; *Encyc. Bib.*, III, 3439–49. *Cf.* also Biblical introductions. 2. Life in the Arabian desert. Palmer, *The Desert of the Exodus and Wilderness Wandering;* Stanley, *Sinai and Palestine;* Doughty, *Wanderings in Arabia*, I, 70–159. 3. The late priestly tradition of the ark. *St. O. T.*, IV, 149–51; Hastings, *D. B.*, I, 149–51; *Encyc. Bib.*, I, 300–9.

§ XXVIII. **The Attempt to Enter Canaan from the South.** GENERAL QUESTIONS: 1. Why did the Hebrews not go at once from Egypt to Canaan? 2. What is the history and the significance of the journey of the spies? 3. The evidence that certain tribes entered Canaan directly from the south. 4. Causes and nature of the rebellions against Moses's authority. 5. Effect of the wilderness life and of Moses's activity upon the character and faith of the Hebrews.

SUBJECTS FOR SPECIAL RESEARCH: 1. The three different accounts of the journey of the spies. *St. O. T.*, I, 215–18. 2. Palestine under the rule of the twentieth Egyptian dynasty. Breasted, *Hist. of the Anc. Egyptians*, 360–4, 373–4, 375, 378; Paton, *Early Hist. of Syria and Palestine*, 144–50; Breasted, *Hist. of Egypt*, 465–6, 470, 512–19; Hastings, *D. B.*, I, 662–3. 3. In the light of the oldest records was Moses's great work accomplished by natural or miraculous means?

§ XXIX. **The Journey from the Wilderness, and Balaam's Prophecy.** GENERAL QUESTIONS: 1. Describe the events in the journey about Edom. 2. The different traditions regarding Balaam. 3. Meaning of his oracles. 4. Their probable date. 5. Trace in early Hebrew life the development of the belief that Israel was a people with an unique destiny.

SUBJECTS FOR SPECIAL RESEARCH: 1. The territory of Edom and Moab. Smith, *Hist. Geog. of the Holy Land*, 555–72; Hastings, *D. B.*, I, 644–5, III, 403; *Encyc. Bib.*, II, 1181–4, III, 3166–71; Libbey and

APPENDIX

Hoskins, *Jordan Valley and Petra*, I. 2. Ancient oracles. Smith, *Religion of the Semites*, 133, 177–81; Hastings, *D. B.*, III, 629; *Encyc. Bib.*, III, 3516; Gray, *Numbers*, 345–8, 350–7, 360–71. 3. Did other early peoples believe that they were under the especial protection and care of their gods? *Cf. St. O. T.*, II, 495.

§ XXX. **East-Jordan Conquests and Moses's Farewell.** GENERAL QUESTIONS: 1. What was the significance of the victory over the Amorites? 2. Meaning of the ancient song of victory? 3. Nature of the east-Jordan territory. 4. The death of Moses. 5. Moses's relation to the book of Deuteronomy. 6. Moses's work as prophet, leader and judge. 7. The essence of his message.

SUBJECTS FOR SPECIAL RESEARCH: 1. Literary analysis and contents of Deuteronomy. Hastings, *D. B.*, I, 596–603; *Encyc. Bib.*, I, 1079–93; *St. O. T.*, IV, 33-4. 2. The variant traditions of Moses's farewell. *St. O. T.*, I, 250-2. 3. The religion of Moses. Hastings, *D. B.*, extra vol., 631–4; Marti, *Religion of the Old Testament*, 36–71.